W9-BFQ-059

Happy holidays—
and great gardening.
love,
Anne

Christmas 1987

FRUITS AND BERRIES
FOR THE HOME GARDEN

FRUITS AND BERRIES FOR THE HOME GARDEN

LEWIS HILL

Drawings by Mary Azarian

A GARDEN WAY PUBLISHING BOOK

Storey Communications, Inc.
Pownal, Vermont 05261

A Garden Way Publishing Book

This quality paperback edition is published
by arrangement with Alfred A. Knopf, Inc.

Printed in the United States by Capital City Press

Fourth Printing, May, 1986

Copyright © 1977 by Lewis Hill

The name Garden Way Publishing is licensed to Storey
Communications, Inc. by Garden Way, Inc.

All rights reserved under International and Pan-American
Copyright Conventions. Published in the United States by
Alfred A. Knopf, Inc., New York, and simultaneously in
Canada by Random House of Canada Limited, Toronto.
Distributed by Random House, Inc., New York.

LIBRARY OF CONGRESS CATALOGING IN PUBLICATION DATA

Hill, Lewis, 1924–   Fruits and berries for the home
garden.
Includes index.
1. Fruit-culture.   I. Title.
SB355.H65   634   76-47534
0-88266-168-X paper

To Nancy . . .
and to all our customer friends
who inspired this book
by their fruit-growing
questions.

ACKNOWLEDGMENTS

In addition to my own more than thirty years of fruit-growing experiences, the knowledge and skills of many other people have been utilized freely in writing this book. I wish to thank Dr. Lyman Calahan, Dr. Richard Klein, Dr. Daniel Meador, Dr. Norman Pellett, Gertrude Catlin, and many others, as well as organizations such as the American Pomological Society, the Brooklyn Botanic Garden, the New York Fruit Testing Cooperative, the North American Fruit Explorers, and the Worcester County (Massachusetts) Horticulture Society, all of whom helped immeasurably in compiling and checking the information.

I appreciate also the many nurseries and nursery folks who furnished information and helped locate trees; especially Stark Brothers, Fred Ashworth, Tyra Thorene, the Burpee Seed Company, C & O Nursery, and the Burgess Seed and Plant Nursery.

I am extremely grateful to Jane Garrett, my patient and understanding editor, who has been a tremendous help and encouragement; Mary Azarian for her artistic illustrations; William Maier for his inspiration and valuable advice; all the encouraging customers who helped me better understand what information the beginning fruit grower is seeking; and to Nancy who contributed the recipes in the Appendix.

I'm indebted also to my forebears who were responsible for the magnificent old orchard that gave me a treasured appreciation for the fine fruits of yesteryear. And I'm also grateful to some special friends of long ago who introduced me to the fascinating pleasures of plants and soil: Mrs. Fred Pleasants of Montclair, New Jersey, and Mrs. Luther P. Eisenhart of Princeton. The former carefully taught me the discipline necessary for gardening, and the latter showed me how to thoroughly enjoy it.

Lewis Hill

CONTENTS

PREFACE

One of the best things about starting school when I was six was cutting through our old and rather decrepit orchard and picking pocketfuls of apples to eat on the way. The early Yellow Transparents and Tetoskys were ready on the first day of school, and even a child could eat a lot of them without feeling stuffed. Later the "heavier" apples ripened—the zippy flavored Duchesses, the Astrachans with their waxy red skin, the golden Peach apples with a rosy bloom, and finally the Wealthys. Even later were the Bethels, Pound Sweets, and Russets. There were lots of other apples too. We didn't even know their names, so we called them by their flavor or appearance: the pear, pumpkin, banana, sugar, or whatever. All the kids in the neighborhood knew where the best apples in each orchard grew, and when they were at their best. Like the raccoons who stole them at night, we could go unerringly to the choice trees.

Even with all those wonderful kinds to choose from, we would continually hear the old-timers speak fondly of other varieties they had grown long ago. They remembered the Alexanders, Baldwins, Fameuses, Pearmains, Strawberries, Seek-No-Furthers, and many others of earlier years. They would tell of cellars stashed with barrels of cider and boxes of apples that would keep all winter. "Can't seem to grow fruit anymore," they would say sadly.

Our old orchard died and fell apart a few years after that. Soon not a tree was left, and most of the other farm orchards disappeared too. Only here and there an occasional tree stayed alive and bravely produced fruit. Most folks were buying their fruit in bags, and their apple pie mix in cans.

But I remembered how much better I had liked the home-grown fruits and was already sentimental about the stately old orchard. Why couldn't we grow fruit anymore? The soil was still there, and still good. The weather wasn't any worse, and maybe it was even better, to hear the venerable citizens reminisce.

So without having any idea of how to go about it, I began planting fruit trees. I couldn't find any of the old favorites that I remembered or had heard about, so I had to order new kinds from tantalizing catalogs sent by faraway nurseries. Their assortment at that time was small, consisting mostly of the same varieties as the fruits that were displayed in our local stores each fall: Red and Yellow Delicious, Rome Beauty, Jonathan, Winesap, and Grimes Golden. I planted a few of each, and soon, just as my neighbors had predicted, every one of them died.

"Course we always grafted our own," a senior citizen told me one day. "We never bought fruit trees. There was always somebody who traveled around, and he sold grafts. We'd have him stick them on some of the seedlings coming up all over. Next year we'd move them into the orchard, and most of them grew. That way you knew both the top and the root were hardy." Here was the first clue that I was doing many things wrong. Right away, I bought a book about how to graft and care for fruit trees, and soon things began to look up.

After some friends saw my beginner's luck with the first grafts, they began to show more interest in the project. Soon people were telling me about old trees here and there that were still bearing the fine old fruits. I quickly found that while it was not nearly as easy to make a graft from an old tree grow as well as one from a younger, more vigorous specimen, it could be done. Within a few years we had quite a few fruits and berries bearing well, just as in Grandpa's time. I found out many other things that the catalogs or books about growing fruit don't tell you. Some I learned the hard way, some from talking with neighbors who remembered things their parents said or did.

One reason for the success of the early orchards was the care the old-timers took of them. The orchard, a century ago, was as important to them as their grain, animals, poultry, wood lot, or vegetable garden. Annual fertilizing and pruning were never neglected. Neither was insect control, even though it might consist only of flinging wood ashes through the trees now and then, or perhaps an occasional spray of soapsuds and water. The farm animals were fenced out, except perhaps in the fall when they were let in to pick up the unused fruit in which insects and disease could overwinter.

I also learned that when I bought fruit trees it was wise to study the catalogs carefully, because a tree recommended for Oregon might not be happy in New England. When catalogs promised something was hardy in the North, it might mean northern Missouri, North Carolina, or northern California. It was only by buying or grafting the kinds that were actually suitable for our area that I finally got the orchard going.

Growing apples was a stepping stone to trying other fruits, and in a few more years we were harvesting plums, pears, grapes, cherries, and a large assortment of berries, just as our ancestors had done. No longer do we have to depend on the small selection in the supermarkets. The dozens of different kinds of fruits growing in our back yard give us an exciting variety of good eating. And unlike Grandpa and Grandma, we have the advantage of a home freezer that lets us enjoy the produce all year. It seems good not to have to wash a raft of sprays, fumes, and waxes off our fruit before we eat it, or worry about whether our apple pie contains more preservatives than vitamins.

In fact just about everything connected with fruit growing is a pleasure, and especially the harvest. When I pick the first red strawberry of the season, or the first juicy ripe raspberry, or the first apple, the battles with insects and weeds are quickly forgotten. Thoughts instead are of boyhood memories of a majestic old orchard laden with fruit . . . and hopeful anticipation of all the fabulous harvests ahead. It took me about twenty years to reach this stage—to learn how to grow good fruit. I hope this book will help you accomplish it in less time. A whole lot less.

FRUITS AND BERRIES
FOR THE HOME GARDEN

1 / WHAT TO GROW?

"As the twig is bent, so the tree is inclined." The old saying is very true. Several old fruit trees on our place lean very heavily and will eventually topple over. There are other trees suffering badly in the shade of large maples, and a few are struggling where the soil is far too wet for part of the year. We even have one large crab apple in the front yard growing up into the telephone wires. All are sad monuments to my early days of planting and pruning, when I had little idea of how to do it.

No one told me back then about tree nutrients, and how grass and weeds would likely steal them all while the poor tree suffered from malnutrition. I just kept heaping on the wrong combinations of fertilizers, awaiting the amazing results that didn't come. Nor did I know that winter's sun could be as responsible for frost injury as winter's cold, or that pollination was necessary to get fruit, and that I could even help the bees, if necessary. It took a while to learn that when a tree looked sick it wasn't always bugs or disease at all but sometimes a physiological difficulty that sprays couldn't help. I found there are ways to get trees to bear larger fruit, and at an earlier age, and even ways to get them to produce a good crop each fall instead of every other year. Even with harvesting there seemed to be many techniques to be learned.

Knowing what you are doing is very important because the first years in the orchard set the course for the next fifty or more, and are usually the key to success or failure. Gardeners are sometimes uncertain about how to begin growing fruit, or even if they should attempt it at all.

Every spring the same couple comes to our nursery to buy vegetable and flower plants. They always look longingly at the little trees and say, "If only we weren't so old we would put in a few fruits and berries." The trouble is, they have been saying that for over fifteen years. If they had planted their little orchard the first year, they could already have harvested a dozen crops! Some people hesitate about getting involved in what they consider a long-term project. Others have planted a few trees at one time or another, had them die, and decided not to try again. Still others think fruit trees are expensive and take a lot of room. I also meet a surprising number who feel that fruit growing is the pinnacle of gardening and a higher level than they care to attempt. They feel that it takes too much skill and time and should

3

be left strictly to the experts. Many have been frightened, too, by tales of twice-a-week spraying with deadly poisons. Some extension services in the past have even advised gardeners that it was more practical to buy fruit than to bother with a small orchard.

All of this is most unfortunate. The truth is, if you pick the right varieties of fruits (and many beginners don't) and give them a suitable place to live and a little care (and again, many beginners don't), fruit trees and berries require no more care than most other growing things, and often less.

You can still plant and enjoy your produce even if you are along in years, or if you have no plans to live on the same piece of land for generations. Dwarf fruit trees begin to bear within two or three years; many small fruits get into good production within three years; and you can pick everbearing strawberries the first year. If you do have to move, you can take pleasure in the fact that fruit trees will add tremendously to the sale value of your property.

We have only a small area in fruits, but last year we put hundreds of packages of various fruits and berries in the freezer, besides all the ones that

A country home and a fruit tree seem to go together.

got preserved in other ways, or went into our root cellar. Of course, all summer and fall we eat lots of pies, shortcakes, berries and cream, drink lots of fruit juice, and give away fruits and berries of all kinds. (No mention will be made of the amount we eat right off the trees and bushes while we are picking.) Naturally this amount and variety of fruit would cost a tidy sum in the local market, if it were available. The increasing price and continual shortage of many fruits makes us appreciate our orchard, berry patch, and vegetable garden more every year.

Fruit plants are not much of an initial investment in light of all the future dividends you get from them. A fruit tree can cost as little as a bushel and a half of good fruit, and berry plants are only a few cents each. Even a small family with their own garden and orchard can easily save over $700 a year on their annual food bill. Why buy tropical fruit drinks when you can make your own? Why spend hard-earned money on commercial wines and all the taxes? Now $700 is a lot of money, but don't forget the extra savings in taxes too. Except for seed, plants, and fertilizer, your home-grown food hasn't cost you anything, so it is tax free. If you had shelled out the $700, you would have needed an additional income of at least $1000 just to pay the federal, state, and other taxes on it. So the savings are substantial, and more and more people are realizing it.

If you have only a small lot you can still grow fruit. Many dwarf trees grow to full size within an 8-foot circle. Strawberries grow in crocks, hanging baskets, pyramids, and barrels. A few feet of raspberries will produce quarts of fruit every year. Blueberry, elderberry, currant, and gooseberry plants can be substituted for ornamental foundation plants and hedges around the house. Fruit trees can replace flowering trees and shrubs, and nut trees can be planted instead of shade trees. While our orchard bears little resemblance to Kew Gardens, we find a satisfying pleasure in growing something that is beautiful in all seasons and also produces a product that can be put into a tasty pie or a tantalizing jug.

Getting Acquainted with Your New Tree

One day a prospective customer exploded, "Why don't you just come right out and make us file adoption papers when we buy a tree!" Come to think of it, maybe that's not a bad idea. Anyone who has ever raised a tree from infancy to adolescence hates to send it out into the world to be treated with no more attention than one would give a newly set birdbath or flag pole. So naturally when I spot a novice orchardist I inquire about his planting plans and make some suggestions.

Of course everyone wants trees that grow and produce, but a surprising number of people forget that a tree is a living, growing thing and needs care. Many times along country roads you've seen abandoned farms where there are dozens of sturdy old apple trees growing miles from civilization. They obviously get no care whatsoever, yet they appear to be growing well and producing fruit. It is very likely that sometime, someone helped those trees get off to a good start. You'll want to help your fledgling fruit trees begin in the same way. It's easy. All you have to do is think from the tree's point of view.

Choosing the Right Variety

Getting off to a good start in life is important, so be sure you begin with a good tree. Not only do you want a healthy tree, but you'll also want to get the right kind of tree—one appropriate to your location. If you're going to buy a dog, you're not likely to select a Mexican Hairless to romp with you in the snow of upper Alaska, or an English sheep dog for your tropical island retirement. Yet each spring the express offices, United Parcel depots, and post offices up north are piled high with peach, fig, apricot, walnut, pecan, and sweet cherry trees that have no more chance of survival than a walrus caravan crossing the Sahara.

Gardeners in the warmer parts of the country can have trouble too. Many trees need a certain amount of winter or they will die. Each variety of apple, pear, peach, and similar fruit has a chilling requirement that must be met or the tree won't survive. In frost-free or nearly frost-free areas, most ordinary varieties are unsuitable; only especially developed kinds with low winter chilling requirements should be planted.

Because so many plants that are being sold are not hardy for the climate where they're planted, thousands of dollars, tons of fertilizer, and hours of work are wasted each year, not to mention the shattered dreams of would-be back-yard orchardists. Many disappointed gardeners never try again. Others keep at it year after year, thinking they did something wrong. But the cards are always stacked against them. So get things in your favor by choosing trees that are right for your climate. The chapters on the various fruits and the suggested varieties will help you make a good choice.

After your carefully selected tree arrives, treat it well. Many people aren't aware that because baby trees are newcomers to the world they need special attention. Almost no one would buy a puppy and dump him in the back yard to shift for himself; yet gardeners often buy a helpless little tree, plant it far too quickly and carelessly, and promptly lose interest in it. Unlike the pup, the poor tree can't go hunting for food and water, or even howl to remind you it's being neglected. You'll want to plant it carefully and see that it never has a chance to dry out.

What a Tree Needs

Your tree has the same basic requirements as any living thing:

A place to live. The ground will be its permanent home, so make it pleasant. The soil should be able to accommodate the huge root system of the mature tree and, with a little help from you, also keep it well fed. It shouldn't be too wet. Fruit trees detest wet feet and quickly get sick if this condition persists for more than a few days at a time.

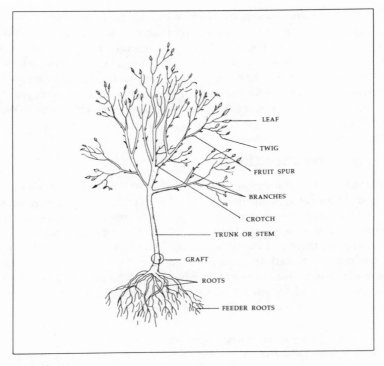

Parts of a tree

Air to breathe. Trees need air too. Instead of oxygen, trees breathe in carbon dioxide and breathe out oxygen, so they freshen our air. Remember how nice the woods smell.

Food and water. Like any youth, a tree needs the most food when it is growing the fastest. A tree grows mainly in early summer. Its roots take in nourishment dissolved by water in the soil. Nitrates, phosphates, and potash are high on its list of favorite foods, with sprinklings of other minerals. You can provide these with applications of dried manure, compost, mulch, or some of the many chemical or natural fertilizer mixes you can buy. Chapter 5 on soils will tell you how.

Keep in mind that a tree likes to eat, so every spring you should set out a hearty meal for it. Soil alone is seldom rich enough to sustain a growing tree for long without extra help.

Sunlight. Most plants need light, and fruit trees need a great deal—practically all day long in the North. Sunlight converts the minerals brought up from the roots by the sap into organic matter. This mysterious process called photosynthesis is the way leaves convert the minerals from earth and fertilizer into tree growth and fruit. Be sure buildings or other trees won't block out sunlight either now or in the future, or your tree will grow poorly and the fruit will ripen late.

Room to grow. A tree shouldn't be crowded. Be sure not to plant it too close to other trees, highways, overhead wires, paths, or buildings. And there is as much of a tree underground as there is above, so be sure the roots have plenty of room to grow. Deep, rich soil is necessary for successful growth.

Protection. A grown tree can stand a little neglect, but a young tree must be carefully protected. Animals, insects, machinery (especially lawn mowers), children, and weather all take their toll of newly planted trees each year. Keep an eye on your young tree and be ready to spring to its rescue whenever danger threatens.

Two Trees for the Price of One

Unlike shade and forest trees, a good fruit tree is almost never grown from seed. Even seeds from the best apples, plums, peaches, and pears are likely to grow into trees that produce poor fruit. Johnny Appleseed's widely renowned trees weren't good for much of anything except cider.

It may surprise you to know that the little Jonathan apple tree that you got in the mail or picked up at a nursery is very likely two trees in one, and it is possible that neither was grown from seed. The part that will be above the ground and produce fruit was started from a tiny piece of branch called

The graft of this fruit tree is very obvious. Most are not quite so distinctive (University of Illinois).

a scion (pronounced *sion*), which was taken from a large Jonathan apple tree. This scion was selected because of its ability to produce good fruit. It also determines what the size, color, and quality of that fruit will be. The part of the tree under the ground, the rootstock, which may also include a short piece of the trunk, determines the general size and shape of the tree, its vigor, and the type of soil in which it can best grow. The root may have been grown from a seed, or it may have been a root division of a larger tree. Both the rootstock and the top should be suitable for the climate where it will be planted.

The two parts of your tree have been joined together by a surgical operation called a graft. If you have gardened before, you may already have had experience with grafted plants such as tea roses, two-colored cactus plants, red-leaf maples, and copper beech trees. You can locate the graft on your young fruit tree easily. It will probably show as a good-size bump or bend in the stem, at ground level or a few inches above or below it. As the tree grows the bump will gradually disappear, but if the graft was made above ground the two different kinds of bark will often be quite noticeable even years later.

Keep in mind that everything below the graft is probably a poor quality tree. If it were allowed to grow into a mature tree, it would not be likely to produce fruit worth picking. If sprouts grow from below the graft, they should be cut off immediately. They may grow very quickly and could soon crowd out the good part of the tree. If mice or rabbits chew the bark and kill the tree above the graft, any growth coming from below will also be worthless. Unless one of these sprouts can be regrafted with a scion of a good variety, the roots should be dug out and the tree replaced.

This is the tree that will be living with you for the next forty or fifty years. It is a beautiful example of what mankind working with nature has produced, and a masterful improvement over the fruits that the early Greeks began cultivating. Now it is ready to enrich your life with its beauty and bounty, asking only a little care and attention in return.

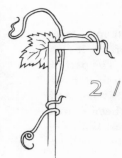

2 / PLANNING YOUR FRUIT GARDEN OR ORCHARD

When you are involved in a project like fruit growing that will quite likely last a lifetime or more, you naturally want to do it right. Mistakes made early have a way of coming back to haunt us. If you plant your vegetable garden with the plants growing too close together or in the wrong spot, or if you choose the wrong seeds, you lose only one season. But if you make a similar mistake with fruit trees, it may be years before you find it out and decades before you can remedy the damage. That's why I like to plan our fruit-growing areas on paper before I plant trees in the ground.

Even if you can't plant everything you want the first year, it's an excellent idea to make a plan so you will have the best possible trees growing in the best possible locations. Then put it in a safe spot where you can always find it. Keeping your plan up-to-date throughout your gardening or orchard-ist career will pay dividends because labels will no doubt be lost, and whenever a tree begins to bear you'll want to know what it is. Also, if a tree does poorly or dies, you'll want to know the variety so you can decide whether to replace it with the same kind or try another.

If you have only a small lot you don't have much choice about where the trees will be planted. But within the boundaries you have, you will want to place them where they will have full sun and plenty of room to grow. Also make sure that they have well-drained soil; tree roots can't grow well in heavy, wet soils.

Before you choose the exact location of your future orchard, stop a moment, look into your crystal ball, and try to decide what's likely to happen in the future. Are the neighborhood teens apt to hold motorcycle or snowmobile rallies where you envision your fruit trees? Will the location become a shortcut used by the whole neighborhood? Is it possible that in the future someone will have to dig up the area to repair a cable, water pipe, or sewer line? Will the orchard block off an area where service vehicles may have to go someday? Will your neighbor's row of little oak trees grow to powerful heights and shade it, or will his horse get loose and graze it to the ground? Perhaps heavy rains and melting snows sometimes form pools of water there that could drown it. Maybe in the winter drifting snow collects in alarming depths, or road salt drains onto it.

Sometimes it seems like the whole world is out to get a newly planted tree, so you'll want to make sure it is protected as much as possible. In fact, it's good insurance to plant it near the house so you can keep a watchful eye on any troubles before they get too serious. Probably George Washington wouldn't have cut down his father's cherry tree if it had been where his mother could have kept a better eye on it. Fruit trees planted too close to the road, on the other hand, are tempting to passersby, and you will probably have competition for your bounty from all the neighborhood kids. Better reduce the temptation by planting your trees in a less convenient place.

Another point to keep in mind is that certain fruit trees are susceptible to disease and insects and may need spraying during the summer. If vegetables and berries which may be ripening at that time are planted too close, it may be difficult to avoid spraying them when you spray the fruit trees.

Even if you can't meet every requirement for perfect placement of your trees, it's nice to consider all the possibilities so that you can avoid obvious pitfalls in advance. A large tree is hard to move and a disappointment to lose.

How Many Trees?

Before you start making a blueprint of your future fruit garden or orchard, decide roughly how many trees you are going to plant. Often the

Suggested planting plan for a small orchard

number of trees you have in your garden or orchard is determined by the space available. If space is limited you should resist the temptation of crowding in too many trees. Even gardeners with large lots shouldn't let enthusiasm get the best of them. In the quiet of winter too many of us succumb to colored catalog pictures and tantalizing descriptions of fruits and berries. Soon, with little rhyme or reason, we have made out quite an order. When the trees arrive in the spring we realize, too late, that not only our area but also our time and energy were vastly overestimated. Keep in mind that a few trees well cared for will be far more productive and satisfying than a larger orchard partly neglected.

It's almost impossible to suggest the right number of trees for every family's needs. Each family has a different taste preference. And it makes a difference, too, whether all the fruit will be consumed fresh or if some is to be preserved. The following suggestions are offered as a guide only, for no two gardeners would ever have the same reasons for choosing their assortment.

For a family of four who will do some preserving:

Apples (full size or semi-dwarf)	3–6
Apples (dwarf)	4–10
Apricots	2–4
Cherries	2–3
Nectarines	2–4
Peaches	2–4
Plums	3–5
Quinces	1–2

Disease Resistance

From time to time I'll mention varieties of fruit trees and berries that are disease resistant. Even resistant varieties can sometimes have problems, however, and you should keep in mind that fruit gardening, like every other form of agriculture, is a legal way to gamble. You are only stacking the odds a bit more in your favor by planting disease-resistant varieties.

Planting Distances

Different varieties of fruit trees grow in quite different ways, so it's difficult to say for sure how wide each tree will eventually grow. Some grow upright, like the Yellow Transparent apple and the Dolgo crab. Others are very spreading—the McIntosh, for instance. And trees grow differently in varying soils and climates.

If possible, plan your orchard so that no tree will touch any other tree, even when they are full grown. They should also be planted so that they will not eventually rub buildings or overhang highways, sidewalks, or property lines.

The following are approximate diameters of some full-grown fruit trees. When you plant them, allow enough additional room so that you can walk between them and light can reach all the outside of the tree.

FRUIT TREES

Apple (standard size)	25 to 35 feet
Apple (semi-dwarf)	15 to 20 feet
Apple (dwarf)	7 to 10 feet
Apricot (standard)	18 feet
Apricot (dwarf)	8 feet
Peach (standard)	18 feet
Peach (dwarf)	8 feet
Pear (standard)	18 feet
Pear (dwarf)	8 feet
Plum (standard)	18 feet
Plum (dwarf)	8 feet
Quince	12 feet

NUT TREES

Butternut and Black Walnut	35 feet
Chestnut (Chinese)	30 feet
Filbert	15 feet
Walnut and Hickory	35 feet

If standard (full-size) trees are used, the space between them need not be wasted the first few years. If necessary spraying is done carefully, vegetables, strawberries, or other temporary crops can be grown there. As long as adequate fertilizer is used, you'll do no harm to the fruit trees.

Some people like to plant extra fruit trees (called fillers) in their home orchard, intending to take them out as soon as they begin to crowd each other. It's difficult for most of us to cut down a healthy producing tree, however. Unless you can be very ruthless I don't recommend this method, for filler trees must definitely be removed when the time comes.

Shopping for Trees

All over the country there are many reliable nurseries and garden centers offering excellent assortments of high-quality stock, so a better selection is now available to the home gardener than there was a few years ago. Even so, too many supermarkets and garden shops selling fruit trees show little interest in local conditions. They often buy their trees from a large grower hundreds of miles away who has no idea what kinds are suitable. Wholesalers are as likely to send the same assortment of plants to northern Maine as they do to southern Kentucky.

Traveling salesmen usually also offer a poor choice. They often know very little about fruit growing and are more interested in making a sale than in filling your needs. "We sell dreams to people," one told me candidly. To make your dreams come true, buy your trees if possible at a nearby well-established nursery that does its own growing. Unfortunately, these are few and far between. Mail-order houses that graft their own trees are your next best bet if they are not too distant and if they offer good varieties on suitable rootstocks. Reliable garden centers that offer acclimated and disease-free stock are equally good.

When you're shopping for trees you may wonder what size to select. Fruit trees come in all sizes, from 8 inches tall to 10 feet and more; they may be either one, two, three, or four years old. They are priced accordingly. Lots of people think that if they plant a large tree they will be guaranteed large crops sooner, but it isn't necessarily so. A young tree can usually get established sooner, grow faster, and bear earlier than a large tree, which may need some time just to get its big root system re-established. But, very small trees are difficult to protect from lawnmowers and other hazards. They are also hard to train to a single stem, often growing instead into a funny-shaped large bush. So the smallest sizes are not usually your best buy, either.

For the most part, trees with a single stem or lightly branched, from 4 to 7 feet tall, one or two years old, are best for the homeowner to buy and to plant. They also cost less and ship more safely than the larger trees.

There are a few nurseries that get rather carried away in their catalogs, using superlatives a bit too generously. Words like *biggest, best, sensational, tremendous crops, astonishing size* abound in their literature, along with colored photos of trees that only Madison Avenue could grow. I suspect that many of the barkers who once worked for P. T. Barnum and his circus are now writing nursery catalogs.

TREES FOR SUMMER PLACES

Many home orchardists live in city apartments and have to do all their fruit growing during vacation months. If you are one of these, choose varieties that will ripen before you have to return to town. Early apples, plums, cherries, and various berries are ideal for summer gardeners.

Since fruit trees need a little attention at other times of the year, perhaps you can find a year-round resident to help you out if you aren't able to manage occasional working weekends at your place. Late winter pruning, spring feeding, and possibly dormant spraying will benefit your fruit crop.

If you are an absentee orchardist for most of the year, it will be even more important for you to choose the most reliable, easiest to grow, and most disease-resistant varieties you can find.

5-IN-1 TREES

Colored nursery catalogs often display gorgeous "orchard-in-one-tree" photos with several varieties of fruit grafted on a single tree. Usually it is wise for a beginning orchardist to avoid these 3-in-1, 5-in-1, and other multiple-grafted fruit trees. The different varieties seldom grow at the same rate and they are difficult to prune. We used to have a tree in our back yard with several kinds of apples growing on it. Each year I grafted a few more branches. By the following year I had forgotten where the various varieties were and cut off some of them while pruning the tree, so I never gained anything. Except for being a local curiosity, it had no practical use.

On the other hand, if you want something really unusual or if you have only a small space, and if you're willing to give it the special care it needs, the multiple graft tree may be perfect for your back yard.

PATENTED TREES

Sometimes in catalogs you may see a fruit tree listed with U.S. patent number thus-and-so. You may have been surprised to find that trees can be patented. Over the years quite a few thousand members of the plant world have been developed which were unusual enough to be registered in the patent office. This of course does not mean that they are superior in every way to any other variety, but only that they were unique and that they can now be propagated only by the person or firm holding the patent or by those licensed to do so.

Shade trees, roses, and fruit trees are the plants most often patented. Because perennials, shrubs, and small fruits can be started so easily, a patent on them would be difficult to enforce.

Over the years some great fruits have been patented. Stark Brothers Nurseries, which has pioneered in the introduction of many outstanding fruits, often pay handsome prices for new varieties. They sometimes even build a huge iron cage over a new tree to prevent damage or theft. Then, to ensure their rights to start more trees from it, they take out a patent.

Some nurseries, especially Stark Brothers and the C & O Nursery (see addresses in the Appendix), list patented kinds of fruit in their catalogs that the homeowner may want to consider planting in his orchard. Many patented fruits, however, have been developed especially for the lucrative commercial growers market, so the beginning orchardist will want to consider carefully also the old varieties that have been grown for years, as well as some of the newer unpatented kinds that have been developed by university experiment stations.

Choosing Varieties

If you're a beginning fruit grower it's wise to choose fruits and berries that are easy to grow. While it may be tempting to try French Wine Grapes, Granny Smith Apples, Red Peaches, Sweet Cherries, Japanese Plums, and English Walnuts, it makes more sense to start with varieties that need less painstaking care.

For your first attempt at growing tree fruits, you may want to try some easy-to-grow apples and plums. Raspberries, strawberries, currants, gooseberries, and elderberries are good small fruits that are almost certain to succeed. Of course, if you have been successfully growing things for years, go ahead and plant grapes, blueberries, peaches, and anything else that will grow well where you live.

After you have decided on the fruits you want to grow, the next step is to pick out the varieties of that fruit best suited for your geographical region. The chapters on the different fruits and berries will offer help, and also be sure to consult the State Extension Service nearest you, listed in the Appendix.

It's always an excellent idea to talk with local fruit growers who have been at it long enough to know what they are doing. They are often better sources of helpful information than all the books, extension pamphlets, and fruit magazines ever written. They can help you decide which trees are best for your climate and give you advice on what insects and diseases are bad in your area so you can buy the most resistant trees.

One word of warning, however: avoid advice from the know-it-all neighbor, relative, or friend who doesn't garden very much but is an "authority" on the subject. Listen politely to those people who have read a good article, had a gardening ancestor, or known of someone who always had wonderful success by doing thus and so—but let common sense be your guide. We have met many otherwise intelligent gardeners who dumped unreasonably large quantities of borax, Epsom salt, alcohol, kerosene, sawdust, superphosphate, ammonium nitrate, and even hot coffee on their trees just because someone told them to.

If you are unable to locate any local help in choosing easy-to-grow varieties for your area, the following list may be helpful, although it is in no way complete. Spot your growing zone on the map on pages 30 and 31. Remember that conditions sometimes vary widely within each zone. For instance, if you live on a high hill in Zone 4, you are probably getting Zone 3 weather. Similarly, a good sheltered spot near a large lake in Zone 4 could make your growing conditions like those in Zone 5.

FRUIT VARIETIES SUGGESTED FOR BEGINNING GROWERS

Zone 3

APPLE. Astrachan, Connell, Dolgo Crab, Duchess, Peach Apple, Prairie Spy, Quinte, Wealthy, Yellow Transparent
PEACH. None
PEAR. Golden Spice, Luscious, Mendall, Parker, Patten
PLUM. La Crescent, Pipestone, Redcoat, Waneta
PLUM CHERRY. Compass, Sapalta
SOUR CHERRY. Meteor, North Star

SWEET CHERRY. None
NUT. Butternuts

Zone 4

Growers in this zone should be able to grow everything listed for Zone 3 plus:

APPLE. Cortland, Imperial, Lobo, Lodi, McIntosh, Northwest Greening, Regent
CHERRY. Richmond
PEACH. Reliance (in favored spots)
PEAR. Flemish Beauty, Kieffer, Seckel
PLUM. Green Gage, Monitor, Stanley
SWEET CHERRY. None
NUT. Black walnuts (hardy strains)

Zone 5

Growers in this zone should be able to grow everything listed for Zones 3 and 4 plus:

APPLE. Delicious, Empire, Gravenstein, Northern Spy, Prima, Priscilla, Rhode Island Greening, Yellow Delicious
PEACH. Stark Frost King, Stark Sure Crop, Sunapee
PLUM. Burbank, Damson, Earliblue, Italian, Santa Rosa, Shiro
SOUR CHERRY. Montmorency
SWEET CHERRY. Bing, the Dukes, Stella, Windsor
NUT. Carpathian walnuts, filberts, hickory

Zones 6–8

Many varieties that will grow in the colder zones will also do well here, although certain kinds of fruits developed especially for the colder climates may not be satisfactory for these zones.

APPLE. Grimes Golden, Rome, Stayman, and Winesap should all do well here, too. Apples that grow best in Zone 3, including those of the McIntosh family, are not recommended.
CHERRY. All should do well.
PEACH. Candor, Elberta, Halehaven, Madison, Redhaven
PEAR. Anjou, Bartlett, Bosc, Clapp Favorite
PLUM. Most should do well
NUT. Chestnuts plus the hardiest pecans and walnuts are worth a trial.

3 / FRUIT GARDENING ON A SMALL SCALE

Would-be homesteaders in crowded areas are often frustrated that local restrictions forbid many forms of farming. It is comforting to know that while both the neighbors and the local zoning commission might raise a ruckus about your keeping a flock of chickens and a few pigs in the back yard, no one is likely to find an ordinance prohibiting a tree or two. In fact, planting a tree almost anywhere is encouraged.

In recent years mini-gardens have become very popular everywhere. Gardening on a small scale, which has always been a necessity in tiny back-yard city lots, is now a common practice in suburban and even rural lots because the sizes of the lots have become so much smaller. It's not always the size of the lot that causes people to plant on a mini-scale, either. Some people prefer to keep their plantings small because they have only a small family or because of limited time to spend on a garden.

For years tiny gardens of dwarf peas and midget sweet corn have been grown in suburban back yards, and miniature roses and dwarf evergreens have landscaped small front lawns. It was inevitable that dwarf fruit trees for miniature orchards would also be developed. The big trees of the past are simply not practical on a small lot.

Though the word "orchard" may stir up visions of acres of well-spaced fruit trees, or at least a dozen big old gnarled specimens around Grandpa's house in the country, an orchard can also be two or three little dwarf fruit trees on a half-acre lot.

Dwarf Trees

The development of the dwarf tree, whereby fruits are grafted on a rootstock that grows a tree less than a quarter of the diameter of a regular tree, has opened up a whole new dimension for home orchardists. Not only can gardeners who formerly had too little room now grow fruit trees, but those who once had room for two or three trees can now grow ten or twenty in the same space. This means a greater variety of fruit and less work. Older people and acrophobiacs who don't care to climb ladders can now prune, spray, thin, and harvest while standing firmly and safely on the ground.

Dwarf fruit trees are still fairly new, but many varieties are available.

Many of these trees grow only 6 or 8 feet tall and spread about the same width. Nearly all dwarf trees have the nice habit of growing quite rapidly when they are young and then slowing down. Not only is pruning easier on these smaller trees, but less of it is required. Another good point: dwarfs usually bear at an earlier age than the standard trees, and their fruit is just as large and good. Of course a dwarf tree produces considerably less fruit than a full-size tree, but since so many more trees can be grown in the same space, the yield per acre may actually be much more.

Since many catalogs now give customers a choice of dwarf rootstocks as well as varieties, a list of the most commonly used is included in the Appendix to help you make a better decision if several choices are available.

Unfortunately there's a gloomy side too. Most dwarfs are grafted on the roots of imported, shrubby trees that keep the fruit trees small. Many of these rootstocks are of English origin and are not as hardy as those used for standard trees. You are likely to have trouble growing them in Zones 3 and 4. So if you live in a cold part of the country, check the recommendations of the local extension service before you order dwarfs.

Dwarf trees are practical, not only for small lots but also for country places and even commercial orchards.

Comparative sizes of dwarf and full-size
fruit trees. Twelve or more dwarf trees
can be grown in the space it takes to grow
one standard full-size tree.

Dwarf fruit trees can be planted in
large tubs, planters, pots,
or boxes for use on terraces.

Espalier trees take little room
and are very attractive.

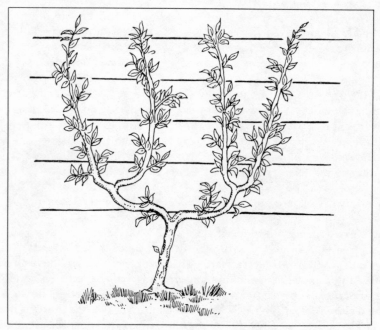

20

Some dwarf trees are rather brittle, too, and tend to break easily in high winds. Where snows get very deep they may not be practical because lower branches cannot be kept high enough to prevent excessive breakage. Also, in some areas they appear to be somewhat more susceptible to diseases and insect damage than native-grown rootstocks. Despite these possible drawbacks, the dwarfs are a great addition to the world of fruit growing and certainly worth considering if you have the right conditions for growing them.

Espaliered Trees

Remember how I cautioned you not to plant trees too close to buildings? Well, with espaliered trees you can disregard that advice. They not only grow well in close quarters but are especially attractive and, when well cared for, will produce an abundance of fruit.

Espalier means trellis, but to gardeners it has come to mean a tree that is being grown as a vine, flat against a building, wall, or fence. They are widely used in Europe where gardens are small and land is scarce. In America, espaliers are also grown in tiny yards, but they are often planted, too, because of their beauty. I know a farmer with several hundred acres of land who delights in his several beautifully espaliered trees.

Are espaliers difficult to grow? Naturally, when you are trying to force a tree to grow in a completely different manner than it otherwise would, you will have to go to extra pains. It is not at all hard, though, and not nearly as exacting as grafting or bonsai growing.

You can save yourself a lot of time and effort by buying a tree that has already been started as an espalier. See the list in the Appendix or look in garden magazines, which often list nurseries who sell these. Since all the difficult preliminary shaping has already been done, it is quite easy for you to continue the training.

If you want to start your own and grow it in an artistic pattern that is exclusively yours, why not? First you should decide on what kind of design you want. The candelabra is one of the most commonly used espalier shapes, but there are countless others. Designs can range from a simple bean pole with the tree being grown to a single stem only, to complicated forms that only a mathematician could devise. After you decide on yours, shop for the kind of tree that can be grown that way with the least trouble. If possible, go to a nursery where you will have a good choice of trees from which to choose.

Next you must decide whether you want to start with a full-size or a dwarf tree. If you are going to plant it against a house that is two or more stories tall, you'll want the standard or full-size one. You will have an impressive-looking espalier, but picking and pruning will have to be done from a ladder. For most spots, a dwarf or semi-dwarf will be a better choice. Be sure to take a close look at the trees. You will want to select one that has branches already growing in the right directions if possible. These can be used to spread out for the espalier effect. If nothing like this is available, take the best you can find, prune it back to a single stem, and start from that.

Planting is, of course, done at the proper time and in the usual way, with all the necessary fertilizer and watering. Set the tree so the trunk is about one foot from the building or wall. Avoid planting it under overhangs, since the tree will need both skylight and rain. Also, the tree should be placed where it can get nearly half a day of sunshine.

Training the tree is often accomplished by driving nails into the building or wall and guiding the growth by fastening the branches to them. However, a much easier and neater way is by using wires. After the planting is completed, a guiding trellis is installed behind it. Start this trellis by putting in some strong posts 7 or 8 feet high, close to the wall or building, at the ends of where your espalier will grow. These posts should be set in the ground about 2 feet deep so they will be secure. Staple strands of smooth wire on the posts to make a fence of four or five strands. The bottom wire should be about 2 feet from the ground, and the top three each about a foot apart. Make sure all are securely anchored to the posts so they won't sag.

As the branches begin to grow, snip or rub off all that are not headed in the right direction. As the proper branches grow in length, pull them down and fasten them to the wire so they will form the pattern you want. Use durable plastic, rawhide, or cloth strips to hold the branches. String or wire will cut into the tender bark.

Getting the espalier well established may take two seasons or more. Don't get discouraged if it doesn't look like much the first year. Check it every few days to make sure all the branches are growing the way you want and not sneaking out toward the yard. After your tree is well shaped, the wire trellis can be removed.

PRUNING MATURE ESPALIERS

Whether you buy your espalier trees or create your own, you will find that the pruning process goes on forever. Don't expect the tree to submit to its new role in life without your help. It will constantly try to grow branches in all directions all its life just as nature intended.

You'll be doing most pruning in the summer although other fruit trees are usually pruned during the late winter. Perhaps pruning isn't even the best word, since you will actually be pinching off adventuresome sprouts and thereby preventing growth from getting started in the wrong places. Be very sure that when you snip back all this unwanted growth you are not also cutting off all the spurs or short branches where the flower buds will form, or there will be no fruit.

Pear and apple trees probably make the best espaliers because they are easiest to train. We once had a lovely red flowering crab apple espaliered on our white barn, until we decided to paint the barn red and the tree had to be removed. Peaches, nectarines, and apricots can also be espaliered with a little additional care. It's possible to espalier even cherries, plums, and quinces, but this is so contrary to their bushy habit of growth that it is seldom worth the effort to try to train them. Certain small fruits—blueberries, trailing blackberries, grapes, and even gooseberries (if you don't mind working among the thorns)—can be espaliered in small places where a larger tree is impractical.

As with shrubbery and flowers, if espaliers are planted under the eaves of a building, some protection against ice and sliding snow may be necessary in snow country. Also, additional fertilizer will probably be necessary since rain from the roof usually leaches nutrients from the soil at a more rapid rate than it does when they are not being subjected to the additional wash.

In addition to being planted against buildings and walls, espaliers can be planted in a row to make a living, fruit-producing fence. They are grown just as they would be if they were planted against a wall, except the ends of the limbs of each tree are grafted to the limbs of the next to form one continuous tree. Espalier fences are a beautiful, productive novelty, but they take a lot of work. It's best not to attempt too long a planting if your time is limited.

Two-Story Gardening

Much has been written in favor of two-level or two-story gardening, whereby a crop of berries or vegetables is grown beneath the branches of fruit trees. In some cases this may be possible and even practical, but in most cases it is not. It is difficult to fertilize the soil in such a way that both the tree and the under crop get properly fed, and usually neither enough sun nor rain gets through the tree branches for good growth.

A further danger in growing plants under a fruit tree is that sprays necessary for controlling fruit pests may have to be applied at the time when berries or vegetables growing beneath it or near it are ready for use. Whenever there is room, it is better to give both trees and other crops all the space they need for best growth, and to plant them far apart to avoid contamination.

Landscaping with Fruit

One nice way to enjoy fruit on a small lot is to use fruit trees and bushes instead of ornamentals and shrubs. If you are landscaping a home for the first time or replacing some plantings, why not substitute fruits for the traditional shrubbery?

Most fruit trees can be just as lovely as flowering trees and large shrubs. After all, they bloom too, and their fruit crop gives the effect of a second flowering. We have a Dolgo crab apple in the front yard that thrills us with a profusion of white blossoms each spring and is covered with gorgeous bright red apples every fall—plenty for us, our friends, the freezer, and the migrating Canadian birds who have put us on their route south.

Blueberry plants, currants, and gooseberries all make attractive foundation plants around the house. Put the sun-loving blueberries on the east and south sides, and currants and gooseberries on the west and north. Elderberries make a fine hedge or screen. They will grow in areas that are usually too shady or too moist for other fruits, so they can often be grown on the north side of your building. They grow quite tall, so leave them plenty of room.

Strawberry plants can be used as an edging for flower beds and can be grown in a host of other ornamental ways. I've seen them in hanging baskets, window boxes, jars and pots, barrels with large holes drilled in them (see below), and pyramids. The everbearing varieties that produce fruit the first year are best to use where plants cannot be wintered over in their containers. All of this is beauty you can drink in with your eyes first, and eat later on.

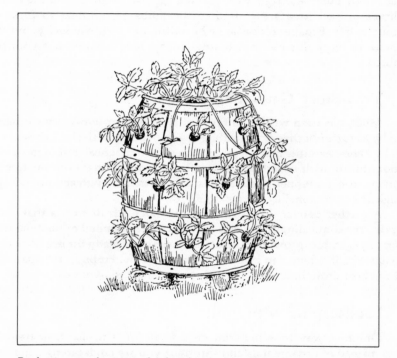

Everbearing strawberries can be planted in barrels, window boxes, hanging baskets, or flower borders to make use of limited space.

4 / OUTWITTING JACK FROST

A friend from Mexico who visited us recently said, "You spend lots of time talking about the weather. We hardly ever mention it at home." It's true. The weather plays an important part in our lives, as it does with most gardeners. About twenty years ago I began keeping a daily record of weather and temperature, hoping that the information would help us better plan our growing program. Now, after two decades, all I really know for sure is that New England weather is cussedly unpredictable, which any Yankee could have told me in the first place.

Weather may change several times a day here, or it can get bogged down and stay the same every single day for six weeks. The last frost of spring can come in late April or in late June. The first frost in fall may come in late August or early November. Snow can arrive first in mid-September or in late December, and snowstorms of a foot or more have descended upon us in late May.

Nearly every part of North America has surprises on the weather scene. Each year we hear of crop failures in one area or another due to unusual weather. In Georgia, Idaho, Minnesota, and even the Deep South, hard winters or late spring frosts can ruin the fruit crop. Few sections of the country can be certain of a good harvest every year.

There are many ways in which cold weather can affect trees. Extremely low temperatures often damage them, but surprisingly it isn't always the low winter temperatures alone that do the most harm. Injury to the limbs and trees is sometimes most severe during mild winters. Even experts are puzzled by some forms of winter injury. Sudden changes in weather can damage trees as much as low temperatures. A long January thaw may cause the tree to begin to grow, or a warm sun in March may heat the tree's brown bark to quite high temperatures. In both cases the sudden return to below-freezing temperatures is a severe shock and is often fatal.

The duration of cold can hurt the tree too. Like animals and humans, a tree can often stand quite considerable cold for a short period, but it will suffer if the situation continues for hours or days. Even though trees are suitable to the area, almost any place can have a prolonged exceptionally cold spell that causes frost damage.

The damage to tree wood can show up as whole limbs that fail to leaf out in the spring. Or you may notice large cracks in the bark. This bark later loosens and falls off, exposing the bare wood underneath and creating ideal conditions for fire blight, cankers, rots, or other infections to enter the tree. Openings in the bark should be sealed with a good tree paint as soon as possible to keep out air and bacteria. Prune back any damaged limbs that cannot be repaired as soon as the damage can be determined in early spring before much sap movement has taken place.

What Is a Hardy Tree for Your Area?

As much as possible, select trees that will stand the weather expected for your region. If you have extra room it is fun to experiment with a few trees intended for a warmer zone, but you'll want to stack the odds somewhat in your favor. You're much more likely to have success if you choose varieties carefully.

To be successful in your orchard, a fruit tree has to meet several requirements. First, it must be able to make its growth during the first part of the growing season, then settle down and harden up before the first frost. It should also be able to ripen its fruit before autumn's killing frosts ruin it. Finally, during the winter the entire tree—fruit buds, branches, trunk, and roots—should be able to withstand the coldest temperatures for their likely duration and not start any growth during winter thaws.

In addition to the other factors that determine hardiness, different parts of the tree or plant have different tolerances to cold. Often the roots and tops of some plants are perfectly hardy but their blossom buds are tender. Strawberries, for example, have very tender buds that are formed in late summer within the crown of the plant. They must be covered for the entire winter in many parts of the country to protect the forming fruit buds and ensure a good crop. Not only are strawberry buds susceptible to winter injury, but the blossoms are also especially sensitive to spring frosts. Strawberries, peaches, plums, and pears tend to bloom early, which makes them a special target of Jack Frost. Even later-blooming fruits like grapes and nuts can be hit because the blooms are so sensitive to even a light frost.

Many people think a tree's hardiness is determined only by the cold temperature it can stand. To the contrary, a short growing season can often limit the choice of fruit varieties you can grow even more than the lowest temperatures. Certain peaches, plums, and nuts are often advertised as being hardy to 20 degrees below zero. This may be true, but what is unsaid is that the trees need a long growing season to properly harden the wood so that it can stand those low temperatures. Some tree fruits, as well as many grapes, nuts, blackberries, and blueberries, are still growing when the first fall frosts hit in certain areas of Zones 3, 4, and 5. Their new wood is often soft and green and the growing cells are killed.

Although the requirements for a successful fruit tree might seem to limit your chances for good growing if you live in a cold region, you don t have to worry. Many varieties of fruits will thrive in each zone, and you have

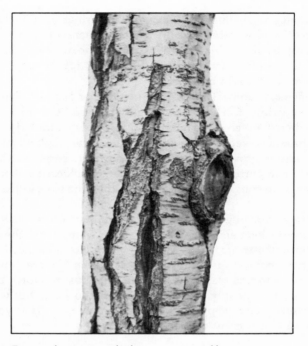

Frost cracks open wounds that can cause trouble later on (University of Illinois).

only to discover which ones are best in your area. The chapters describing each fruit offer help in making your choices.

Older gardeners sometimes complain that trees don't grow as well as they used to. Granted, in the good old days the virgin soil might have been more nourishing and there were fewer weed, insect, and disease problems. The real reason, however, that trees probably grew better several decades ago is because they were usually bought from a nearby nursery that grew them on the spot. Or they were grafted by a local horticulturist who could join good tops to native wild seedlings with apparent ease.

By planting trees that had originated in the same neighborhood, the grower was certain he had trees suitable to his area. Now many of us have to depend on nurseries that may grow their trees hundreds of miles away. Worse yet, many nurseries, garden centers, and sales yards buy their trees from huge wholesale nurseries in the South and Southwest. The high price of northern land and the fact that a tree can be grown faster in the warmer areas have forced many northern nurseries to stop fruit tree production. Many now concentrate on growing the more profitable ornamental shrubs.

Difficult as it may be, the home fruit grower should try to find out the point of origin of the fruit trees he buys and, when possible, select the ones grown in climates most similar to his own. This brings up a lively argument. People disagree over whether it really matters where a tree was grown. Is a McIntosh tree grafted on a Malling rootstock in Alabama really different from the same variety grafted and grown in Quebec? I feel that the ones grown closest to home always do better.

We once saw some Tennessee-grown Sugar Maples planted in Vermont as an experiment. The southern-grown trees held their leaves for a month after their Yankee companions had lost theirs. Similarly, a few years ago some Christmas-tree growers in northern New England planted some Balsam Fir seedlings grown in other states. They were surprised the following spring when the imported trees started to grow much earlier than the native ones, and were also considerably upset when the June frost killed all the new growth.

Can trees from one zone acclimate to another? Often they can if they are able to survive long enough. Both the Sugar Maples and the Balsam Firs imported from warmer areas are becoming more like their northern cousins each year. Trees that are vastly unsuited for another climate, however, have little chance of adapting. Nectarines may never adjust to North Dakota, and the gooseberry will probably never grow well in Louisiana. But we gardeners love to experiment, and keep right on trying out new kinds as you probably will too. It's part of the joy of fruit growing.

Micro-Climates

Although it helps a great deal to know your growing zone, every gardener realizes that within each zone there are many micro-climates where a small area may be a zone or two warmer or colder than the surrounding area. High elevation, air drainage, fog, inversions, frost pockets, prevailing air currents, proximity to bodies of water, and many other conditions cause these variances. It makes frustrated gardeners bemoan the fact that they can't grow a certain plant, while the Joneses who live ten miles away can grow the same variety beautifully with no trouble whatsoever.

Artificial Climates

In Iceland, Alaska, and in much of northern Europe, many fruits and vegetables are grown in glass or plastic houses. With the generous supply of land and excellent transportation system in the continental United States, this method of growing is seldom done seriously. But many gardeners have built hobby houses and enjoy growing varieties of fruit that wouldn't ordinarily grow in their zone. Greenhouses make it possible to grow dwarf peaches, pears, cherries, and grapes even in Zone 3.

There are many types of structures suitable for this. One kind often used consists of a frame built around and over the trees. Sometimes an above-ground swimming pool is also included. During the summer the trees are allowed to grow naturally with only usual care. In late summer, before the nights begin to cool off too much, the frame is completely covered with clear four or six mil polyethylene plastic. This keeps the trees frost-free until late November. During the winter the ground and even the pool are allowed to freeze, but since temperatures are greatly modified inside the building, neither freezes to a great depth. In early summer when all danger of even a mild frost is over, the plastic is removed.

Usually no artificial heat is needed because the ground and pool, if one is used, soak up the daytime heat and release it during the cold nights. In areas of extreme cold, two layers of plastic, one outside and one inside the frame, may be necessary. Covering the side walls with fiberglass, which is left on all year, saves part of the work of replacing the plastic. It also shelters heat-loving plants from cool winds during the summer. Water and ventilation must be provided all the time the building is entirely covered. On sunny days, even in midwinter, the temperature may go well over 100 degrees. Opening a window or having a fan that works on a thermostat can provide ventilation.

Some problems may occur in this artificial climate. Disease and insects may be more prevalent since most natural controls are missing. Of course, some provision must also be made for pollinating the early-blooming trees. If there are bees in the neighborhood you can simply open the door when the trees are blossoming. Without bees, you'll have to pollinate by hand.

All in all, fruit growing in a greenhouse can be an interesting hobby. Whether or not it is worth the time, money, and work involved is up to you. Most of us will probably choose to do our gardening outdoors, facing the weather head-on. Whether we live in Bismarck or Tallahassee, Bangor or Spokane, it is not likely that every fruit and berry we grow will have a vintage crop every year. With good planning and care, however, there should be enough successes to far outweigh the failures, making it all worthwhile.

I can't overemphasize the fact that you shouldn't make any large plantings of fruits for yourself or as a commercial venture until you have grown a few of them successfully in the same area for six or seven years. This advice comes from bitter past experience—my own failures and those of many other gardeners I've known.

To sum up, you can use various schemes to protect your trees from frosts and you can repair winter damage, but the best way to outwit the weather is to choose fruit varieties that are as hardy as possible for your climate. This means searching out the trees that will grow in the length of growing season you have as well as the ones that are temperature hardy.

The zones of plant hardiness (based on USDA *map)*

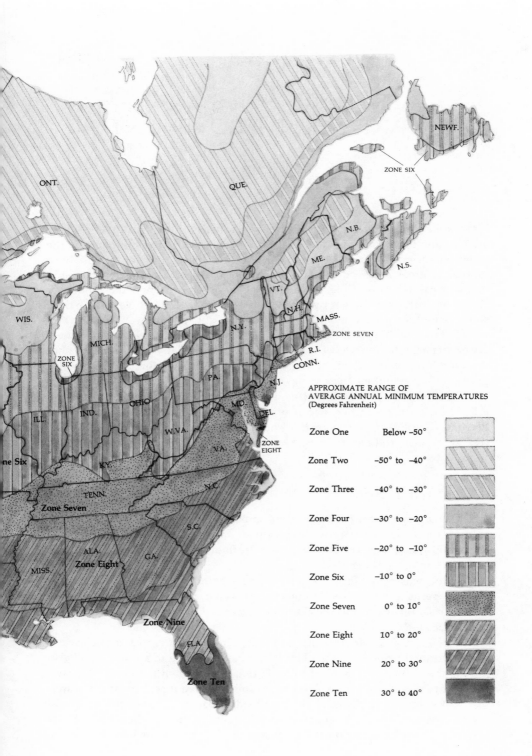

ONT.

QUE.

NEWF.

ZONE SIX

N.B.

ME.

N.S.

VT.

N.H.

WIS.

N.Y.

MASS.

ZONE SEVEN

MICH.

R.I.

ZONE
SIX

CONN.

PA.

N.J.

OHIO

MD.

ILL.   IND.

DEL.

W.VA.

ZONE
EIGHT

ne Six

VA.

KY.

N.C.

TENN.

Zone Seven

S.C.

ALA.

Zone Eight

GA.

MISS.

Zone Nine

FLA.

Zone Ten

APPROXIMATE RANGE OF
AVERAGE ANNUAL MINIMUM TEMPERATURES
(Degrees Fahrenheit)

Zone One	Below −50°	
Zone Two	−50° to −40°	
Zone Three	−40° to −30°	
Zone Four	−30° to −20°	
Zone Five	−20° to −10°	
Zone Six	−10° to 0°	
Zone Seven	0° to 10°	
Zone Eight	10° to 20°	
Zone Nine	20° to 30°	
Zone Ten	30° to 40°	

5 / ORCHARD SOILS
AND SOIL IMPROVEMENT

How was your diet yesterday? If all you had was a little weak tea, chances are you don't feel too much like an evening of square dancing or painting the spare bedroom. If you had three healthy meals, you're much more likely to be feeling great and ready to take on anything. Nobody considers a steady diet of weak tea as sensible, but a great many home gardeners feel somehow that their fruit trees can get by nicely on even less. Often people tell me their trees are looking poorly and ask what could possibly be wrong. "What do you use for fertilizer?" I ask. "Fertilizer?" they say, looking puzzled. While there are gardeners who overfeed their trees and are continually giving them a shot of something or other, many more seem to neglect feeding altogether. Or perhaps they give their trees some preparation that is of little nutritive value.

When you plant a fruit tree, keep in mind that with proper care and a little luck with weather, it can produce a good many tons of fruit in its lifetime. The soil around your tree contains the elements that will make the tree grow and produce its fruit. You'll want to understand that soil.

What Is Soil?

Years ago I mentioned to a group of gardeners that they should mix manure with the dirt before planting their trees. A lady immediately protested. "Dirt is something you sweep off the floor," she said indignantly. "Soil is what you are talking about."

She was right. Probably dirt farmers should be properly called soil farmers because soil is definitely not the same as dirt. Soil is something special. It is full of life and provides the right conditions for plant life to grow and thrive.

Soil contains mineral nutrients, clay, sand and other rock particles, and humus formed from decaying plant life, plus moisture and air. Good soil also has an abundance of beneficial bacteria that break down the organic matter, and plenty of earthworms to loosen the soil and give it texture and fertility.

If you have gardened at all you already know that soil comes in several layers. The top layer is the most important because that is where most of the action is. Topsoil has the most humus and fertility and is the loosest. It is the layer where most root activity takes place. The subsoil, the next layer down, is usually quite hard. It contains mostly minerals and possibly traces of organic material from long ago. Often it's filled with lumps of clay, veins of gravel or sand, and large rocks. Roots of trees, particularly deep-rooted trees, do penetrate this subsoil and get many mineral nutrients from it. Farther down is the hardpan, which is a thick layer of clay. Roots cannot penetrate it easily and, except for breaks or faults, water cannot move freely through it.

The depths of both the soil and the subsoil vary greatly from place to place. Very few sections are blessed with deep fertile soil of just the right texture, moisture-retaining ability, and alkalinity. Most of us have to doctor up our soils. Therefore it is very important to diagnose soil problems and correct them, not only when you plant your trees but every year.

Organic and Chemical Gardeners

Some scientific gardeners regard soil as something that merely holds up the tree and acts as a temporary repository for the nutrients and moisture. They find out all the nutrients a tree is supposed to need, mix them in the correct proportion, then feed the concoction to the tree in somewhat the same way a critically ill patient is fed in the hospital.

Organic gardeners have a completely different viewpoint toward soil. To them, the soil is a living thing. They believe it should have an abundance of decaying organic matter plus any necessary additional minerals in natural form. They dislike leaving it bare and, whenever possible, try to protect this valuable soil by making sure it is always covered with mulch, grass, or some other living crop. They also like it to be loose, spongy, and full of earthworms.

Organic gardeners believe that if a tree has available an abundance of nutrients in natural form, it will select the kinds and amounts it needs for best growth. They think that chemical gardeners tend to "force" their trees to take the highly soluble plant foods whether they need them or not, causing uneven growth and consequently a weak tree. Since they believe that the main functions of disease and insects are to eliminate the weak, they feel that trees grown in a "natural" environment will be more pest-resistant. It follows, they maintain, that people who eat food grown on healthy trees and plants are healthier people.

Since chemical and organic gardeners are kilometers apart in their thinking, naturally there is a third group who feel that the truth is somewhere in between. The middle-of-the-roaders don't think of the ammonium nitrate growers as mad scientists out to destroy the world with test tubes. Nor do they see the smelly compost makers as narrow-minded activists standing in progress's four-lane highway with pitchforks. Instead, they try to use the best methods of both groups. They believe in good healthy organic soils, deep mulches, and recycling garden wastes, but they feel no guilt about adding a little chemical fertilizer if the tree seems to lack something. Nor do they mind reaching for the spray gun if bugs mount an attack. In recent years this third group has attracted a great many followers.

Your Soil and How to Improve It

To help understand what is going on beneath the surface of the orchard, let's divide the properties of soil into three important parts: structure, condition, and fertility.

Soil structure can mean the general makeup of the soil—whether it is sandy, clay, rocky, marshy, or worn-out powdery dust. Because trees need considerable room to freely spread out their roots, neither rocks, heavy clays, nor wet mucky soils provide good growing conditions. Neither does pure sand, since it dries out too fast.

It's no secret that soil structure is one of the hardest things to improve. If you are stuck with a thin layer of soil over solid rock, there is little you can do short of hauling in many loads of topsoil. New house owners often have a real soil problem because builders usually scrape off all the good topsoil and put back only a few inches for a lawn.

Wet areas may sometimes be drained by ditching, but if the area is very wet it may not be worth the trouble to adequately drain it.

Sandy soils can be given more fertility and moisture-holding capability by working in shredded bark, manure, leaf mold, peat moss, or compost. Heavy loam soils can be lightened in the same way, and also by adding large quantities of sand. Clay subsoils can be broken up by deep plowing or dynamite, although neither of these methods may be feasible for someone who owns a small piece of land.

Mulches can gradually improve soil by preventing erosion from sun, wind, and rain, and by adding nutrients and humus. If you're working with a large area, plowing under crops of green material such as clover, oats, or winter rye can add humus and tilth to the soil, a process called green manuring.

A home orchardist should never despair if his soil is not the best. If you can grow a vegetable garden or a lush lawn, the soil can usually be put in shape for berries and fruits. If it is not deep enough for the root systems of full-size trees, dwarf trees may do very nicely there.

Soil condition can be regarded as the pH, or alkaline-acidity, of the soil, and is caused by the breakdown of water molecules in the soil into positive and negative ions. The soil's mineral and organic materials affect this breakdown. For example, the presence of calcium limestone causes alkaline soils, whereas the presence of peat, sulfur, or aluminum causes the soil to be acid.

All plants and trees seem to have a certain pH at which they can best use fertilizer. When soil becomes too acid (sour) or too alkaline (sweet) for the plants, the fertilizer nutrients remain locked within the soil and the plant can't get at them. It is something like a hungry man with his hands tied to the chair at Thanksgiving dinner!

Some plants—certain weeds and grasses, for instance—can grow over a wide range of soil pH. Others have a very limited range and are very fussy. Most cultivated soils range from 4 to 8 on the pH scale. Seven is neutral, being neither acid nor alkaline. Anything below 7 is acid and anything over is alkaline. Blueberries will not grow at all well unless the soil is very acid (4½). Plums and peaches prefer about 6; apples like 6½ to 7. Strawberries and blackberries grow best at the 5 to 6 range, and raspberries like it slightly higher.

These pH scales shouldn't cause you any worry because, except for blueberries, most fruits will grow well in ordinary garden soils, which usually test from 5½ to 7. If you are in doubt about your own soil, the little soil acidity test kits are simple to use and inexpensive to buy. Many garden supply houses have them. For a little more money you can get a complete testing kit that will also show your soil's fertility.

Soil condition is easy to improve. Acid soils can be made more alkaline by the use of lime. For fast results, lime can be worked into the earth by cultivation or rototilling; or it can be spread evenly on top to be carried in by rains. The pH of the soil can be raised one point by applying 10 pounds of lime per 100 square feet (a square area 10 feet by 10 feet or a circle area about 12 feet in diameter). Avoid overdoses of lime, however. Because it is cheap, it is tempting to add large amounts. But too much lime, like too little, locks up the fertilizer and stops tree growth. It can also cut off the flow of nutrients to the growing fruits and cause a good number of them to drop before they are fully ripe.

Lowering the pH is seldom necessary since acid soils are far more common than alkaline ones. But if it is necessary, 3 or 4 pounds of powdered sulfur per 100 square feet will lower the pH one point on ordinary soils. On sandy soils, aluminum sulfate often works better than sulfur. Follow the directions on the package. For organic gardeners, quantities of cottonseed meal, composted oak leaves, peat moss, or mulches of pine needles all help in acidifying soil and keeping it acid.

Soil fertility is determined by the amount of nutrients in the soil and their availability to the plants. Despite what you may hear, it is difficult for even an expert to look at a soil and guess how rich it is. But it is safe to assume that ordinary soils are so badly depleted both by erosion and use that most orchard and berry crops will need some additional fertilizer every year.

Here are the main elements needed for plant nutrition:

Nitrogen. This is one of the nutrients most needed for good fruit tree growth and the one usually lacking in most soils. Gardeners who use vast quantities of greensand, wood ashes, granite dust, and rock phosphate often fail to realize that none of these supply much nitrogen. Nitrogen is supplied naturally in small amounts from the air. Thunderstorms make larger amounts available to nourish the earth—you've probably noticed how plants spruce up after a summer shower. The gardener can also add nitrogen by using certain nitrates and other chemicals, manures, or butcher shop wastes such as bloodmeal, bone meal, and tankage.

35

Phosphorus. This necessary element is supplied by rock phosphate, bone meal, manures, superphosphate, and other organic and chemical fertilizers.

Potash. Greensand, granite dust, and wood ashes supply organic gardeners with this element. Chemical-minded growers rely on potash salts of various kinds.

Trace elements. Dozens of other elements, from boron to zinc, are used by trees and plants in various amounts. Home owners seldom have to be concerned because usually the soil alone can supply the minute amounts needed. Manure, compost (especially composted leaves), and greensand can usually supply the rest. Trace elements are also available commercially. These are sometimes fritted on small particles of glass that release them slowly. Many trace elements are needed in such tiny amounts that there is still not much known about their effect on plant life. It is quite certain they should be used sparingly because if they are present in the soil except in minute amounts, many are very poisonous to plants.

How to Feed a Tree

While slow-acting organic fertilizers and mulches can usually be applied safely any time of year, I am a firm believer that very early spring, as

How to feed a tree. Fertilizer is spread in the shaded area
where the feeding roots of the tree are located.
Heaviest feeding should be toward the outside of the circle.

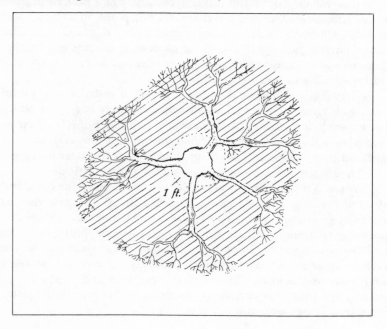

soon as the ground thaws, is the best time for applying all fertilizer. The second best time is late fall, just before the ground freezes. Fertilizers that are spread early can get into the soil quickly while it is still moist. The spring rains can work it down toward the tree's roots, ready for the tree to use just when the need is greatest for growth and setting its fruit.

The tree root zone covers just about the same area as that of the branches, and it looks much the same. As with the branches, the large roots are near the trunk and the small fibrous hair roots that actually pull in the nutrients are farther away. The roots that feed the tree are therefore in a circle beginning about a foot or two from the trunk and continuing to the outside spread of the branches. The fertilizer you put too close to the trunk or spread much outside the branch area is likely to be wasted (see page 36).

Neither fertilizer nor lime should be spread on frozen ground unless it is heavily mulched, for melting snows or rains can easily wash it all away. If you mulch your trees, it is better to pull off the mulch and spread the fertilizer directly on the soil. Then replace the mulch and add more if necessary. Mulched trees need much less fertilizer and lime than cultivated ones because they are better protected against erosion. In fact, if you add enough new mulch each year and the soil is reasonably good, this may often be all the fertilizer a tree requires.

Since most soils are worn out or badly eroded, fertilizer is something they always seem to need. It can be bought, collected, or made. Home gardeners have developed so many methods of acquiring fertilizer that garden magazines continually list new ones.

Those who are ecological-minded use large quantities of farm manure when it is available, and they compost kitchen and garden wastes. Such varied things as hair from the local barber and night soil find their way into orchard and garden. There is a considerable argument over recycling human wastes in the production of human food, but many people think that if it is composted a year or more, all dangerous bacteria is destroyed.

When commercial fertilizer is purchased, whether chemical or organic, the analysis is always printed on the bag as required by law. It is listed in numbers, such as 5-10-10. The first number indicates the percentage of nitrogen by weight; the second, phosphorus; and the third, potash. Thus a 100-pound bag of 5-10-10 fertilizer contains 5 pounds of nitrogen and 10 pounds each of phosphorus and potash, all in compounds that can be handled safely and will break down rapidly to furnish fertility to the plants. Most of the other weight consists of a filler of inert ingredients, sometimes lime. A 50-pound bag, the size you'd usually buy, contains half as much of each element.

A complete fertilizer contains at least some of all three of these prime elements. An incomplete one would have only one or two. Thus rock phosphate could be listed 0-30-0, some superphosphates as 0-20-0, and bone meal as 4-20-0. The actual analysis—that is, the percentage of each element present—may be higher than is listed on the package since most companies do not want to get into trouble by listing their formulas too low.

In selecting an orchard fertilizer, choose one that contains all three ingredients plus any others your extension service may recommend. Because there are so many kinds of fertilizer available to collect or buy, an enthusiastic gardener may be tempted to overfeed his trees. Keep in mind that twice as much is *not* twice as good.

The following list contains some of the more common fertilizers and the approximate analysis of each. The "amount to apply" listed here is meant for one application per year, unless otherwise stated. Naturally, these amounts are only to serve as a guide to new orchardists. As you gain experience you'll use slightly more or less than the suggested amount, depending on your soil and the demands of each tree.

ORGANIC FERTILIZERS

Animal tankage. A byproduct of the meat industry; 8 percent nitrogen, 20 percent phosphorus. Rather smelly, even when dried, but it does make things grow. Use 3 pounds per 100 square feet.

Bloodmeal. Dried animal blood. Good fertilizer and deer repellent. Use with wood ashes or greensand in combination with bone meal or rock phosphate for a complete fertilizer. Use 1 or 2 pounds per 100 square feet.

Bone meal. Finely ground animal bones. Use with greensand or wood ashes. Steamed bone meal is sometimes available and works faster. Use 3 pounds per 100 square feet.

Cottonseed meal. Good on acid-loving plants such as blueberries; 7 percent nitrogen, 3 percent phosphorus, 2 percent potash. Use 5 pounds per 100 square feet.

Cow or sheep manure (dried). 5 percent nitrogen, 3 percent phosphorus, 5 percent potash. Use 10 pounds per 100 square feet.

Greensand. Material from ocean deposits. Use with another fertilizer that contains nitrogen, such as bloodmeal, cottonseed meal, or manure; 2 percent phosphorus, 6 percent potash, and many additional trace elements. Use 5 pounds per 100 square feet.

Poultry manure (dried). Another strong smeller. Some gardeners think trees grow just to get away from it. This is more powerful than cow and sheep manure, so less is needed. Use 6 pounds per 100 square feet.

Raw manure. Fresh or aged raw manure is sometimes available from farms or homesteads. If fresh, it is better not to work it into the soil without composting (see end of chapter). Fresh manure can be put on top of the ground around trees or berries or under mulches if applied in early spring or late fall after fruit is harvested. Cow, sheep, horse, and pig manure can be applied at the rate of 100 pounds per 100 square feet. Poultry manure can be applied at 30 pounds per 100 square feet.

Rock phosphate. Natural phosphate rock ground very fine; 30 percent phosphorus. Becomes available to trees extremely slowly; should last three years. Use with nitrogen and potash fertilizers. Use 5 pounds per 100 square feet.

Wood ashes. Used to make soil more alkaline; 7 percent potash. Combine with fertilizers that contain nitrogen and phosphorus. Use 5 pounds per 100 square feet.

LIQUID ORGANIC FERTILIZERS

Fish emulsions and various commercial products such as liquid Fertril are available to give plants a quick start if necessary. If you have manure at home you can make a good liquid fertilizer, manure tea (sometimes called manure tonic water). Just mix manure—either fresh or dried—and water.

DRY CHEMICAL FERTILIZERS

5-10-10. The most commonly used commercial fertilizer. It is sold under many trade names with a wide range of prices. Start with 1 or 2 pounds per 100 square feet per year.

5-10-10-2. Same as above with 2 percent of another chemical added, one that is recommended for certain crops or soils that require larger than average amounts. Boron, magnesium, and manganese are most often added. Get the formula that is recommended for your area and crop.

10-10-10 or 15-10-10. Fertilizers with two or three times as much nitrogen as the 5-10-10 formula. These should be used very sparingly by the beginning gardener, if at all. As well as the danger of burning plants, overfertilizing can cause excess foliage growth and delay bearing. It can also lead to poor coloring in the fruit on older trees.

LIQUID CHEMICAL FERTILIZERS

Many liquid fertilizers such as Rapid-Gro are available. These can be used on newly transplanted trees to ease planting shock, and for stimulating growth early in the season. As with all chemicals, they should be used carefully, according to directions on the container.

SLOW-RELEASE FERTILIZERS

To give chemical fertilizers some of the advantages of organic ones, quite a few control-release fertilizers such as Magamp and Osmocote are now on the market. These are much more expensive than ordinary fertilizers, but they release their nutrients over a period of weeks or months, assuring a long season of even feeding for the tree. They also reduce the likelihood of burning from using too much fertilizer, and leaching is less likely to occur with these products. Also on the market are fertilizers in a "pill" form that orchardists can bury near their trees for long-time, slow-release feeding.

You can make your own slow-release fertilizer by putting half a cup of 5-10-10 fertilizer in a plastic bag and punching two or three holes in it with a pencil Two bags—one on each side of the tree and near the outside spread of the branches—can feed a mature dwarf fruit tree all season. Six or more bags would be required for a mature full-size tree.

MULCHES

You probably won't want to mulch your fruit trees if they are part of the landscaping on your front lawn. But if your orchard and berry plants are in a less developed part of your lot, a mulch is such a great advantage in growing trees you'll want to use it. Mulches suppress weeds and grasses that steal soil nutrients. They control moisture by preventing evaporation. They protect against soil washing away. They encourage earthworms. They guard against too rapid freezing and thawing of the ground. And when they rot they add humus and fertility to the soil.

To mulch, you spread a layer of organic material several inches deep to cover the soil around the tree, from the trunk to the outside spread of the branches. Renew it whenever necessary, which usually means at least once a year. The mulch can be leaves or bark or peat or any number of things (see box).

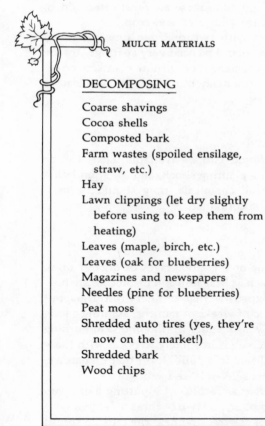

MULCH MATERIALS

DECOMPOSING

Coarse shavings
Cocoa shells
Composted bark
Farm wastes (spoiled ensilage,
    straw, etc.)
Hay
Lawn clippings (let dry slightly
    before using to keep them from
    heating)
Leaves (maple, birch, etc.)
Leaves (oak for blueberries)
Magazines and newspapers
Needles (pine for blueberries)
Peat moss
Shredded auto tires (yes, they're
    now on the market!)
Shredded bark
Wood chips

NONDECOMPOSING

Black plastic
Crushed rock or gravel
Flat rocks or slate
Marble, granite, or asbestos
    rock chips

Mulches are also good for berry bushes, but those of a long-lasting nature such as shavings and wood chips shouldn't be used on strawberry beds which will be plowed back into the soil within a year or two because they'll damage the soil. Straw or leaves make better mulches for them. Besides all the other advantages, mulches keep rains from spattering dirt on the ripening berries.

Nonorganic mulches are sometimes used on trees and berry bushes. They often look better and usually do most of the things organic mulches do, except add much humus or fertilizer. Blueberry growers often spread black

A mulch suppresses weeds, helps retain moisture, and helps prevent frost heaves.

plastic around their plants, and some suburban gardeners like the clean appearance of crushed rock, flagstones, marble chips, or slate. These mulches are less of a fire hazard and, except for the plastic, all of them last for many years.

LEAVES AS FERTILIZER

One of the best fertilizers I have ever used is also one of the cheapest: leaves. If you are lucky enough to live in an area where they lie in large heaps on the ground every fall, consider them a gift from nature and scoop them up. Leaves are an excellent soil conditioner. They contain all the nutrients a growing fruit tree would ever want, because they come from large trees whose roots reach far into the subsoil, getting trace elements that shallow-rooted trees and plants would miss.

Leaves can be composted for a year or more before use, or they can be shredded with a shredder and added immediately to the soil, or they can be used as a mulch. They work well in any way. If you mulch with them, simply pile them around the tree several inches deep as soon as they are gathered, letting the composting take place under the tree. The autumn winds

POSSIBLE SOURCES FOR FREE
OR LOW-COST FERTILIZERS FOR COMPOST AND MULCHES

MANURES

Farms
Kennels
Packinghouses
Racetracks
Stables
Zoos

VEGETABLE AND FRUIT WASTES

Processing plants
Restaurants
Stores

SHAVINGS, BARK, CHIPS

Furniture factories
Paper mills
Wood plants and sawmills

LEAVES

Country roads
Parks
Street departments

PAPER AND CARDBOARD

Newspaper offices
Rubbish collectors

HAY AND STRAW

Farms (spoiled hay is sometimes very low-priced)
Seaweeds, marsh hay (sometimes available in garden stores)

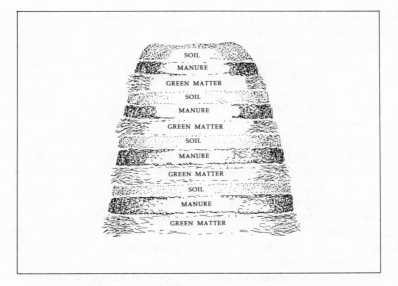

*A compost pile is made of alternate layers of manure, soil,
and green waste matter. The drawing shows layers after compressing.
Keep the pile moist and covered to hasten decomposition.*

will likely blow them away unless you find a way to hold them down. Hay, shredded bark, or shavings are all good for this purpose. After a few months the leaves will decompose and turn to leaf mold, one of the most wonderful fertilizers there is. An abundance of earthworms will appear, and hundreds of new root hairs will begin growing.

Some people feel that all leaves are acid. It is true that oak leaves are. Maple leaves are not, however, and neither are the leaves of most other common shade trees. A little lime or wood ashes can neutralize oak leaves if they are used.

Leaves can be gathered from forests, along back roads, or neighbors' lawns—if no one minds. Municipal crews are often glad to have a place to dump their leaf collections. Since the leaves of one mature maple tree are estimated to contain about $20 worth of fertilizer, rake on and watch your trees grow lavishly.

COMPOST

Composting does in a faster and more controllable way what nature does all the time in gardens, fields, and forests. It is the rotting of organic waste material which provides humus to grow more plants and trees (see page 42).

Gardeners and orchardists make their compost piles by piling wastes in heaps to increase the heating process and therefore speed up decomposition. It works best to alternate layers of soil 1 or 2 inches thick, layers of manure 2 or 3 inches thick, and layers of green material (leaves, garbage, garden wastes) 5–8 inches thick (before compressing; see page 43).

The piles can be enclosed in neat pens you can buy ready-made; or you can construct your own bins from stone, boards, or cement blocks. Some people don't enclose their compost at all. There are some towns that forbid open compost piles, so it is well to check local laws. Of course you can always make compost on a small scale in large covered garbage cans in a garage, basement, or outdoors.

Compost heaps should stand about 2–3 feet high after settling has taken place. Be sure to keep the pile flat so rain will soak in and not run off. If they are properly made, there will be no unpleasant smell either when the compost is rotting or while it is being used.

Most gardeners like to have three compost piles: one which is being made, a second in the process of rotting, and a third being used. In most areas it takes a full year to rot compost properly, but keeping the heap wet during dry weather speeds up rotting. Bacteria activators are also available if you want faster decomposition.

It is possible to develop a good soil, even if nature willed you something less. With all the possibilities for free and low-cost fertilizer, it needn't be expensive, either, and will make all the difference between puny, struggling plants and thriving, healthy specimens.

6 / PLANTING THE TREE AND GETTING IT OFF TO A GOOD START

Every spring we used to observe Arbor Day at our little country school. If every tree planted over the years had survived, the school would now stand in a forest. Instead it has very few trees around it today.

The tree-planting ceremony was quite impressive. After a salute to the flag, someone especially chosen would dig the hole and another would plant the tree. A decree which had gone out from the Governor was duly read, and someone always recited "Trees" by Joyce Kilmer, and it went on and on. Finally the group would sing an appropriate song, completely off-key. The tree seldom lived. The ceremony was well organized and the poetry more than adequate, but we were all a little deficient in our planting ability. Although we were mostly from farm families experienced in growing vegetables, grains, and hay, few of us had planted trees. Our ancestors had spent years clearing the land. To them, a tree was something for an Indian to hide behind.

Looking back on those days, I'm surprised that any of our Arbor Day trees ever survived. No one considered that the tree might be planted too shallow or too deep. No one thought it might be suffering more than we were, as the poems and readings went on, both they and the tree getting drier and drier. No one ever thought to wrap the tree's roots or to bring a pail of water. Thousands of trees later I still meet many people who think that ceremony is more important than proper planting. Some people check the phase of the moon but forget to water. Some worry about whether the tree should face the same direction it originally grew, or if perhaps it should be planted before sunup for the best results. They are more fascinated by ritual than by good soil and fertilizer. Planting success can never be assured merely by bowing thrice toward the fruit goddess Pomona, but it can be helped along by attention to seemingly minor details.

Many times gardeners hurry the planting operation too much. Trees they've ordered during winter's leisure arrive during the spring rush. Often their new owners unwrap them by pulling off the strings too hastily and scraping their bark in the process. Then the defenseless trees are allowed to lie in the sun and wind while a too-small hole is quickly dug for each one. Roots are crammed in, the soil is heaped over only part of them, and the tree is left to its own devices. "Why did my tree die?" the owner puzzles. "Must be it wasn't any good to begin with."

Lots of puttering is unnecessary when setting a tree into the soil, but each one should be handled and planted carefully. If the tree comes bare-rooted—that is, without soil surrounding the roots in a pot or a ball—remember to treat it like a fish. It can't live long without lots of moisture. Potted or balled trees should never be allowed to dry out, either.

Most mail-order trees will be shipped bare-rooted, packed in moisture-retaining wrapping. Trees purchased at a local nursery or garden center may also be bare-rooted, or they may be potted or balled. Balled or potted trees can be planted successfully at any time of the year when the ground isn't

A common mistake in planting is to dig too small a hole. The roots should not be crowded and should have plenty of loose soil to get started in. This hole should have been at least three times as large.

frozen. It's best to plant bare-rooted trees in the spring before growth starts in northern areas. In Zones 6 and warmer they usually can be safely planted in the fall.

Bare-rooted trees are almost always the cheapest to buy. They were probably dug in the fall, stored in controlled temperature and humidity during the winter, then wrapped and shipped in the spring. They are likely to be quite dry when they reach your doorstep. Your first and very important step when they arrive is to unwrap them at once and soak the roots for several hours in a tub or a pond of water (see page 48). Don't worry if they arrive on a cold day. Even if the roots are frozen, there is no problem as long as they thaw slowly. Put the package in a cool basement or garage and let the tree warm up gradually. Then soak the roots. After a few hours of soaking, the tree should be planted.

The planting is done in much the same way for each tree, whether it comes to you bare-rooted, balled, or potted. Since presumably you've already chosen a good location, the next step is to dig a hole much larger than necessary—one the size of a bushel basket should be adequate. Put all the soil that has been taken out in two heaps, with the good topsoil on one side and the poorer subsoil on the other (see page 48).

Mix generous amounts of compost and manure or dried blood with the topsoil. About half soil and half organic matter is a good proportion. A bushel of this mixture is about right for an average-size tree, and should adequately fill the hole you have dug. (Do *not* use any dry granular chemical fertilizer at this point because it is much too strong for a tender new tree.) Enough of this mix should be put back in the hole so that the tree can be set at about the same ground level as it grew in the field or pot. On a bare-rooted tree you can find this level on the tree bark just above the roots. Planting a tree too deep smothers the roots and usually kills the tree; planting it too shallow causes the roots to dry out.

Now hold the tree carefully, making sure it's standing straight and at the right planting depth, with the roots well spread out. Then put back enough of the soil mix to barely cover the roots. Fill the hole completely with water. Allow the water to soak into the soil mix and drive out any pockets of air that could dry out the roots (see page 49).

With the rest of the soil mix, finish filling the hole to nearly ground level. Be careful not to damage the tree with the shovel during the process —the young bark is tender and can't stand rough treatment. It may be necessary to use a little of the subsoil you've dug up too, but most of it should be carted away and discarded. Giving your tree's roots the best start possible is very important.

Remove any plastic wrapping or containers from balled or potted trees, but be sure that the soil that is surrounding the roots is kept intact. I heard of one gardener who shook all the soil off the roots before he planted his potted tree. By doing this he lost all the little roots that make a balled or potted tree superior to a bare-rooted one.

The tree should be staked if necessary and a slight depression or saucer should be left around the tree to trap rain and future waterings. Unless it rains really hard, a newly planted tree should be thoroughly watered two or three times a week. Each time it will take a whole pail of water poured on slowly to reach the bottom of the roots. Keep watering until the tree is well established, at least a month. This watering cannot be emphasized too heavily. It is the cheapest, quickest, and most dependable way to get your tree off to a fast start. One nursery furnishes a packet of tablets with each tree and gives the customer instructions to put a tablet in a pail of water and to water the tree every other day. The tablets, like the doctor's sugar pills, do nothing. But they often accomplish their purpose by reminding people to water.

Right: bare-rooted trees
and bushes should be soaked
in a tub of water
for several hours before planting.

Below: when planting, dig a hole
more than large enough to contain
all the roots without crowding (A).
Put the good topsoil on one
side of the hole, the poorer
subsoil on the other. Mix compost
or manure and peat moss with
the good soil and put enough back
into the hole so that the tree
can be planted at the same depth
at which it grew before being
replanted (B). *Pack the soil firmly.*

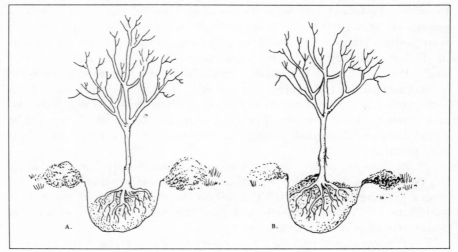

Even though water is beneficial for your young tree, don't follow the example of one of our neighbors. He left the hose running on one small tree for an entire weekend. By Monday morning his poor tree had drowned. Overwatering is definitely not a good idea.

If you like you can add manure or a small amount of liquid fertilizer such as fish emulsion or manure mixed with water to every other watering to feed the tree and give it a faster start (see page 39).

A good deep soil is very important if you want a healthy tree. If you hit a rock ledge or hard clay when you dig the hole for it, seek out another location. The tree's roots can find their way around small rocks, but if the soil is too shallow, your planting will be doomed from the start. Digging a pocket in a shallow vein of clay to plant the tree is not recommended either. Water is likely to collect there and drown the tree. Attempts to break up subsoil are usually frustrating and should be done as a last resort only if no other location is available. If absolutely necessary, iron bars, pickaxes, tractor subsoilers, and even dynamite can do the job.

Pruning

After the tree has been planted it should be pruned immediately if you received it balled or bare-rooted. (If the tree has grown in its pot for a year or more, no pruning is necessary.) The reason for pruning at this early stage is so the top will balance the roots. When your tree was dug before you got it, some of the roots were cut off and a corresponding amount of top should be cut back to compensate for this loss. If the tree is not pruned, a lot of little branches and leaves will begin to grow faster than the roots are growing

Slowly pour a whole bucket of water into the hole (A). Fill the hole nearly to the top with the remaining soil-compost mix. Leave a slight depression to catch rain and future waterings (B).

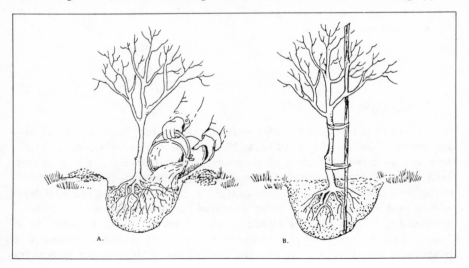

A.   B.

to support them. By holding back this top growth you encourage the roots to keep ahead of the top and thereby make a stronger tree.

Some people like to prune severely and cut the tree back to a stub, as shown below (A). Others remove only the weakest branches, leaving the rest. Personally, I prefer to trim all the weak and broken branches, cut back the strong ones at least half, and then cut back the top to about three-fourths its original height and just above a strong, fat bud. The tree will look pretty well chopped up, but it will grow and thrive far better than if it were planted with all its branches intact (B).

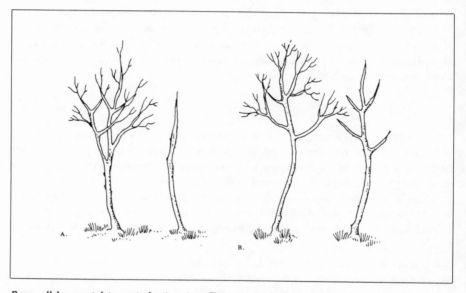

Prune all bare-rooted trees at planting time. Tree A *is cut back to a whip. Tree* B *has all limbs partly cut back.*

Staking

Newly planted, standard-size fruit trees seldom need staking if they are carefully set in and pruned back. However, in very windy areas the trees may lean with the prevailing winds unless they are given some help in their early years. Another exception is dwarf trees, which are extremely shallow-rooted and often benefit greatly from staking. If you need to stake, first drive a large post in near the tree. Wrap a strip of burlap around the tree trunk—some use cloth or a piece of strong plastic or even stockings or panty hose. Then secure the wrapped part of the tree to the post. Avoid using any kind of string or wire that may cut into the tender bark of the tree. As soon as the trees begin to grow and their roots become well anchored, staking will probably no longer be necessary.

Mulching

Unless your tree is living in a well-manicured lawn, you will probably want to mulch around it after it is planted. As explained in Chapter 5, a mulch will help hold moisture, suppress grass and weeds, and help feed and protect the tree. Mulches are best made of organic matter that can rot and gradually add fertility to the soil.

Make a Chart

If you haven't already done so when you planned your orchard, be sure to make a chart as soon as you finish planting. Varieties, dates, and any other information should be recorded. When the tree arrives it may have labels wired on its limbs. These should be removed to prevent girdling the tree as it grows. Even plastic or paper labels will soon fade and fall off, so a permanent chart in a safe place is your only sure way of knowing what you planted.

The First Years

After its initial pruning your young tree will need very little additional pruning until it begins to produce fruit. Only some frequent minor clipping or pinching of branches is necessary to get it to grow into a good shape. Although there is something special about a gnarled, spreading, twisted old dooryard fruit tree, if you want it to attain its maximum fruit production, some shaping is essential in infancy.

Some varieties seem to grow naturally into a nice shape with little care. The Dolgo crab apple, for instance, shapes itself beautifully. Other trees, such as the Yellow Transparent apple, seem bent on growing as many tops as possible. The extra tops should be pruned back to encourage a more spreading tree. Many plum trees grow so wide that the outer branches hang on the ground unless they are snipped back occasionally.

I carry a pair of small hand-held pruning shears while walking by the trees. That way I can remove growth headed in the wrong direction as soon as it starts. Frequent light pruning is ever so much better than having to cut off large limbs that have grown in the wrong places. Frequent pruning also conditions the orchardist to the pruning habit by developing both his attitude and skill.

Overbearing

As a beginning fruit grower anxiously awaiting my first crop, I was always delighted to find a tree blooming the first or second year after planting.

As the little fruits grew it was even more exciting to see how many of them the young tree was producing. Actually it wasn't good at all for the tree, as I have since learned. If your tree is growing extra well and is in good rugged condition, it may not hurt it a bit to bear a fruit or two the second year after planting. But be careful. Some varieties tend to bear far too early and too heavily. If a tree produces when it is very young, or if it bears more fruit any one year than its strength can stand, it may become so weakened that it won't produce another crop for several years. Or it can even get infected with some disease at that point and die an early death. Usually a standard-size tree shouldn't be allowed to bear until the third year after planting, and then only if the tree is in vigorous growing condition.

If your tree is precocious and wants to bear before its time, you can easily curb its ambition by picking off most of the small fruits as soon as they appear. How many you leave, if any, should depend on the number of fruits you think your tree can safely mature and at the same time still make good growth for even bigger production in the years ahead.

7 / POLLINATION

Despite all those legendary childhood lectures about the birds and the bees, pollination is still a mystery to many would-be fruit gardeners. People ordering trees usually know they should do something about it, but they are often unsure whether they will get the best results by selecting two trees of the same variety or two completely different kinds. They're not positive whether pollination will change the variety of fruit, or if planting several kinds of berries near each other will result in a grand mix-up of them all at some future time. They wonder, too, whether a plum can pollinate a cherry, or if European plums can cross with the Japanese ones; and if apples will mate with stone fruits or with pears, or even if all the hundreds of varieties of apples are compatible with each other in every instance.

Tree salesmen, either from lack of knowledge or outright dishonesty, often take advantage of an amateur's ignorance of these matters and sell him trees he neither wants nor needs. Therefore, before you order your trees it is practical to know a little about the mysteries of pollination.

Like almost everything else in the advanced forms of plant life, the fruit tree's prime duty is to reproduce itself. It does this by blooming and bearing fruit, which contains seeds. As in the animal world, two separate genders are involved. Both the male and the female parts of the blossom have to join together if offspring—fruit and seed—are produced. The perfect flower is bisexual, both male and female.

Some plants—like holly, bittersweet, and certain tropical trees such as dates—have imperfect flowers; that is, each plant is either all male or all female. A date orchard is usually planted with each male tree surrounded by dozens of female ones, like a sultan and his harem. Likewise, only female holly plants produce the colorful berries, but males must live in the same neighborhood to produce the pollinating pollen or else—no berries. These all-male or all-female plants are not common in the plant world. Most fruit trees have both the male and female parts on the same flower.

Sex and the Single Tree

Even with perfect flowers, your fruit tree is probably going to need a mate. Although a few varieties are self-fertile, which means they can polli-

53

nate themselves nicely and bear very well alone, most kinds produce few if any fruits without a partner nearby.

This is how it happens: In a perfect flower, the male portion is the cluster of several little uprights in the center of the flower called stamens (see below). These are covered with a yellow or orange powder called pollen, which is the stuff you get all over your nose when you smell a flower up close. The female part of the blossom, the pistil, is the long slender green tube slightly taller than the stamens and in the midst of them. The pollen from a flower on one tree must be moved to a flower on another to bring about cross-pollination or cross-fertilization. In other words, pollen from the stamens of Tree A must move to the pistil in Tree B.

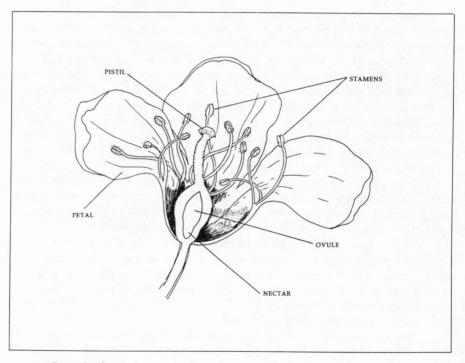

Parts of a flower

In order to cross-pollinate, the trees must be in the same family group. Apples cannot pollinate pears, nor can pears pollinate plums. You should have at least two of each species of the fruit tree that you plant to ensure good bearing. In other words, if you want to grow pears, you should plant two pear trees. If you want to grow apples, you will need two apple trees, and so on.

There is one more catch. The trees have to be two *different* varieties. Having two alike won't work. The reason for this is simple. Let's suppose you want to plant two Jonathan apple trees. Since all the true Jonathan trees in the world came originally from one tree, every Jonathan is really part of the same tree divided millions of times. Since a tree can't fertilize itself, having two trees that are just alike is no different from having only one tree. You need to plant two separate varieties—a Jonathan and a Delicious, for instance. Similarly, if you want to grow plums, you should plant two different kinds of plums. If you want to grow pears, you need two different kinds of pears, and so on. That way you can be sure of true cross-pollination.

How does all this pollen get around? Most forest trees—pines, maples, oaks, and so forth—are pollinated by the wind, as are most grasses and grains such as corn. With most ornamentals, vegetables, and fruit trees, however, the means of bringing the two flowers together is the bee. That is why the two trees need to be within easy flying distance of each other. Although bees

Peach blooms. The pistil and stamens are clearly visible (USDA).

can and do travel much farther, as a rule the busy little fellows should not be forced to fly more than several hundred feet to bring about the mating of these blossoms.

The bee is, without doubt, an innocent party to these goings-on. She accidentally effects the fertilization of the flower as she goes about her business of gathering nectar to take back to the hive. In reaching deep into the throat of the flower where the sweet stuff lies, she has to wiggle past the pollen-laden stamens, picking up lots of the abundant yellow stuff on her fuzzy body. As she goes from tree to tree, flower to flower, a great quantity of pollen gets moved from the stamens of one tree to the pistils of another. On a good day one bee may visit 4000 or 5000 blooms.

When a grain of the proper pollen hits the head of the pistil it is absorbed in a tiny opening and moves down a tube to the ovary. There it joins with the ovules to produce a growing cell which, in a short time, develops into fruit and seed. For fruits with a single seed or pit, only one grain of pollen is needed. Apples, which have ten seeds if they're perfect, need ten grains. If only five or six pollen grains are taken in, the fruit will probably be lopsided.

Don't worry that the quality of your fruit will be affected by the pollen of your tree's partner. The mating tree influences only the genes in the seed and therefore any plant grown from that seed. The fruit is merely the carrier for the seeds and will stay the same whether the bees bring pollen from a sour wild seedling or a high-quality grafted tree. The trees grown from the seeds, however, will vary widely, each producing fruit different from its parents and from each other.

Here is some general information on the pollination requirements of various kinds of trees; more information is given in the chapters on each specific fruit. Even though two varieties are not always needed for pollination, many orchardists feel that trees do better if several are planted together. Not only the pollination but possibly even the companionship of the other trees may be beneficial.

Apples. Two or more different varieties are recommended for best pollination. Northern Spy and Baldwin are poor pollinizers, so a third variety should be planted with them to ensure that something happens. If several apples all belonging to the same family group—such as Delicious, Starking, and Starkspur—are all planted together, they should have another variety nearby that is not closely related to them—such as Duchess, Dolgo, Greening, or any of many others. Otherwise cross-pollination may not take place.

Peaches. Although many peaches are self-fertile and will bear quite well by themselves, many of the most popular kinds are not. Mikado, J. H. Hale, Elberta, and others need a mate. Usually it is a good idea to always plant two different varieties for best production.

Pears. Two or more different varieties are recommended for good crops. Bartlett and Seckel do not get along too well together pollenwise, so a third variety is needed if those two are to be planted.

Plums. More gardeners seem to have trouble with plum pollination than with any other fruit. Often they complain that even though the trees bloom heavily they set little or no fruit. Plums bloom so early that sometimes bee colonies have not yet built up to full strength, and as soon as the more fragrant apple blossoms burst open, the few bees sometimes ignore the plum blooms and go to the apples. Two different varieties of plums within the same family are usually necessary for good pollination. The families are explained in Chapter 16 with suggestions about their pollination.

Sour cherries. Sour cherries are one of the few fruits that will nearly always self-pollinate really well, so one tree is all you need.

Sweet cherries. Two or more cherry varieties are necessary. Sour cherries are not good choices to cross-pollinate with them because they seldom bloom at the same time.

Helping Out the Bees

When only one variety of a fruit tree is blooming and there appears to be no suitable partner blossoming anywhere in the neighborhood, you can help the bees produce some fruit by pulling a fast one on nature. Here's how we do it: If only one pear tree is in bloom, we drive across town to an abandoned farm where a big ancient pear tree is blossoming away, borrow a few flowers, and bring them home. We put them in a bucket of water under the tree and the bees take over from there.

Some gardeners who have no room to plant additional trees graft another variety on the limb of their tree for pollination. This method, like the bouquet-in-a-bucket one, is sort of a last resort. Two different trees growing near each other are a much more reliable way to get consistently heavy crops.

Bees are so important that if you own a hive or have a neighbor who raises them, count yourself very lucky. In cold wet years the wild bees are seldom numerous enough to do a good job, especially for the early-blooming trees. Fruits that have been poorly pollinated will usually drop soon after forming, if they form at all.

People with frost problems will also appreciate a strong colony of bees nearby. Flowers that are pollinated soon after they bloom seem to be more resistant to a light frost than the virgin blooms. The pistil, which carries the pollen down the flower, is delicate and easily damaged. Apparently if pollination has already taken place and the pistil no longer is needed, the bloom can stand a lower temperature than if it were unpollinated.

Artificial Pollination

To supplement the sometimes rather unreliable work of the bees, orchardists have experimented with do-it-yourself ways of gathering and spreading the pollen. In some cases a kind of vacuum cleaner has been used to gather pollen, which is then distributed over other trees. Hand- or motor-driven dusters, sprays, airplanes, and even shotguns have been used for this spreading, but most of them have not proved too successful. Hand-pollination works best.

Although the idea may at first seem silly, if the bees are very few and fail to do their duty, we small growers can actually pollinate quite a lot of fruit by hand. Take a small soft paintbrush such as those used by artists and dust the flowers with it, knocking the pollen into a teacup. Then brush it carefully onto the blossoms of an adjoining tree. You can mark the limbs to show which ones have been treated, and if you have the energy you can pollinate the entire tree. Actually quite a few dwarf trees can be pollinated in an hour or so since not every single blossom needs to be pollinated; dusting only one bloom in a cluster is plenty. There's no need to start a big crop of fruit that will need thinning later on.

Obviously this system is impractical on a large scale. Nevertheless, the home orchardist with a free weekend, if he finds very few bees among his blossoms, can often salvage a good part of the fruit crop by personally buzzing about his trees with a camel's hair brush. The bees, though well organized, apparently have no strong labor unions, and so far we have run into no difficulties at all by usurping some of their duties. This is lucky, because we always try to keep on the good side of the bees.

For those who don't want to go to all the trouble of gathering pollen, there are several companies that gather and sell it. This pollen can be hand-spread or placed in special inserts that can be put into beehives. Bees, on their way out of the hive, walk through this pollen and pick up generous amounts to spread around the trees.

These three companies supply pollen and inserts commercially:

Antles Pollen Supplies, Inc.
Box 1243
Wenatchee, Washington 98801

McCormicks Fruit Tree Company
1315 Fruitvale Boulevard
Yakima, Washington 98902

Pollen Products
255 East Milgeo Street
Ripon, California 95366

8 / SPRING AND SUMMER

Although the harvests of autumn may be what fruit growing is all about, I really enjoy the rest of the year in the orchard too. Even watching the orchard come to life is exciting. The sap of the fruit tree begins to move early in the spring, but not as early as in the willows or maples. In the North, days will have to warm considerably and the ground be thoroughly thawed before the swelling of the buds becomes noticeable. Not long after that the leaves appear, and then the flower buds.

Few strolls are more pleasurable than one through an apple orchard when it is in bloom. The rich, sweet fragrance of a perfume no chemist could possibly capture is unforgettable as it blends with the freshness of a spring day. It is delightful to the eye, too, for a fruit tree is strikingly beautiful whether it is a small new tree bravely blooming for the first time, or a gnarled heavily laden ancient specimen now well into its second century.

An orchard in bloom is pleasurable to more than two senses. The birds also like to stay near the fragrant beauty, and their songs and chirps blend cheerfully with the thousands of buzzing bees. No fruit grower should ever become too busy to pause for a few minutes or even hours to enjoy this experience. Soon the petals will fall and the new fruits will begin to form. The birds will start to build their nests, and the insects will commence to hatch. Everything is at work and so, too, must be the orchardist.

Check over the orchard frequently to see that insects, disease, animals, or any other dangers are not threatening it. Insects and disease can increase rapidly with favorable warm weather conditions, and scavenging animals can swiftly pass the word to their many friends to come and join in the feast of young succulent twigs and forming fruits.

Also make sure the trees have a good supply of nutrients at this time when they are growing their fastest. And not only should plenty of fertilizer and moisture be available, but be sure the trees get first chance, before the weeds and grass. Now and then someone asks if I can tell him why his little fruit trees are doing so badly. We walk into his back yard and he says, "Just a minute, I'm sure they're in here somewhere." Some minutes later among rank growing weeds and grass that stands nearly up to our waists, we locate his puny little trees. And he still can't figure out why they aren't growing.

I mentally compare those trees to a small child at a family reunion where everyone is outreaching him at the table. He'd like a plateful of the food, but long before the crowd stops grabbing, everything is gone. There's not even a glass of water left for him. Likewise, no healthy, green-blooded, all-American weed is going to be Mr. Nice and share his dinner with your tree. After all, he was probably there first. The only way to deal with weeds and tall grass is for you to be firm. Demand that they leave the area. Keep them mowed, or pile on a heavy mulch to smother them.

Now is the time for you to encourage plenty of birds in your fruit grove. Soon hundreds of egg clusters will be hatching on the ground, under loose bark and among the leaves; and hordes of insects will begin to devour your trees. Birds can be your best ally in your battle with the bugs, but even so, some spraying will probably be necessary. Chapter 9 will help you plan your pest control program.

A light pruning is usually beneficial to keep young trees growing in the right direction and to stop them from getting too wide, from developing too many tops, or from growing lopsided. And all sucker branches springing

Apples in need of thinning

from the roots and the lower part of the trunk should be removed as soon as they sprout.

Thinning

Here's a trick little used by home gardeners that can make you the envy of your neighbors: If you want your tree to produce its best fruit and bear big crops every year, don't ever neglect to thin the fruit. It's a difficult task for many people, so even if they know about thinning, they often just won't do it. They think it is wasteful or contrary to nature.

But if you stop to think about it, Mother Nature herself does a lot of thinning. Immediately after the fruit sets, a mature tree will usually drop hundreds of tiny fruits, and a few weeks later, when the fruits are the size of marbles, another drop usually occurs. This is known as the May drop, June drop, or July drop, depending on where you live. Don't be alarmed. The tree is merely getting rid of the extra fruit it can't grow to maturity. Since the tree's

Apples after thinning. Each has room to develop to its fullest.

only interest is to produce a big crop of seeds by maturing a large number of fruits, filling up your pantry shelves doesn't enter into its plans at all. It wants only to scatter lots of seeds over the countryside, perhaps even only every other year. As seeds are not your main interest, you merely continue what nature started and pick off a good part of the tiny fruits that are left after the second drop. The tree's strength and energy are then diverted to the remaining fruits, so they grow much faster and larger (see below).

How many should you pluck? One of the best rules seems to be to leave about 6 or 7 inches between each fruit. In years when a tree bears

Small apples result if the fruit set is too heavy.

heavily, this often means picking off 70 or 80 percent of your crop, which is a real shocker for most folks. If you have ever heard that a Yankee gardener is so tight-fisted he has to bring in a neighbor to thin his turnips, you should see us squirm when we have to thin our fruit. But thin them we do, painful as it is to pick and throw away perfectly good apples, pears, and peaches. You will, too, when you see how much bigger and better the fruit is when you thin, and when you find that you actually have far more bushels than otherwise. And almost all of the fruit will be topnotch, with few culls, since as you thin you naturally remove any imperfect or insect-damaged ones.

Since hand-thinning is such a laborious task, many commercial growers use a specially developed spray early in the season to thin the fruit in their orchards. Quite a bit of skill is required for proper and safe chemical thinning, so you'll probably be lots better off by doing it in the safe, reliable, old-fashioned way.

Some apples such as the McIntosh do a pretty good job of thinning themselves with early summer drops, if they have been properly pruned. On the other hand, many apples such as Wealthy, Yellow Transparent, and others have a tremendous desire to overproduce, and heavy thinning is almost always necessary, not only to ensure large fruit but sometimes even to save the tree from bearing itself to death.

We have found that peaches, apples, pears, and the large fruited plums all benefit from thinning, but we never bother to thin cherries, crab apples, the small canning pears, small fruited plums, or any of the small fruits except bunches of grapes.

Besides producing better fruit, thinning provides other benefits. One of the frustrating things about fruit growing has long been the bad habit of many trees to bear every other year. With some trees such as York Imperial and Baldwin apples this tendency is normal. Even severe thinning doesn't completely correct it. With most trees, though, pruning excess branches and thinning the surplus fruit will promote fairly regular bearing every year.

Since the seed contains the potential of all the future trees, as you might expect, it takes more of the tree's vitality to produce the small seeds than the large flesh of the fruit. Therefore, cutting down on seed production saves a tremendous amount of tree energy, even if the total weight of fruit is more. Suppose, for example, your apple tree has 1000 small fruits on it. Each one contains ten seeds. If you pick off 800 of them, your tree is going to mature only 2000 seeds instead of 10,000. Quite a difference! Naturally it will feel more like trying again next year.

Try not to feel guilty about thinning. Like disbudding your roses for bigger blooms or thinning your carrots, it is a perfectly nice thing for you to do for your tree. Just remember to clip or pick the small fruits carefully so you don't damage the limbs and remaining fruits. If picking and throwing away so much of your crop is more than you can bear, do as I do and spread the operation over several days. It is less painful that way. After you see the results, it will become easier each year, and soon you will be tempted to thin even more heavily to get those larger blue-ribbon type fruits. Each variety of fruit has a built-in size limit, however, and even overthinning will not increase size beyond this maximum. In fact, if a large tree bears only one fruit, that fruit will get no larger than its own built-in potential.

Late Summer Care

Toward the end of summer, fruits begin to rapidly increase in size. Insects and disease may still be a problem, especially in years that are unusually wet or dry, so spraying may still be necessary. Check your bearing trees frequently to see that the crop is not overloading the branches. Some years a large tree may produce nearly a ton of fruit, so take a look now and then to see that the limbs are not in danger of breaking from the weight. If this seems likely, wide boards or planks of the proper length can be stood upright on the ground to prop up sagging branches until the fruit is harvested.

Be sure to resist any temptation to use fertilizers in the late summer to increase the size of the fruit. Tree growth must not be stimulated at that time since the tree is getting ready for its long winter nap.

Getting the feel of the orchard can only be accomplished by actually being there and seeing what is taking place week by week. When you do get in tune with your trees and begin to feel the beautiful cycle of the fruit tree, what might have once been a difficult chore performed nervously and cautiously will become a delightful experience, and your trees will thrive. "The footsteps of the owner are the orchard's best fertilizer," according to an old English saying.

9 / DISEASE AND INSECT CONTROL

Every little while we hear someone say, "I'd love to plant a few fruit trees if they weren't so much work." This often comes from someone who seldom complains about other garden work. What they usually mean by work is that they are worried about spraying. Most gardeners believe that commercial orchardists spend most of the summer spraying one chemical or another on their trees, and think this has to be the fruit grower's way of life. They are also frightened that most of the chemicals are violent poisons in the rankest form, and even opening the package may be risky. This used to be true, but not anymore. In recent years there has been a shift away from this separate-chemical-for-every-bug craze. Also, many trees are now being sold for home orchards which are much more disease- and insect-resistant than varieties formerly offered. Many new, safe, and easy controls for orchard pests have been discovered, too, and more natural ways of thwarting the pests are being found every year.

The lethal arsenics, DDT's, Dieldrin, Parathion, and Chlordanes everybody used so carelessly a few years ago are now banned or severely restricted. With good sanitation, spraying may not even be necessary in many years, if you live in an isolated location. When it is necessary there are now some effective pesticides that even organic gardeners can use with a clear conscience. What's more, these new sprays are packaged in small sizes with directions that are especially written for home orchardists.

Home orchards that usually have only a small number of trees and several different varieties are certainly not as inviting to epidemics of bug and disease as are acres and acres of trees of the same kind. Still, if you grow fruit year after year, sooner or later there is a good chance that some pest will find your trees desirable and perhaps decide to make them his summer project.

Please don't get scared reading this chapter. It is here if you need it to help you cope with the little surprises nature continually tosses at us to make life more interesting and to keep gardening from getting too boring.

Determining What's Wrong

Fruit trees can look sick for a variety of reasons. Many times the trouble is physiological and caused by environmental conditions that no spray can help at all. If a tree is not happy with its climate, moisture, soil, fertilizer, or light conditions, or if it is starved by weed and grass competition, it is not going to do well, and no amount of spray can help. Likewise, if a tree has been damaged by animals, chemicals, salts, or machinery it is going to look less than thrifty and again, even the best all-purpose orchard dust will do no good. So diagnosing the problem correctly is most important.

When you've determined that a tree has problems not caused by its environment or by things such as animals or machinery, check the leaves and bark for insects. Sometimes insects can be easily seen, sometimes not. Tent caterpillars, Japanese beetles, and even aphids can be spotted easily and identified. Others, such as mites and scale, are very small and hard to see, even though the damage they do can usually be recognized. Still other insects spend a lot of their life out of sight either underground or beneath the loose bark of a tree. Then there are those that fly around the orchard at night, laying eggs that hatch inside the fruit. Naturally, every insect that you see in your orchard is not an enemy. Most will be quite harmless, and some even beneficial. Since you never know what to expect, however, be ready to cope with an invasion of bugs should it appear.

Diseases are easier to identify. Whoever named them used terms so descriptive that even beginners can often recognize them. How could you not identify brown rot, powdery mildew, leaf curl, scab, sooty blotch, fire blight, black knot, rust, or leaf yellows?

Before you reach for the spray can, then, spend some time trying to determine which problem you have. Chapters on the specific fruits list particular problems that bother each species, but a list of the common physiological ailments, diseases, and insects that could arise in your orchard is included here for ready reference.

PHYSIOLOGICAL PROBLEMS OF TREES

It is often impossible for anyone to identify what is causing a tree's problem by simply looking at the symptoms. If the leaves are yellow, for example, it could mean any number of things might be wrong. By listing many possible causes of physiological problems, I hope to help you determine the one most likely affecting your plant.

Lack of sun. Often a trouble in northern areas. Fruit trees need to get almost full sun to grow well and to mature fruit properly. Don't hide them behind large buildings or large shade trees.

Too much sun. Sometimes a problem in the South where certain small fruits can get more heat than is good for them.

Too much water. Most fruit trees need good soil drainage. Their roots do not like soil that is constantly wet.

Too little water. A problem on poor or sandy soils, especially in dry seasons.

Overlimed. Too much lime locks up soil nutrients and may cause fruit drop, poor growth.

Underlimed. Too little lime also causes poor growth because the tree can't utilize soil nutrients.

Overfertilized. Fertilizer burn shows up as a browning, scorched look on leaves and may kill the tree. Moderate overfertilizing may cause the tree to grow too fast and not produce, or to produce fruits with poor color.

Underfertilized. Weak growth. Leaves look yellowish or pale green.

Weed and grass competition. Same results as when the plant is underfertilized.

Late frost injury. Buds fail to bloom, or blooms fail to set fruit.

Animal damage. Bark rubbed or chewed. Twigs snapped off.

Mechanical damage. Branches or bark torn or scrubbed off. Mowers or machinery may be to blame.

Road salt. Weakening of the tree and drying out of the leaves are caused by melting snow and salt runoff from roads and driveways.

Soil compacting. Poor growth results from soil that is very hard and difficult to dig into. Can be caused by worn-out soil, by heavy machines, or by excessive foot traffic through the area.

Too little soil. When large rocks or subsoil are close to the surface, poor growth results since roots can't grow enough to feed the tree.

Electrical leakage. Underground cable sometimes ruptures and heat cooks the tree.

Sewage burn. Leaking sewer pipe allows chemicals and sewage to "burn" tree. Trees planted near a septic drainfield may have fruit flavor spoiled by fertilization with raw sewage.

Excessive suckering. Some rootstocks send up lots of little plants below the graft. Cutting them off regularly is the best remedy.

Water sprouts. Clumps of new branches often grow upright around a newly pruned limb. These should be removed. Moderate pruning annually rather than severe pruning every two or three years helps prevent water sprouts.

Winter injury and sunscald. In both the North and the South, low temperatures and sudden temperature changes can be a real problem, especially to younger trees. Winter sunscald is caused by the warm sunshine on the dark-colored bark, which raises the temperature of the wood considerably higher than the surrounding air. The sudden drop in temperature as night falls or a cloud covers the sun causes extensive cell damage to the bark, often causing it to split and come off. A similar injury may occur during the hot days of summer. Orchardists have found that a white latex paint sprayed on the east and south side of the tree trunk helps reflect the sun and prevent this injury. Allowing the branches to grow close to the ground when feasible also provides additional shade for the tender trunk bark and helps prevent this.

Diseases

Diseases can be spread by wind, rain, insects, and pruning tools. Like human genetic diseases, they may also be inherited and passed on through

Sunscald injury has developed into a large wound.

scion or rootstock. Some are very hard to control—fire blight and raspberry mosaic, for instance. Others, such as certain scabs and rots, are quite often easily kept in check by careful and frequent spraying.

Apple scab is the most common apple disease, attacking both leaves and fruit. It forms olive-colored splotches on the leaves, often making them warped and curly. Fruits are covered with dark, hard, unsightly blotches, and sometimes with cracks. Fruit infected early in the season may fall before maturing. Those infected later are often unfit for use. Early spraying is important to prevent these later infections, which are frequently spread by rain.

Scab may not be a problem at all in dry years. In seasons with a lot of rain, spraying may have to be continued until a week or two before harvest. Dormant oils can help prevent early infestations, but fungicides such as Captan will likely be the only way to have good control all season. The disease often overwinters in apples and in leaves on the ground.

Black knot can be recognized by the thick, fleshy excrements on limbs of cherry, plum, and other stone fruits. It begins in summer as sticky secretions, but is most noticeable in winter when trees are bare. The best control is to remove infected limbs in summer as soon as it is spotted. All wild plums and cherries nearby that are infected should also be removed.

Brown rot attacks the growing fruit of all the stone fruit family. Plums and peaches are often affected the worst, with the fruit becoming a mushy rot just before it ripens. Like scab, it is spread by rain, so is worse in wet summers. It also overwinters in decaying fruit on the ground. As with scab, regular spraying with Captan gives good control.

MAJOR INSECTS AND DISEASES

DISEASE	ENEMY OF	ATTACKS
Apple scab	Apple	Leaves, twigs, fruits
Black knot	Plum, cherry, other stone fruits	Branches
Brown rot	Peach, plum, apricot, nectarine	Fruits
Canker	All trees, some bush fruits	Trunks, limbs
Cherry leaf spot	Sweet and sour cherry	Leaves
Fire blight	Apple, pear, quince	Branches, twigs
Peach leaf curl	Peach and nectarine	Leaves
Peach scab	Peach, plum, nectarine	Leaves, fruits
Powdery mildew	Many fruits, berries	Twigs, leaves
Root gall	Tree fruits	Roots
Rust	Apple, quince	Leaves, twigs
Wilt	Tree fruits, berries	Leaves, branches

INSECT	ENEMY OF	ATTACKS
Aphid	All fruit trees, especially apple	Leaves, fruits
Apple maggot	Apple	Fruits
Borer	All fruits, especially peach	Trunks
Cherry fruit fly	Cherry	Fruits
Codling moth	Apple, pear	Fruits, leaves
Curculio	All fruits except pear	Fruits
Mitey	Apple, peach, plum, nectarine	Fruits, leaves
Oriental fruit moth	Peach, apricot, plum	Leaves, fruits
Pear phylla	Pear	Leaves
San Jose scale	All fruits	Trunks, twigs, fruits, leaves
Tent caterpillar	All fruits	Leaves

Canker in its various forms may bother fruit and nut trees as well as small fruits. Apple blister canker, bleeding canker, blueberry canker, butternut melanconis dieback, camellia canker, currant canker, grape dead arm disease, and nectria canker are some of them. While the list sounds rather depressing, probably none will ever bother your orchard.

Canker is a very noticeable diseased section of the woody part of a tree or bush, and it may even be an open wound. In some cases it may spread all around the trunk and kill the tree. Often it results from injuries that were left untreated. If canker does get started, the best method of treatment is to cut out all the diseased wood and seal the cavity with a tree sealer or cement. Sterilize all tools after use with a Chlorox solution or a 5 percent solution of formaldehyde.

Apple scab—the disease attacks leaves, twigs, and fruit (Gertrude Catlin).

Cedar apple rust is one of the worst of several rusts that bother fruits. Rust attacks leaves and fruit. The disease needs nearby Wild Juniper (Red Cedar) to complete its cycle, so elimination of that plant when feasible controls it beautifully. Where this is difficult, Ferbam sprayed as directed on the package will give good control.

Cherry leaf spot, as its name implies, attacks cherries. It overwinters on fallen leaves and is spread by spring winds. It is worse in damp weather. Raking and composting leaves each fall gives some control. Captan is the recommended spray.

Fire blight is a deadly disease that fortunately presents a real problem only to certain fruit trees. Many varieties of pears and some apples are very vulnerable. Planting disease-resistant kinds (listed in their respective chapters) is the best precaution. You can also control it by promptly sealing all new

Black knot, a disagreeable disease on plums and cherries (USDA)

Cherries badly infected with brown rot (Gertrude Catlin)

tree wounds with a tree compound and pruning away all infected parts as soon as they appear.

Most other plant diseases are caused by virus, but fire blight is caused by bacteria, which are spread most often by wind, insects (especially bees), and pruning tools. An especially prepared streptomycin is sometimes used in commercial orchards for treatment. The disease is curious in that it can be very bad in certain years and then disappear entirely, apparently for no reason, even with no treatment.

Peach leaf curl overwinters on the tree twigs, spreading rapidly in the spring. Infected leaves are curled, crinkled, and thickened. Ferbam is a good spray for its control, and should be applied before the buds begin to open in the spring.

Left: canker on an apple twig. Right: canker on a peach tree (both by Gertrude Catlin)

Peach scab attacks both peaches and plums, causing velvety blotches to appear over the mature fruits. Captan gives good control.

Powdery mildew, a white velvety disease, covers leaves, twigs, and fruits of tree fruits, currants, and grapes. Wettable sulfur has long been the standard control. Karathane or Dikar are also used. Benomyl (Ben-Late) gives by far the best control, but it is a systemic and I'm always a bit fearful about using them (see page 85). Sanitary measures, not crowding the plants, sufficient pruning, and careful disposal of infected parts are the best controls.

Root (crown) gall is a bacteria disease causing large swellings on roots of fruit trees and bramble fruits. No known cure. Plant only certified healthy trees and plants.

Wilt occurs in several varieties that may bother tree fruits and berries. Besides the obvious one that occurs when there is not enough water in the soil, there are others caused by diseases that suddenly shut off moisture to part of the plant. Verticillium wilt is most common, attacking fruit trees and berries, vegetables, and shade trees. Control is especially difficult. It is well to plant fruits and berries away from vegetables if the disease is present in the garden, and to cut out the diseased limb and burn it at once. All pruning tools and shovels used in digging out infected plants should be sterilized immediately after using, to prevent spreading the disease. A good disinfectant can be made by mixing one part Chlorox with nine parts water.

Cedar apple rust lesions on apple leaves and an apple (Gertrude Catlin)

Far left: fire blight injury on an apple twig (Gertrude Catlin)

Left: powdery mildew affecting the top of a young apple tree (Gertrude Catlin)

Lower left: verticillium wilt on a strawberry plant (Gertrude Catlin)

Below: peach leaf curl (Gertrude Catlin)

Aphids on new growth of an apple tree (Gertrude Catlin)

INSECTS

One day in high school biology class our teacher confided in a hushed voice that a single insect could produce 100,000 or more descendants in a few weeks. While all of us were showing the proper degree of amazement the teacher expected, the boy sitting behind me whispered fairly loudly, "Imagine what would happen if she ever got married!"

That little remark stayed with me, and I think of it each spring as cocoons burst and larvae proliferate. No longer do I feign amazement at the procreative ability of bugs. I truly *am* amazed. And I've also learned why early control of orchard pests is so important. It saves much, much trouble later on.

Here are some insect problems that may show up in your orchard. Control programs are suggested later in the chapter. There are many types of insects, and they attack fruit plants and trees in different ways. Some chew leaves or burrow into the wood or bark. Others suck nutrients from the leaves or branches.

Aphids of various kinds attack bark, leaves, or fruit of almost every tree. The insecticides commonly used now control them very well, luckily. Many of the leaf aphids are spread far and wide by ambitious ants who like the sweet substance they secrete. The tight curling of new leaves at the end of branches on young trees is often a result of heavy aphid colonies sucking out the plant juices. Small infestations can often be knocked out with a few light squirts of House and Garden Raid, or a shaking of garden Rotenone dust. Both are easier than mixing up a tank of orchard spray. Treatment should be in two installments. A week after the first treatment you should repeat it, to catch any new insects that may hatch later.

Apple maggots are easily one of the meanest insects in the fruit world, and many a crop of apples has been wrecked by these persistent pests. They're known as the "railroad worms" and can quickly reduce a beautiful

The adult apple maggot sits beside some of his handiwork.
Top: External injury to an apple. Bottom: internal injury (all by Gertrude Catlin)

apple to a pulpy brown mess. The damage is caused by an insect closely resembling a house fly but slightly smaller, which lays its eggs in the growing fruit by piercing the skin. The larvae, often in large numbers, hatch and tunnel through the fruit. Larvae live in fruit that falls to the ground in the orchard during the fall, then burrow underground for the winter, ready to emerge the following summer. Swarms of these flies can often be seen under fruit trees in late summer in unsprayed orchards. Cleaning up all the old fruit is one of the best controls. A good spraying program (see pages 88–89) carried on through most of the summer will almost completely control this maggot if he's a problem in your orchard.

Borers are small worms that burrow into the trunks of trees, often near or just above ground level. A pile of sawdust and excrement, together with the weakened condition of the tree, indicate the presence of this fat, alien

Peach tree borer in a tree trunk (Gertrude Catlin)

invader. Usually brutally punching the fat grub with a wire is the most effective means of disposing of him, since sprays frequently fail to reach him. Tree wraps can help discourage this creature and keep him from getting started, but unfortunately trees received from nurseries occasionally already have the young larvae in them. We have imported them twice to our area that way. Better look closely at the trunks of all new trees when they are first received to make sure no borers are at work. Even one can soon weaken a tree enough so it will break off at ground level.

Codling moths cause the wormy apples everyone knows so well. The fat white or grayish grub and its excrements about the hole in the fruit are solid indicators of the insect at work. The codling moth is fond of laying its eggs in the flower at blooming time, so practically the only way to control this pest is to spray (see pages 88–89) between the time the bees leave—when the

Adult codling moth and injury (Gertrude Catlin)

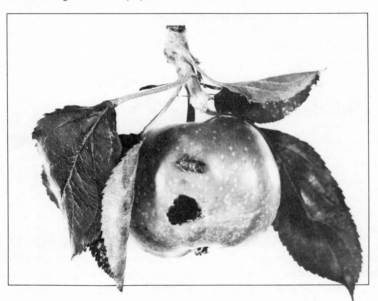

petals have fallen—and the time the new fruit has formed protection for the hatching egg. Sometimes there is a second or third generation the same year, all infecting the crop. Codling moths like to overwinter in sheltered spots, a favorite one being the space under the loose bark on older fruit trees.

Curculios are small insects that puncture forming fruit and lay eggs, often causing the fruit to drop prematurely. Dark blotches around the punctures are clearly visible on the fruits that remain on the tree. Spraying regularly with a good orchard spray (see pages 88–89) is about the best control.

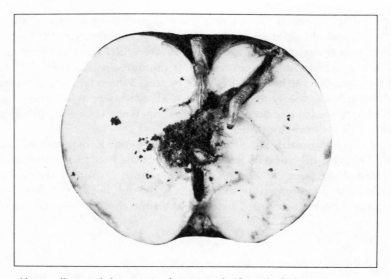

Above: codling moth larvae at work in an apple (Gertrude Catlin)

Right: plum curculio on an immature cherry (Gertrude Catlin)

Mites are small sucking insects that attack leaves and fruit. They may never become a nuisance in most home gardens, but sometimes show up in dry summers. Ordinary orchard sprays (see pages 88–89) control them.

Oriental fruit moths occasionally become real pests on peaches and nectarines. They attack twigs and fruits, often having four or five generations in a summer in warmer climates. Early and repeated spraying is the best control (pages 88–89).

Pear phylla is the most common pear insect. A small creature, it can strip the leaves off a tree and soon ruin a crop unless it is controlled. It can also beget several generations each summer, so early spraying is important. Black sooty secretions cover the fruit and leaves when phylla is present.

San Jose scale, despite the name, is not a skin disorder or musical term but an insect so tiny you need a magnifying glass to see it. It works under a scale it has built up for protection and, along with its numerous relatives, sucks nutrients from the twigs in such quantities that the branches often die. Few fruit trees are immune from this pest, but luckily the standard orchard spray program (pages 88–89) controls it very well.

Tent caterpillars, cankerworms, and webworms create cobweb masses that are a familiar sight in hedgerows. All of them cause similar injury to leaves during the summer months. Here again, the standard spray program (pages 88–89) controls them very well and prevents future generations from building up; or the big webs may be cut off and burned if you choose.

Natural Controls

Rather than spray, natural or organic gardeners prefer to use natural controls and orchard sanitation to fight insects and disease. For instance, releasing ladybugs or praying mantises (warmer areas only for mantises) will control aphids and certain other insects. They can be purchased from many mail-order nurseries or from advertisements in garden magazines.

Another natural control has the descriptive name "Tanglefoot." A sticky goo, usually available in garden stores, it can be spread in a band around each tree a foot or so from the ground. This will prevent the insects that usually crawl up the trunk from doing so. It particularly discourages ants from carrying aphids up to the leaves.

Planting insect-repellent herbs and flowers throughout the orchard is a method some growers use as a natural control. They have used, with some success, tansy, wormwood, marigolds, peppermint, nasturtiums, petunias, horseradish, and others.

Sanitation Methods

Whether you prefer chemical or natural pest control, or a combination of both methods, you will probably want to follow certain sanitation practices.

1. Pick up all unused fruit. Bury it in the compost pile or destroy it. Many bugs and diseases overwinter in old fruit.

2. Prune the trees regularly. Cut out all infected wood and dead or broken branches where trouble could start.

3. Thin out the branches to allow better air circulation, which helps cut down scab, particularly in humid or wet summers when the disease is at its worst.

4. Rake up and compost leaves where scab and other diseases can linger.

5. Keep loose bark scraped from the trees so insects can't overwinter in it.

6. Isolate the planting if possible. If you have the only fruit trees within miles, hopefully the worst bugs and disease may never find you. Small growers have it easier than commercial orchardists because large plantings are

very attractive to insects. If there are other small orchards in your area, see if you can all work together to discourage bug hospitality.

7. Mix up your plantings. Like isolation, it's another way to make things tough for the bugs. Whereas large growers want all their varieties together for convenience in picking and spraying, small growers don't need to group them. As one of our friends put it, "If a bug finds one of my plum trees, I'm not going to make it easy for him to find the next one."

One of the very best disease and insect controls is to plant resistant varieties of trees (see the lists in the following chapters on fruits). Many are of superior quality but are not well known or widely planted because they are not suited for commercial use.

Bug Traps

Electric bug traps are quite successful at trapping flying insects, particularly those that move by night. A. M. Leonard and other companies have them for sale (see addresses in the Appendix). You can make your own by shining a light bulb with a reflector on it into a shallow pan of water that has a film of kerosene. The light will attract the insects and they'll subsequently die in the kerosene (see below).

A homemade bug light

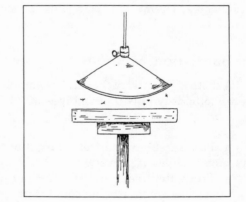

People who object to electric bug traps say that they kill good and bad bugs alike and also attract insects from great distances. Also, houseflylike insects, such as the apple maggot, may not show any interest in them at all, since they're more likely to be abroad in the daytime.

Gallon glass jugs with a pint or so of vinegar in them attract and trap large numbers of fruit flies.

Paper cups with a bit of molasses in the bottoms, hung among the limbs of apple trees, are used successfully to trap egg-laying codling moths in the spring.

Black paper tied around tree trunks will provide a shelter for some harmful insects. By removing the paper at intervals you can kill the insects under it.

A hedgerow helps encourage insect-eating birds. Birdhouses, feeders, and waterers also help bring birds to the area.

Keeping the grass mowed discourages places where insects and disease can hide out and increase.

Toads eat vast quantities of insects that spend part of their life cycle on the ground. Clay pots with a hole broken in one side and pans of drinking water encourage these beneficial and friendly fellows.

The Case for the Messy Orchard

I don't want to leave the subject of insects and disease without a word about a completely different cultural method that is growing in favor—the messy orchard.

Old-time orchardists had little time for the niceties of orchard neatness and sanitation. The prunings too small for firewood were allowed to stay on the ground, rot, and return to the soil. The farmer spread manure generously under the trees in early spring, kept a hive of bees, let the geese roam there, and allowed the pigs to go in and pick up unused fruit in the fall. He didn't mow or spray, but he seldom had diseased or wormy apples either.

It's true that pests weren't as widespread in the old days, but some "natural" gardeners wonder if the old-time cultural methods didn't help keep out insects and disease. The old-timers believed that orchard grass would help prevent fire blight. Years of not mowing turned it into a short-growing thick thatch similar to a heavy mulch. Bug-eating birds, mice-eating weasels, and pollinating wild bees all had a place to live.

This lazy man's orchard, as it is sometimes called, is far from that. In no way is the orchard neglected. Wounds and broken limbs are promptly taken care of. Little trees are heavily mulched from the time they are planted until they begin bearing heavily. Fertilizing must take place too—in fact, it actually should be increased, since both tree and thatch must be fed. Trees should be pruned, but the prunings may be cut fine or chipped to decompose faster. Fruit must be thinned to increase size and to encourage annual bearing.

This method of growing is mentioned only because it apparently works. In no way do I recommend it over the conventional method, especially if your orchard is a city or suburban lot. But if you have plenty of room in the back country and if you want to pioneer in the old style—it's your orchard.

Spraying: How, When, and What

Most gardeners, including many organic gardeners, have resigned themselves to the fact that they will probably have to spray if they want consistently good fruit. Rather than guess if the pests are going to be prevalent any one year, they suspect the worst and carry out an annual spray program.

Just as nurseries have finally recognized a need for home-grown fruit varieties, at last large chemical companies have begun to notice the needs of the home gardener. Sprays and sprayers are now being manufactured especially for us. No longer do we have to buy 10 pounds if we only want one, or use a slide rule to change the formula for mixing enough for one acre into the amount needed for a single tree.

Timing is very important to the home orchardist. Whether you use chemical or organic sprays, you'll want to get them on at the right time. As mentioned before, many insects can produce several generations during a single summer, so knocking out the first one saves much grief later on.

The amount of spray you use is also important. Most home orchardists tend to scrimp and often cover only a small part of the tree. For good pest control, thorough coverage is necessary right into the inner branches. Commercial orchardists sometimes use 10 or more gallons of spray mixture for one large tree.

COMMON ORCHARD CHEMICALS

INSECTICIDE

Used for controlling insects. Common ones for orchard use are Malathion, Methoxychlor, Lindane, Sevin, Pyrethrum, and others made by numerous companies. There are also many brand-name insecticides such as Cythion, Imidan, Lorsban, and others.

FUNGICIDE

Used for the control of disease. Captan is most widely recommended. Lime sulfur, bordeaux mixes, sulfur, Ferbam, Zineb, and others are also used.

HERBICIDE

Used for controlling unwanted weed and brush growth in the orchard. A herbicide known as 2-4-D is often used for controlling broadleaf weeds. Princeps, Roundup, and Casaron are some that were developed for grass control, and Silvex to kill woody brush.

Choose a day with no wind. We prefer to spray in the early morning when the air is usually quiet. Pick a nice day, because rain within a few hours is likely to undo all your efforts. Cold, rainy seasons are difficult ones for the orchardist.

Wear protective clothing. Even with the safer sprays it's a good idea not to breathe the chemicals or get them on your skin, eyes, and hair. Wearing a raincoat, goggles, rubber or plastic boots, and a cap are good precautions. Also remember to always stand well behind the spray. If you accidentally get any chemical on you, wash up immediately and thoroughly. No matter how harmless a pesticide is supposed to be, you can be sure it's not going to do your body any good.

SYSTEMICS

A few years ago scientists found that certain chemicals absorbed into the plant's system make it repulsive to attacks by disease and insects. This has given growers a whole new way to attack plant troubles. All they have to do is to mix some of the chemicals into the soil to be taken up by the plant's roots, or spray it on so it can be absorbed by the leaves. One treatment lasts all year.

Understandably, the government has hesitated about declaring these chemicals safe for all uses, so some have not yet been cleared for use on fruit trees. Still, some growers are using them.

I think a lot more research is necessary before one can be sure the systemics are safe for food crops. I have misgivings about eating food that a bug finds obnoxious, so I'll make no recommendations for their use. I have found that some systemics have proven excellent for keeping leaf miners off birch trees and lilacs, and a host of small bugs off roses; but I would never consider using them on fruit, berry, or vegetable plants, or even on shrubs that produce berries for the birds.

Systemic insecticides include Cygon, Di-syston, Metasystox, Rogor, and Systox. Benomyl is one of the systemic fungicides.

SPRAYING EQUIPMENT

Sprayers for the home orchardist range from small trombone types that spray from a pail and cost only a few dollars to very large, expensive, power-driven machines. The trombone sprayers are easily cleaned, have few parts to wear out, are convenient to store, and are often ideal for someone having only a few trees.

Trombone sprayers are unhandy to move around, however, so an easy-to-carry sprayer is better if you have more than a dozen trees. The compressed-air tank type works well and is perfectly satisfactory if you have low-growing dwarf trees. They may not spray high enough to easily cover full-size trees.

For more serious orchardists there are back-pack sprayers, both power and hand-operated; power sprayers that can be pulled behind garden tractors; and on and on. Choose the one best suited for your use. I would avoid the power-operated ones unless you are a large operator and a good mechanic.

Some caution on sprayers is necessary. Avoid buying a very cheap model, and be sure to keep it clean and in good shape. Replace any worn gaskets immediately so that the spray doesn't squirt out on you. Be careful not to open the pressure tank before the pressure is relieved, or it will likely blow insecticide all over you. Old spray dries and forms crusts that plug the tiny spray orifices, so immediately after use be sure to clean out all your equipment with generous amounts of detergent and water. Then dry the sprayer thoroughly before putting it away so rust won't form.

ORGANIC VS. CHEMICAL SPRAYING

Orchardists tend to split along organic-chemical lines when it comes to opinions on sprays, just as they do with fertilizers. The chemical crowd likes to take advantage of a century of progress and believes today's problems need today's answers. Natural or organic gardeners, on the other hand, believe that a lot of today's problems are the result of misguided progress and that a return to old-time cultural methods will result in fewer insects and less disease. They believe chemicals also knock out natural controls by killing both good and bad insects, birds, and other wildlife.

As with fertilizers, there is a third group standing somewhere in between. They are organic-minded and reject a spray-happy existence, but

An inexpensive sprayer, suitable for the home orchardist (University of Illinois)

are willing to rely on modern chemistry rather than put up with wormy or scabby fruit; similarly, they might reject a penicillin shot for a common cold, but would probably snap it up fast if they had double pneumonia.

SPRAYS FOR ORGANIC GARDENERS

The insecticides Rotenone, Pyrethrum, Ryania, and biological cultures are available in many garden houses or natural food stores. These seem to be the safest sprays for pest control. All are used by organic gardeners, although the purist may reject them all.

Unfortunately there are no fungicides, including Captan and Ferbam, that meet with approval from the purists. Bordeaux mixtures and lime-sulfur sprays used in the past are all viewed by most of them as too toxic.

Organic gardeners sometimes use dormant oil sprays to control the first infestations of many diseases, and often this is enough if they follow other safeguards. Dormant oil spray can be bought ready to mix at many garden houses or can be prepared at home by mixing 2 quarts light motor oil (not kerosene or fuel oil) with 1 pound fish oil soap or half a cup liquid detergent. Mix 1 part of this mixture with 20 parts water as needed. Use at once after you have mixed it with water, because the oil and water will separate if stored for any length of time.

Dormant oils can be used safely on the trunks and branches of trees early in the spring before any growth starts. It should never be used on green leaves, however.

Rotenone and Pyrethrum are insecticides made from plants. They wash off easily and have low toxicity. They kill a large range of insects, but their effective life is so short they need to be applied frequently to be useful.

Ryania, another plant-derived insecticide, gives good control over codling moths and certain other insects.

Tri-excel, a mixture of several organic insecticides, is a good all-around spray for organic gardeners.

Tobacco dust kills many insects and is an especially good control for aphids.

Biotrol and Thuricide are both trade names for Bacillus Thuringiensis, a biological control that kills the larvae of certain harmful insects.

The preceding organic sprays are available at many garden stores and nurseries. Carefully follow package directions for best results.

Wood ashes were used by old-time gardeners, who tossed them through their trees when the dew was on in the morning. They claimed this gave disease and insect control and was a good fertilizer as well.

CHEMICAL ORCHARD SPRAYS

For those who prefer to use chemicals, home orchard sprays are available in most hardware or garden stores. Be sure to follow exactly all the instructions on the package for mixing and using.

Orchardists who want to make their own orchard spray can use the following recipe. It will make one gallon of all-purpose orchard spray that can be used to control most fruit and berry insects and diseases. To one gallon of water add:

1. Captan (buy 50 percent wettable powder)—3 tablespoons
2. Malathion (buy 25 percent wettable powder)—2 tablespoons
3. Methoxychlor (buy 50 percent wettable powder)—3 tablespoons

Mix thoroughly, and stir or shake the sprayer frequently to keep them from separating. The Captan is for disease control and the Malathion and Methoxychlor are for insect control.

Again, I caution home orchardists to use only the recommended sprays and to follow directions exactly. Experimenting with unknown chemicals can be dangerous. Many can cause serious damage to the tree at certain stages of its growth, to say nothing of the effect they might have on you and your grandchildren.

BUY ONLY WHAT IS NEEDED

Shelf life for many agricultural chemicals is limited, so don't buy more than you can use within a year or two. Store in a dry, cool place secure from children and pets and away from all foodstuffs.

Spray Schedule for Most Home Orchards

Before you begin, there are times when you definitely should *not* spray. First, never spray when the trees are blooming, in order not to harm pollinating insects. Second, do not spray within two weeks of picking—humans are important too.

Since trees bloom at different times, the first four sprayings may be at irregular intervals. After that fourth spraying, the whole orchard may be sprayed at one time (Sprays 5 through 7). In order to coordinate these sprays, you may allow seven to twelve days between Sprays 4 and 5. If you wish, dormant oil spray can be used instead of orchard spray for Spray 1. After that, use the orchard spray or your choice of organic sprays.

SPRAYS FOR TREE FRUIT

1. Dormant spray. Use when tips of buds are swelling but before they begin to turn green.

2. Bud spray. Use when leaf buds are just beginning to open.

3. Pink spray. Use when blossom buds show pink and are nearly ready to burst open.

4. Petal fall spray. Use when nearly all petals are off tree.

5. Summer spray. Use seven to twelve days after Spray 3.

6. Summer spray. Use ten to twelve days later.
7. Summer spray. Use ten to twelve days later.

Sometimes additional sprayings are needed. If so, they may be continued at intervals of ten to twelve days until two weeks before harvesting begins.

SPRAYS FOR GRAPES

1. Orchard spray. Shortly before blossoms open.
2. Orchard spray. Just after fruit has begun to form.
3. Orchard spray. Two weeks later.
4. Orchard spray. Two weeks later, if necessary.

This spray program should control flea beetles, curculios, berry moths, root worms, and fruit rot.

SPRAYS FOR RASPBERRIES, BLACKBERRIES, TRAILING BLACKBERRIES

1. Ferbam. Use in the spring, when canes are dormant, to control spur blight. Use 3 tablespoons of 76 percent wettable powder per gallon of water.
2. Orchard spray. Use when new canes are 4 to 6 feet tall for control of anthracnose, tree crickets, and cane borers.
3. Orchard spray. Use directly after berries are harvested.
4. Ferbam. Use after leaves have begun to come off and canes are dormant (same formula as number 1).

SPRAYS FOR STRAWBERRIES

Leaf spot. Use orchard spray at ten-day intervals the first summer following planting.
Cyclamen mite. Use Kelthane, following directions on package.
Weevils and tarnished plant bug. Use orchard spray mix just as bud clusters start to form.

Although the control of orchard problems seems complicated and somewhat overwhelming to read about, it really is not. Don't be discouraged by the long list of possible troubles. As I have already pointed out, with a simple spray program and ordinary care you can control all the fruit pests that are likely to bother you. The beautiful blemish-and-worm-free fruit you harvest will be worth the trouble.

10 / ANIMALS AND OTHER HAZARDS

Despite what some conservationists may say, gardeners and orchardists in many parts of the country have found that all wildlife is not vanishing. In fact, many animals are multiplying far beyond belief. The increase in animal activity these days may have come about partly because there are so many abandoned farms in rural areas where unmowed fields and ungrazed pastures encourage mice and rabbit life. There are fewer hunters and trappers and a decrease in the number of predators, too. Whatever the reasons for the current proliferation of wild animals, they can be one of the fruit grower's most serious problems. If given a few favorable months, some animals—like mice—can multiply astronomically, and sometimes the orchardist isn't aware of what's happening until too late.

If you move to the back country and are surrounded by woods, you rather expect some visitations by wildlife. But nature has adjusted to today's changing world, and city and suburban gardeners also often find woodchucks, raccoons, and rabbits in their gardens. Even deer have been known to occasionally stroll down the streets of good-size cities. So wherever you live, you may face the problem of unexpected and uninvited guests.

Of course, some people plant fruit trees and bushes because they want to attract animals and birds and they know the wildlife will come flocking to them. They love to watch deer eating apples from their trees and birds swooping over the berry patch. However, most of us who toil over our trees hope to have at least part of the fruits of our labors for ourselves.

As one who has tried to garden and grow fruit for three decades on the edge of a wilderness, I sympathize with those who battle the wildlife. Besieged by everything from mice to moose, I've found that the only plant we grow that some form of animal life doesn't relish is rhubarb, and I'm sure the only reason rhubarb escapes is because of its poisonous leaves.

Mice Control

Mice and voles are probably among the worst problems to orchardists, simply because of their sheer numbers. Damage from them can occur anytime but usually is most severe in late fall, winter, and early spring. Particularly upsetting is their habit of chewing the bark off tree trunks beneath the snow where you can't see what is happening until the spring thaws. Even though a girdled tree may leaf out, it will soon die, and there is usually no practical way to save it.

Mice not only girdle newly planted fruit trees but often debark trees up to 8 inches or more in diameter. Some years are worse than others, and since you cannot predict when they'll strike in full force, it's best to be on guard at all times.

A good hunting cat or two is fine control in a small orchard, but it's more reliable to wrap your young tree trunks in hardware cloth, heavy metal screening, or plastic tree guards. These can be left on year-round, or you can wrap the trunks carefully each fall with aluminum foil and remove it in the spring. Guards should extend at least 2 feet above ground to be an adequate protection. If wire or wire mesh is used, make sure it does not constrict tree trunk growth.

Keeping the mice away from large trees is harder, but various paints and repellents have been tried with some success. Commercial orchardists often use poison corn or oats about the trees. The poison used—zinc phosphide—is effective against mice and is apparently quite harmless to most larger animals and pets. Usually the poison is placed under mulches or in small cans to keep the birds from eating it; or it can be scattered about just before the first snow comes.

Mouse poisons are available in many farm stores, such as Agway, Inc., or you can contact the state horticulturist at your state extension office (ad-

Mouse damage. The tree will die because the bark is completely girdled.

Plastic guards, or similar material, protect young trees from rodent damage.

dresses are given in the Appendix). Be sure to order well in advance of when you'll want the poison; sometimes it takes a while to locate a source and get it shipped.

Rabbits, Porcupines, Raccoons, and Squirrels

These small animals were seldom a problem when hunting was more intensive or when dogs ran more freely, but now in some places they cause a lot of grief. Rabbits eat the branches and bark off trees. Porcupines chew the bark and sometimes cut off whole limbs, dropping them to the ground for easier nibbling. Several times these prickly creatures have invaded our garden, cutting down and completely consuming a whole long row of raspberry canes in a single night.

Raccoons and squirrels are more likely to eat mature fruit. The raccoon doesn't wear his bandit mask for nothing! Gray squirrels will often run about an apple tree merrily taking one bite from each apple, ruining the whole crop.

A good dog can help chase away these animals very effectively, but if dogs are impractical or if they must be kept on a leash, other means should be found. Fencing out these persistent creatures is practically impossible, although electric fences do help. Persistent hunting and trapping where allowed may be the only solution. Catching the animals in box traps for release several miles away is a more humane way of handling the situation, but transferring the problem to another neighborhood may not be morally sound, either.

Deer Control

Although bear may occasionally mess up fruit trees in the back country, deer are usually the only large wild animals that bother orchards. In fact, after fighting bugs and mice, the deer seem like monsters. They love both the apple twigs and the fruit, and also seem to get a kick out of scrubbing the bark off fruit trees with their antlers. In many areas it's impossible to grow even one fruit tree without a high fence.

Control of the supersmart deer is probably most difficult of all. They

A high, strong fence may be necessary to keep out larger animals.

are heavily protected by both game laws and public opinion, so off-season harvesting is not encouraged, although sometimes the local game warden will give his blessing if your orchard is beginning to look like a disaster area. Mothballs, dried blood, lion manure (if you live near a zoo), and human urine have all been used as repellents, but they don't work at all when most orchard damage occurs. In fall and winter when other browse is scarce and the cold weather has frozen up the smell-producing products, the deer move in.

A free-running dog can help if you are smart enough to train him to chase out the invaders and return home. But in some areas dogs are shot for chasing deer. Noisemakers, radio music, or flashing lights work, but only for a short time because the deer quickly become accustomed to these mechanical devices and, accepting them as normal, go placidly about their evening meal of your favorite trees.

A high, tight fence seems to be the only answer to the deer problem (see page 93). They will give up on an orchard only when it is made completely impossible and not merely difficult for them. Therefore the fence must be extremely well built, since deer can and will squeeze through the most unlikely places. The larger the orchard, the higher the fence needs to be, apparently. A 4- or 5-foot fence is adequate for a few trees, but a large orchard will probably need a fence at least 9 feet high.

To Hunt or Not to Hunt

Many people who believe that everything in nature is good, find any control of wildlife difficult to accept. "I always plant extra for my friends, the birds and animals," one lady gardener told me proudly. The next week her friends cleaned out her garden, leaving her nothing, and she quickly changed her tune.

Much as I enjoy wildlife in the woods, I have always found it hard to understand why these hungry hordes will walk past acres of wild berries, apples, and tasty plants of all kinds to come a quarter of a mile farther to chew up the ones I have slaved over. Yet every time I suggest violence, there are many who view me as some sort of Genghis Khan.

I do notice that many of our antihunting homesteading neighbors often have a complete change of heart once they've tried gardening in animal country and have seen years of work wiped out in a single night. Some have become quite savage and have adopted punishment to the degree that all wild animals found near the garden are presumed guilty unless quickly proven innocent. Folks around here still speak in awed tones of a woman who, in the midst of an elegant dinner party, heard a noise in her garden. Graciously excusing herself—and still in her dinner gown—she grabbed a .22 rifle, left her shocked guests, and rushed out to dispense with a porcupine who was having his own dinner party in the back yard.

If you live in an area where wild animals are numerous, you may find it a real challenge to cope with them. You may have a degree of success by spraying on some of the commercial bad-tasting repellents, setting up electric fences, or even camping out in the back yard during the worst invasions. Probably you can think of other means.

Other Hazards

Besides animals, fruit growers should expect to encounter certain other problems. In the North, snowmobilers don't always bother to go around young orchards, especially at night. Trail bike and horseback riders sometimes view a new planting as only a bit of brush. Probably one of the biggest mechanical threats to home orchards is the lawn mower. All machinery, including tillers and tractors, should be used carefully around your trees.

In agricultural country, farm animals can be expected to break down even the best fences occasionally and wind up in somebody's orchard or garden. In a few minutes a herd of cows or a few horses can do tremendous damage, and so can wandering goats, sheep, or pigs. Children may thoughtlessly snap off a limb or even a small tree to use for a whip or cane, and pets seem to like to take a crack at young trees. Young puppies trying out their growing teeth or cats playing games can ruin them. If any of these are likely to happen in your back yard, a strong fence with a sturdy gate may be the only answer.

Fences can't keep out bird intruders, though. We welcome birds, and usually they are a great asset as insect controllers in spring and summer. But sometimes they can present a real problem at harvest time. Not only do birds love cherries and nearly all kinds of berries, but they also often ruin large amounts of apples and other fruit. Fruit isn't all they may bother, either. Sapsuckers have been known to bore hundreds of orderly holes in the bark of fruit tree trunks during the winter and spring.

Strips of fluttering aluminum foil, noisemakers, radios, scarecrows, cats, and plastic snakes are all used by gardeners hoping to save their crop. If you use them, put up all bird-scaring devices just before the fruit is mature. If you install them too early, the birds will get used to them; if too late, you'll find that the feathered gourmets have already developed a craving for the stuff and won't easily give up.

A young fruit tree leads a hazardous life, all things considered, and only your constant vigilance can guard it through the formative years and into production.

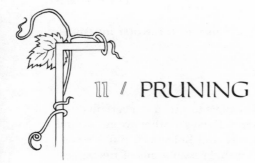

11 / PRUNING

Pruning is a real puzzle to many orchardists. While a few people are happy as larks when they are snipping away at their trees and dreaming of harvests to come, many others prune sparingly or not at all.

Years ago I used to do quite a lot of landscaping work for other people, which included pruning their fruit trees, shrubbery, and hedges. I learned at an early stage that, whenever possible, it was better to prune everything when the owners were away. While everyone liked the results of pruning after it was finished, watching the procedure or actually doing it seemed to many people a bit like slaughtering a steer. "Stop, you'll kill that tree!" or "How can you be so ruthless?" were frequent comments along with frantic hand-wringing.

Should We Prune?

Probably one of the main reasons that Europeans and Japanese are considered such good gardeners is because they are not afraid to prune, and to prune severely when necessary. Americans are learning, but there are still a few die-hard gardeners who are not convinced it's all that great an idea. They stoutly maintain that pruning is contrary to nature and should never be done at all.

This isn't a good argument because nature prunes. She gets rid of dead or surplus limbs by high winds, ice, and snow. Man simply does it neater, more orderly, and with an eye to producing better fruit—things about which nature doesn't always show much concern. No gardener should feel it is wrong to prune, even with the new belief that trees and plants have feelings. If trees could talk, they would probably say, "Please give me a haircut and a manicure." There is no doubt that proper pruning improves a tree's appearance. More important, it conserves its strength for a longer, healthier life and helps it produce larger and better fruit.

There is another group of gardeners who have nothing against pruning but are so afraid of doing it wrong that they can't bring themselves to cut a branch. They feel that if they erred even slightly the tree would never forgive them. Some have read lots of books on pruning, and the more they read the more confused they get. So their tools stay sharp and their trees grow very bushy and thick, producing lots of small fruit every other year, most of which never gets very well colored and goes unused. Gardeners who are too permissive with their trees for whatever reason will likely regret it. Actually, pruning is not at all difficult.

As you approach your orchard, saw and clippers in hand, you'll want to keep in mind some of the reasons for pruning:

1. To remove diseased, broken, or old branches where troubles could start.
2. To decrease the bearing surface of the tree by thinning out extra limbs. A smaller number of fruits will result, but fruits will be larger, the total yield greater, and the tree more likely to bear every year.
3. To remove crossed limbs that rub in the wind and cause wounds, and to prevent bad crotches (forks) that can split when the tree is loaded with fruit or ice.
4. To open up the tree so that more sunlight can get into the inner branches. This allows fruit to grow and ripen there as well as on the outside limbs.
5. To renew bearing wood. By each year removing a few old limbs that have lost vigor and allowing new healthy limbs to replace them, the whole tree can be renewed every decade.
6. To train the tree into a good shape and size so it is attractive, convenient to work with, and strong enough to hold up its fruit load.

When to Prune

For the first few years—in fact, until the fruit trees begin to bear—they need very little pruning. Of course, if you planted a bare-rooted tree you probably pruned it severely at that time. But as your little tree grows, all

Fifteen-year-old semi-dwarf apple tree after pruning (University of Illinois)

*Left: five-year-old sour cherry tree before pruning
and (right) pruned to a modified leader system (both by University of Illinois)*

you'll need to do is correct any bad crotches, keep a strong central trunk (leader), and keep it from getting too wide or too leggy. In fact, overpruning of young fruit trees will delay bearing and cause excessive wood growth.

After the tree begins to bear fruit, however, you'll want to prune more heavily and prune each year. Most orchardists do it in late fall after the leaves have come off the trees, or in very early spring before any growth begins. Trees pruned in late spring will "bleed" badly, which is not good for them. In warmer climates, pruning can be done anytime all winter. But in the North most orchardists don't like to prune when the temperature is below freezing, for they feel it damages the wood cells. Mild, sunny days are much more pleasant to work in anyway.

A few fruit growers like to prune in late summer while the leaves are

Six-year-old peach tree before pruning (left) and after pruning (right). Peaches of this age and older need moderate to heavy pruning to keep them in good production. Note that most of the pruning was done on small branches (both by University of Illinois).

still on but after all tree growth has stopped. They believe that not so much undesirable growth will result the following year if they prune at that time.

We usually do our pruning in late winter or very early spring. Not only is it more pleasant to work on the bright spring days, but I find it easier to see where to cut when the leaves are off. I can nip off any branches that have been chewed by the deer and those that were broken by snow and ice, and I find it's easier to check for fire blight and sunscald at that time too.

You'll find that old-time orchardists love to argue about the best pruning time. Some maintain that they do their pruning whenever their tools are sharp—or any time of the year. But there are lots of arguments against that method. After you have had an orchard for a while, you can choose your own favorite time. At first, however, I recommend late winter or early spring pruning before any growth starts and when the temperature is above freezing.

Methods of Pruning

Just as each orchardist may disagree about the correct time to prune, each has his own method of pruning. If you turned a dozen loose, no two would trim your trees alike, yet each might do a good job.

Home fruit growers often get upset or discouraged at the complicated directions given in pruning books. Some of these give explicit rules for pruning to a leader, a modified leader, or an open vase shape. Don't let these terms throw you. In fact, I wouldn't even worry about them at all, because many veteran fruit growers have pruned for years and never heard of them.

If you want to get technical, pruning to a leader means simply keeping a strong central trunk in the middle of the tree and letting all the other branches come from it. A modified leader means that the central stem is kept partway up the tree, then allowed to branch more freely, growing several tops on the tree. An open vase means that the center of the tree is kept open and limbs are allowed to grow around this open space, letting plenty of sun into all of them.

Generally speaking, trees that produce large fruit—such as apples, pears, and peaches—do better when grown with a strong central or modified leader. Apricots, cherries, and plums, which are less likely to split from heavy fruit loads, are more suitable for the open vase treatment.

Spur Fruits

When pruning, it is well to know something about the fruiting habits of each tree. Some trees produce their fruits along the branches, while others tend to do most of their bearing on short stubby spurs.

Many of the stone fruits belong to this spur-type group, and so do certain varieties of other fruits. In recent years there has been much interest in developing new spur-bearing apples, and some catalogs are now offering them for sale. Commercial growers like them, and they are equally good for the home gardener.

Since the spur-type trees usually make less limb growth they tend to be a somewhat smaller tree—a semi-dwarf. They are likely to bear at an earlier age and require less pruning than a regular tree, and they are more productive than a dwarf tree. Removal of some of the excess spurs will probably be necessary when pruning this type of tree, but be sure not to remove too many or the crop will suffer.

Pruning Tips

When you prune, don't butcher the tree, but don't be stingy either. As in thinning the fruit, my Scottish blood kept me from doing a good job at first. I would prune and prune, yet my trees didn't look like the pictures. Now I have a very effective method. I go out one day and cut off all I dare to, and haul off the prunings. Then I come back the next day and cut off as much more, and that is about right.

Old-timers say that you should open up the tree enough so you could

Right: spur-type apple. These require less pruning than the regular kinds (University of Illinois).

Below: a regular apple tree. These produce most of their fruit on limbs (University of Illinois).

Lower right: sweet cherry tree after pruning to a modified leader system. Usually sweet cherries require less pruning than most other fruit trees (University of Illinois).

grab a cat by the tail and fling him through the tree next July and never hit a branch. I have never heard of anyone actually flinging the cat, but while I'm snipping away I try to keep it in mind. It adds drama and excitement to the pruning job.

Prune each tree according to its growth habit. Every fruit tree grows differently, and it is best to prune them accordingly. For example, Stayman apples are spreading trees, while Delicious tend to grow upward. Pruning has to be adjusted to these habits. On spreading trees the end branches may occasionally have to be pruned so the tree won't get too wide. On the upright-growing trees, correct bad crotches and encourage limbs to spread out in a more open fashion.

Don't allow trees to branch too close to the ground in heavy snow country. Settling snow can break the lower branches. As trees grow and begin to bear heavy loads of fruit, branches that formerly grew upright tend to move downward. To avoid the necessity of cutting large limbs later, don't allow them to branch closer to the ground than you'll want them when the tree is full-grown.

Remove the wood and trimmings and burn them. After your pruning operation, always take the pieces away from the orchard and burn them so insects and diseases won't spend future winters there. Where burning is prohibited or unsafe, taking the prunings to sanitary land fills or cutting them into small pieces for burning in a fireplace or wood stove may be possible.

Prune every year. The tree suffers less shock if it is pruned moderately every year instead of having a large amount of wood taken off every other year or even less frequently.

Avoid chain saws for pruning. Tempting as it is, I would never use a chain saw, even on the large cuts. Even small power saws are hard to control on precision work, and it's too easy to cut into a nearby branch that you don't want to harm.

Be careful not to prune old, neglected trees too heavily. It's a shock for a big old tree to be pruned heavily if it hasn't been touched before. Before restoring an old orchard that hasn't been pruned in years, read Chapter 14.

As you prune, keep telling yourself it is all for the good of the tree. If you're a convincing speaker this may help. And if you have any doubts left, drive past a commercial orchard after it has been pruned and notice how severely they do it. You'll be surprised how much wood they remove.

Tools and Paint

Although the old pruning hooks sound romantic, I don't know of anyone who uses them today. Hand clippers, long-handled pruners, and a fine-tooth saw for large cuts are all the tools necessary. If you have large trees, pole pruners that reach up into trees may be desirable (see page 103).

I like the snap-cut, hand-held clippers better than the kind that has blades cutting past each other like scissors. Snap clippers make a smooth cut, they can be sharpened easily, and on some of them the blade can even be replaced if necessary.

Be sure to keep all your tools clean and sharp so that you can make smooth cuts that will heal over quickly. Be careful, too, when pruning large trees. You may have heard of the tree surgeon who fell out of his own patient.

Whenever I prune I carry with me a can of good tree paint such as Tree Kote. It seals the wounds of large cuts and can be used to fill any breaks or holes you may find in the tree. I think that keeping out weather and bacterial infection is an important part of tree care, but there are expert orchardists who say that tree paint does absolutely no good whatsoever.

Making the Cuts

In pruning, how the cut is made is as important as when. Always cut small limbs back to a bud (see page 103). Young trees or the ends of small branches are pruned this way. Cut close to the bud but be careful it's not so close that it damages the bud. Also, make sure it is an outside bud because branches growing from inside buds will form odd-shaped, ingrown trees. Branches growing from outside buds will develop into spreading trees (see page 104).

Larger branches should be cut back to another limb or to the main trunk. Never leave a stub that has no life in it because it will die, rot, and quite likely get infections that can spread to more of the tree (see page 104).

Make your large cuts in three stages. Fruit tree limbs are heavy and can split into the main trunk easily, often gouging out large hunks of wood. Lighten the load by cutting off the main part of the limb first (see page 104).

Pruning cuts should be made with sharp tools, and close to the trunk or branch.

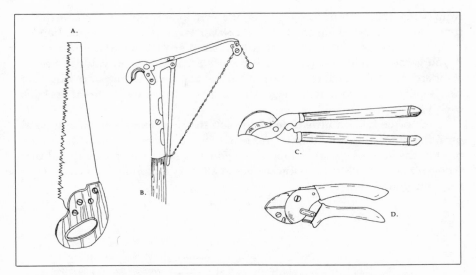

Some useful pruning tools: (A) *saw for making large cuts,* (B) *pole pruners for cutting high branches,* (C) *long-handled pruners for medium-heavy pruning,* (D) *hand clippers or pruners for light pruning*

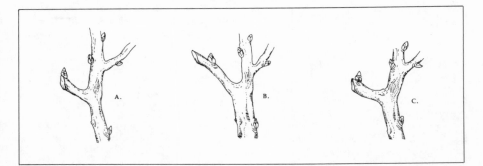

All cuts should be made to a bud. (A) *The cut on the left branch was made too close to the bud and may kill it.* (B) *The cut is too far from the bud, leaving a dead stub.* (C) *The cut is just right.*

Make undercut A first, then B. Make C last, and cover it with a good tree paint to keep out the weather.

Keeping Tall-Growing Trees Low

Occasionally people ask if they can keep their standard-size fruit trees low by pruning. The answer is yes, if you begin early enough and if you're persistent. If you have old trees that have grown very tall, perhaps from being planted too close together, it's a tricky job and not recommended that you try to get them to grow on a lower level. It's too late for them.

If you prefer to grow standard trees rather than dwarfs, however, or if you garden where dwarfs or semi-dwarfs are impractical, you can keep a standard-size tree down to a practical size for many years. Just start when the tree is still short enough to manage, and cut the tallest-growing branches back each year.

It often takes a little time to develop the right mental attitude toward pruning, but being around trees and watching how they grow and how they react to the various cuts will soon make you a master pruner. You'll find that it doesn't take great skill and knowledge at all, only a normal concern for your tree and your larder.

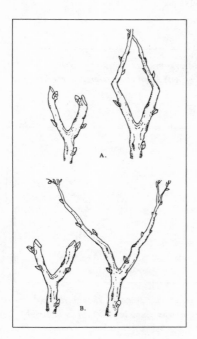

Left: Prune all branches to outside buds. Pruning to inside buds causes ingrown limbs and crossed branches. (A) Pruning to inside buds. (B) Pruning to outside buds encourages spreading of branches and a more open tree.

Make all large cuts in three steps. First make an undercut (A) so the limb won't split. Then cut the limb completely off at B. Make a final smooth cut at C.

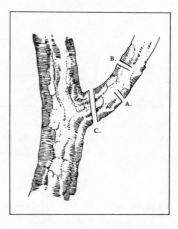

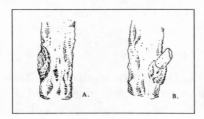

Left: be sure not to leave stubs when pruning. (A) A good cut ready to heal. (B) A stub that will soon die and possibly spread rot into the tree.

12 / THE HARVEST

Although it's hard to believe, a surprisingly large number of gardeners plant all their fruits and berries properly, tend them with great care, and then woefully neglect the very important step of harvesting them correctly. Every year bushels of fruit spoil just because home fruit gardeners are careless or don't know for sure when and how to gather it in.

Picking and using the fruit at just the right time is what home fruit growing is all about. It is the big advantage we have over commercial growers, who must harvest their perishable fruits before they are completely ripe and while they are still hard enough to ship well. Often, too, they have to pick all the fruit on a tree at once because it is inefficient for their large operation to select only the fruits that are really ready for picking.

Every berry and every tree fruit has a time that is best for harvesting. That is when you want to pick it. Not only does tree-ripened fruit taste better and need less sweetening, but it also has more vitamins.

How can you tell when the fruit is ripe? Squeezing and poking is our natural impulse, but it leaves bruises and isn't always a reliable method. Most varieties of tree fruits fall from the tree soon after ripening, so as soon as the fruit will separate from the branch with an easy twist it is ready. Most fruits change color as they ripen. Plums and grapes become covered with a powdery bloom. Cherries, apples, peaches, and pears develop their characteristic color and blush, and you should be certain what that color is. Some of the best-flavored apples are yellow, green, or russet brown in color, instead of red. If in doubt, open up an apple. If the seeds are dark brown, the apple is ripe and ready to pick.

Only pears and a few varieties of peaches should be picked before they are tree ripe. If left on the tree until they are soft enough to eat, they will quickly rot. Pick them just before they are ripe and store them in a cool place; they will be ready to eat in a few days or weeks, depending on the variety.

The taste test is very reliable with most berries. Strawberries become red all over and begin to soften. They and raspberries stay at their prime for only a short time and then deteriorate rapidly, so you should pick them every day during their season. Raspberries slip off their core freely when they are ripe. Blueberries, blackberries, currants, and gooseberries are ready when they have developed their full color and flavor.

Many of the best varieties of apples, peaches, and plums ripen over a long season and should not be picked all at the same time. These are the kinds that commercial growers cannot afford to grow even though they may be of superior quality, but for home orchardists they are perfect. The harvest can be spread out, with each fruit picked at its prime time.

The Picking

Except for eating the fruit, picking is the most enjoyable part of fruit growing. Often the two can come very close together. When we were kids picking raspberries, we were usually given a couple of sticks of chewing gum before we went to the patch. The theory was, if the mouth was full and busy, at least a few of the berries would get to the pail.

How the fruit is picked and how it is handled afterward is as important as picking it at the prime time. Pick on a dry day if possible. If fruit or berries are wet, they will start to spoil much faster than when they're dry. For the

Grapes should not be picked before they are dead ripe. They are one of the few fruits that will not continue to ripen after picking (USDA).

same reason, if berries need to be washed, don't do it until you are ready to eat or to process them.

Get the fruit into a cool place soon after you pick it. We always put berries in the shade as soon as we have a few picked, then move them into a cool room as soon as possible. Baskets or kettles are fine for picking most berries, but raspberries should be picked into small containers. These fruits crush so easily that unless they will be used within hours, only a few of them should ever be heaped together. Pint baskets are best for transporting and storing them.

I like a kettle or small pail that can be easily attached to a belt for picking any of the bush fruits. This leaves one hand free for picking and the other to hold up canes and branches. The best berries often hide under the leaves. Ordinary pails are satisfactory for picking cherries and plums. Even apricots, peaches, nectarines, pears, and apples can be picked in pails. The bags used by commercial growers to pick tree fruits are easy to use and save much possible damage to the fruit. If you have many trees you may want to

These Yellow Transparent apples are developing nicely, and will ripen in a few weeks.

invest in a bag or two. They fasten to your chest, are easy to move up and down ladders, and you can dump the fruit gently into boxes without removing it first.

Speaking of careful handling, all fruit should be treated like eggs. It should always be picked by hand and never clubbed or shaken from the tree. Fruit that has been bruised starts to rot quickly, and the rot can spread to all the good fruit it touches. The old proverb that one rotten apple can spoil a whole barrel is all too true. Any fruit that has been accidentally damaged, as well as all windfalls that fall naturally from the tree, should be used immediately.

The stems should always be left on apples because if they are pulled from the fruit they will leave a hole where rot can start. And be sure not to damage next year's crop by breaking limbs or fruit spurs as you pick.

Look after yourself as well as the fruit. Picking, especially from large trees, can be hazardous. Ladders have a nasty way of tipping when they are leaning against a high branch with a heavy load of picker and pickings. It is always tempting to climb a trifle too high for that luscious-looking plum that's just out of reach. Lifting heavy boxes of fruit can be hard on your back if you aren't used to it. Unless you work regularly as a stevedore, you'd better use containers you can safely handle, and move your loads with a wheelbarrow or garden cart.

After the Picking

Now that your kitchen shelf is laden with beautiful specimens, you'll find that more wonderful things can be done with fruit than with any other food. My favorite way of eating it is fresh off the tree. No middleman—direct from tree to me. But that doesn't mean I don't enjoy applesauce or strawberry shortcake with whipped cream, raspberry ice cream, blueberry pie, apple pandowdy, peach sherbet, or cherry tarts. They are all fit for serving on Mount Olympus on a sunny Tuesday.

We use a lot of fruit and berry juices, both raw and cooked. Crab apple juice, raspberry juice, and elderberry juice are some of our favorites. We stew the fresh fruits, heat the juice with sugar or honey, and bottle and seal it while still hot. They can later be drunk as nectar or mixed into tasty and healthful fruit punches.

Apple cider making with our old Sears & Roebuck press is another fall ceremony we wouldn't want to miss. Each year we not only freeze and bottle large quantities for winter drinking, but put aside several gallons to turn quite by themselves into vinegar.

Many of our friends make a great variety of fruit wines, including apple, currant, elderberry, grape, cherry, and raspberry. Others prefer the rugged hard cider of the old days, and one acquaintance is experimenting with starting an apple brandy business. So far, developing the process has proven to require so much sampling, I fear we may lose him before he finds the secret.

Usually we freeze much of our berry and fruit crop in plastic bags or sealed containers. We have found that the best flavor results if we mix sweetening with it at the time of freezing. Most fruits we freeze raw, with the exception of lots of cooked applesauce, and nearly all of them come out of the freezer tasting almost as if they were fresh. Out of their season we enjoy strawberries that go straight from the freezer into the blender for milkshakes. Just-thawed spiced crab apples on their stems have become a traditional garnish for our Thanksgiving turkey. Pie apples sliced and frozen raw are thawed just enough to break into a shell and bake for spring treats.

Fruits are also easy to preserve by canning in glass jars using the water-bath method. Apples, peaches, pears, cherries, and plums are satisfactory as canned fruits. In fact, I think pears are better canned than frozen. Most berries are not nearly as good canned as they are frozen, but all can be made into jams, jellies, conserves, marmalades, and butters that are superior to the supermarket variety, brighten up the breakfast table when the snowstorms swirl outside, and are perfect gifts.

One of our favorite uses for the big early ripening fall apples is to make them into apple pickles. We use an old family recipe that should never go out of style (see the Appendix, page 243).

Apricots, apples, and peaches can be cut into thin slices and dried either in a warm oven or in the sun. Blueberries and currants can be dried whole, and all the dried fruits can be kept for months on a pantry shelf in an ordinary paper bag.

While we're on the subject of eating, you should be aware of the toxicity of certain fruit seeds. Usually it is not wise to eat seeds of any of the tree fruits. The pit of the nectarine and peach may look and smell like an almond, but it contains hydrocyanic (prussic) acid, a deadly poison. While apple seeds are less toxic—it might take quite a few of them to cause a fatality —they are also quite poisonous.

STORAGE

Many tree fruits can be kept fresh in storage for months. Commercial growers now keep McIntosh apples in good condition until Easter, and home growers should easily manage to keep them at least half that long in a simple, inexpensive, and easily built root cellar.

While home root cellars cannot duplicate the scientifically controlled conditions that the large growers maintain, they make it possible for home growers to eat good fruits and vegetables all winter. We have a simple little one partitioned off in a corner of our basement. It is insulated, has an outside window for ventilation when necessary, and, luckily, has a dirt floor to help increase humidity. We can keep Northern Spy apples there until April if we don't eat them all first. While we can't always maintain the ideal climate of 34 degrees F. and 85 percent humidity, it still keeps our fruits and vegetables remarkably well.

Fruit can often be stored for a short time in an unheated room, too, in cool areas of the country. An old refrigerator in good running condition can hold a lot of fruit and preserve it very well for a long time in warmer areas.

There are many good books now available on processing and storing home fruits. Here are some of our favorites:

Freezing and Canning Cookbook, food editors of *Farm Journal,* Nell Nichols, ed. (New York: Doubleday & Co., 1964).

Putting Food By, Ruth Hertzberg, Beatrice Vaughan, Janet Greene (Brattleboro, Vt.: Stephen Greene Press, 1974).

Stocking Up, staff of *Organic Gardening and Farming,* Carol Stoner, ed. (Emmaus, Pa.: Rodale Press, Inc., 1974).

A list of companies that sell harvesting supplies, home cider mills, and orchard equipment is given in the Appendix. Your local hardware, farm, or garden store will also have many of the items you'll need.

13 / LITTLE TREES
FROM BIG TREES

Once I saw a classified ad in the newspaper asking if anyone had a Yellow Transparent apple tree. Someone wanted permission to dig up a sprout from it to start her own tree. I've often wondered if she found one and, if so, what the results were.

Beginning fruit growers are often puzzled about how trees get their start. Some folks plant seeds from their favorite apples, expecting they will grow into trees that will bear fruit exactly like the original apples. Others, like the woman in the ad described above, believe they can dig up the suckers that often grow about the trunks of larger trees in the orchard. They, too, are sure that these someday will produce the same kind of fruit. Both are usually disappointed.

Over the centuries fruit trees have accumulated a great many ancestors, all of whom have influenced their genes. The seed from any apple can take on the characteristics of any one of its ancestors or any combination of their good and bad qualities. Usually seedlings are most likely to resemble some of the "wild" ancestors, and fruits from them are likely to be small in size, unpleasant in flavor, or inferior in other ways.

This doesn't mean that all fruit trees grown from seed are worthless. Some produce fruit suitable for cooking, jelly-making, or cider. Occasionally a chance seedling is very good. Even more rarely, one produces fruit superior to any existing kind. This lucky chance on nature's roulette wheel is the main method whereby new fruit varieties appear. Every year you'll see new ones listed in the catalogs, but these are exceptions.

Usually fruit tree seedlings are worthy only to be used as rootstocks upon which a good variety may be grafted. This means that suckers or small trees growing from the roots of good ones are not going to bear the same kind of fruit as the good variety. Thus whatever the woman might have dug up from the base of the Yellow Transparent tree were not Yellow Transparent roots at all but those of an entirely different tree.

Trees from Seeds

Seeds from any locally grown, vigorous, good quality fruit will usually grow into seedlings that can be used as rootstocks for grafting. Or you may want to try for the long shot that it might be the one in a million super kind. In either case you can grow them easily.

Simply plant the seeds, stones, or pits as soon as the fruit is ripe in the fall. Plant one or two seeds in a pot and place it in a sunny window. Or, if you want, you can plant them in beds outdoors. Any potting soil can be used, or you can make your own mixture of equal parts of sand, humus (composted aged manure or peat moss), and good garden soil. If planting is to be done outdoors, be sure to protect the seeds from mice and squirrel pilferage. Also be careful to mulch enough to prevent frost from heaving the seeds out of the ground.

The seeds planted indoors should begin to grow within a few weeks; the outdoor ones will most likely be well started by early summer. Allow them to grow a year where they are, whether in pots or in the ground. Then, the following year in early spring, transplant them to a suitable spot so they will have room to grow. In another year or two they should be large enough for budding or grafting. You may even prefer to let a few grow into mystery trees—one you can perhaps patent and name after yourself!

Layering

One easy way to start another plant that is "true to name," or the same as its parent, is by layering. This is a very simple process that is successful

Layering is a simple way to start new plants.

112

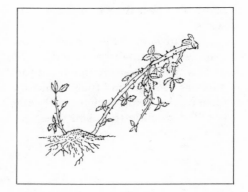

*Black raspberries and trailing blackberries
(dewberries) are started by tip layering the
new plants.*

with most plants. All you need is a good tree or bush with branches close to
the ground.

Simply bend down one of the branches, dig up the soil under it, and
bury a section of the middle part of the limb. If necessary, put a rock over
it so it won't pop back out. Stake the end of the branch so it is pointed straight
up (see page 112).

After a while roots will form on the section of the limb that was
buried. When enough roots have formed to support the plant, cut it from its
parent. The following spring before growth starts, dig up the new plant and
transplant it to its new home.

Rooting can be hastened by cutting a bit of bark from the under part
of the limb that is to be buried in the soil. Then dust the wound lightly with
a rooting compound such as Rootone or Hormodin.

Layering works well with gooseberries, currants, grapes, filberts,
quince, black raspberries, elderberries, and certain other fruits, all of which
often root within a few weeks (see above). Blueberry plants and fruit trees
take much longer, however, and sometimes you have to wait several years.

Be sure to let your spouse and other members of the family know what
you are doing. Soon after we were married my wife "rescued" all the layered
limbs of a currant bush by carefully pulling them up, thinking something
drastic had happened to them.

Division

While it's not practical with tree fruits, division is one of the easiest
ways to start many small fruits. By the time a berry bush is several years old,
new plants have probably already started to form around the original one. If
you want to start as many little ones as possible, the best way is to dig up
the whole plant and split it with your axe, knife, or pruning shears. Just make
sure that each division has a good clump of roots on it.

If you want only two or three new plants, you can sometimes sever
them from their parent with a sharp shovel without much disturbing the main

plant. The best time to make divisions is in early spring before any growth starts.

Currants, elderberries, gooseberries, blueberries, raspberries, and blackberries can all be started by dividing the large plants. If you decide to do this, you can encourage more rooting by piling good soil or compost 2 or 3 inches deep around the parent for a year or two before division. Roots will form on the stems, which can then be dug up and treated as new plants. This is called stooling the plant (see below).

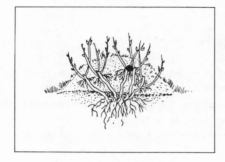

Gooseberries may be started by a form of division called stooling. Soil is heaped over the plant to encourage roots to form on the branches, which are later severed from the main plant.

Cuttings

When I was a child I heard someone say that if you took a small branch off an apple tree and stuck it into a potato in the early spring and planted it, it would grow. Even then I was anxious to start replacements for our diminishing old orchard, and I stuck twigs into potatoes left and right. Then I planted them in a long row and waited.

The "expert" was right. But he had carefully not said *what* would grow. We had a beautiful crop of potatoes that year, with a dead apple branch in each hill.

Over the years I have tried many methods to start fruit trees from cuttings. Most have not been very successful, but with some small fruits I have had great luck using this method.

Cuttings are one of the fastest ways of increasing many plants. Nearly everyone is familiar with the practice of slipping geraniums or chrysanthemums and using the small tips to start new plants. Most of us have also seen people start willow trees by sticking branches into moist ground.

Very few plants start as easily as geraniums or willows, although currants, grapes, and elderberries start quite quickly from cuttings. Gooseberries and blueberries will root, but with more reluctance. Cuttings of most fruit trees are extremely difficult to root.

Usually even hard-to-root plants can be grown from cuttings if they are made at just the right time and are rooted under perfect temperature and humidity conditions in the right media. This ideal environment is difficult for the home grower to provide, however, and even commercial propagators prefer the faster, cheaper, and more dependable method of grafting. Also, some kinds of fruits grow slowly and produce poorly when grown from cuttings.

TYPES OF CUTTINGS

Although tree fruits are usually started by grafting, small fruits are often started from cuttings. Three types of cuttings are commonly used: hardwood stem cuttings, softwood stem cuttings, and root cuttings.

Hardwood cuttings are taken when the plant is dormant in the winter or early spring. Cut the tips of branches from 6 to 15 inches long and store them for three or four weeks in slightly moist sawdust in a cool root cellar. By planting time a fleshy callus should have formed over the cut ends. Treat these callused ends with a rooting powder such as Rootone. Plant them in an outside bed of well-prepared, sandy soil that is rich in humus. The treated ends should be stuck into the soil about 2 inches deep and kept well watered.

In a few weeks both leaf and root growth should start. Allow the cuttings to stay in the bed for a full year, then transplant them the following spring. You can increase their growth by occasional light applications of a liquid fertilizer or manure water. A light mulch of lawn clippings will help hold the soil moisture between regular waterings.

Softwood cuttings are more like the geranium slips. Take these in early summer. When the plant is growing, cut or pinch off some of the new soft

Currants and grapes may be started by softwood cuttings. (A) The freshly cut branch. Note the cut is made on a slant to encourage heavier rooting. (B) A well-rooted cutting

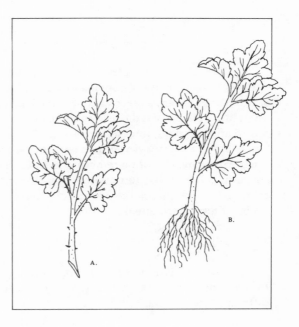

sprouts. These can be 4 to 10 inches long or even longer, depending upon how much new growth has been made. They can be rooted in moist sand, perlite, or sphagnum moss in small pots. The high humidity they need can be provided by enclosing the cuttings in a plastic bag and by frequent watering. Commercial propagators use a mist system to keep their cuttings wet. Mist systems are also available for hobby gardeners if you want to start a lot of plants. Rooting should take place within a few weeks (see page 115).

Carefully move the newly rooted cuttings from their humid mini-climate into an ordinary environment. Frequent watering, and shading them on sunny days, will probably be necessary to prevent wilting. After each cutting is well established in its pot, transplant it into a larger pot to grow into a husky plant that can later be transplanted to a permanent location.

Currants, grapes, elderberries, blueberries, and quinces can all be started by hardwood or softwood cuttings.

Root cuttings are a fast way to grow a lot of blackberry and raspberry plants. They can also be used to increase blueberry, elderberry, currant, gooseberry, and other small fruits. This method is also good for starting dwarf rootstocks such as the Mallings, which can be used later for grafting (see below).

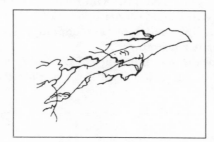

A blackberry root cutting. Sections of root cut into short pieces and planted in early spring will sprout and grow into good-size plants by fall.

To make a root cutting, simply cut down into the plant with a sharp shovel, dig up a mass of roots, and with a knife or small hand-held pruning shears cut them into pieces about 2 inches long. Plant these about 4 inches apart in a well-prepared bed. Lay them flat and cover them with about an inch of a compost, sand, and soil mix.

After a few weeks sprouts will appear from the root cuttings and a new bush will grow. It will be tempting to keep digging them up to see if they're sprouting. Resist the temptation, for they never will grow if you disturb them. After the plants have grown for a couple of years you can transplant them to their permanent location.

Grafting

Grafting is the method most often used in propagating fruit trees, hybrid nut trees, and certain grape vines. It is simply the joining of two different trees or plants by surgery.

Many people think of grafting as a mysterious and magic process that a few gifted individuals are able to perform on inferior fruit trees to make them produce bushels of good fruit immediately and ever after. They seem to think that only these select few are given such power, and somehow associate grafting with faith healing, water dousing, and the ability to bend spoons. The truth is, anyone can graft, but it takes a little patience both to do it and to await the results.

Over the years so many wild stories have been told about grafting that it's no wonder people have a fuzzy idea of what it's all about. Old-timers have told me with complete honesty about seeing, in their youth, large trees that were completely loaded not only with different kinds of apples but with peaches, plums, pears, cherries, and even tomatoes and squashes. Since all scientific knowledge points to the impossibility of such a spectacular event, I suspect someone was pulling a fast one with some wire and a bit of baloney, or else time had dimmed the memory of the storytellers.

Contrary to all the wild stories, only plants that are closely related can be grafted together. Most but not all the different kinds of apples, wild and improved, can be grafted upon each other. Most of the stone fruits—cherries,

GLOSSARY OF GRAFTING TERMS

Budding. A method of grafting using only a single bud instead of a scion or branch.

Cambium. The thin layer of tissue, often green or greenish yellow, between the bark and the wood.

Graft. Union of two different plants or trees by surgery. It is used commercially to propagate large numbers of trees of the same variety, and by home gardeners to start their own fruit trees or change an existing tree so it will produce better fruit.

Grafting Tape. An especially made moisture-proof tape that can be used instead of wax in grafting.

Grafting Wax. Material used to seal grafts so they don't dry out. It is usually a mixture of beeswax, resins, and other ingredients. Today, tree-dressing compounds or grafting or rubber tapes are more commonly used.

Rootstock. The root upon which the scion is grafted.

Scion (pronounced *sion*). The part of the tree that is to be grafted or budded to the rootstock.

plums, peaches, nectarines, and apricots—can be grafted interchangeably and on wild stone fruits. Pears can be grafted on quinces, and vice versa. Pears can also be grafted on apples, but the union is not usually good and the tree will most likely be short-lived. Even tomatoes can be grafted on potatoes since they are so closely related.

Grafting is the best way to propagate most tree fruits for several reasons. It's the fastest way and it also allows the orchardist to choose from a variety of rootstocks. As I said before, the rootstock you choose will determine whether your tree is dwarf, semi-dwarf, or full-size. It can also affect the age at which your tree will begin to bear and how well it will adapt to your soil and climate.

Rootstocks can have other effects on the tree besides changing its growing habits. They can affect the quality of the fruit. I once grafted a branch from a Yellow Transparent apple tree onto a seedling grown from a wild hard green apple. When the new tree began to bear fruit, instead of the soft, mushy Yellow Transparents, the apples were firm, kept longer, and had quite a zippy flavor. I also grafted a McIntosh on a similar wild seedling. The apples it produced ripened late and were rather sour.

Another time I grafted some good plums on a wild chokecherry. The graft was successful but the roots suckered so badly and were so determined to grow back into a cherry bush that the union was completely impractical. Certain apple rootstocks also tend to sucker very badly, as do some wild plums.

Whether you graft your own trees or buy them, it is important to rub off or cut off all growth below the graft as soon as it appears. Suckers take much of the tree's energy, and if left to grow they will eventually crowd out the good part of the tree.

Some people wonder if it is possible to graft large trees. Now and then someone will tell me they have an apple tree 20 or 30 feet high and they wonder if I could graft it so it will produce good fruit. They are discouraged when I tell them that in order to do this each limb would have to be grafted separately, a process that would take years. Even though it is possible, it's usually more practical to start with a new tree.

CLEFT GRAFTING

For a home gardener, cleft grafting is probably the most practical and easiest of the many types of grafting. It can be used for grafting small trees or for grafting new varieties on the limbs of larger trees. The latter is often called top working.

The best time to graft is in early spring just as the leaf buds are swelling and beginning to turn green. Sap is flowing at that time so the new branches cut for grafting—scions—are less likely to dry out before they begin to grow.

The graft is made by cutting off the small tree that you're using for the rootstock a few inches above the ground, or by cutting off the branch of a larger tree wherever you want to put the graft. Be sure to make the cut as smooth as possible.

Next, split this cut end in the middle about ¾ inch deep with a sharp knife or grafting tool. Cut carefully so the knife won't get away from you and completely split the trunk (see below).

Now prepare the scion. Cut a piece from the branch of the good fruit tree you want to propagate. This scion should be 3 to 6 inches long and contain not more than 2 or 3 buds. It should be about the same diameter as the limb or stem it is to be grafted upon, or it can be slightly smaller. In any case it should never be larger.

It is important that the scions do not get dry before the operation. In fact, I like to gather them the day before and put the cut ends into a pail of water so the new grafts will be turgid. Some gardeners like to dip all of the scion except for the cut end into melted wax before it is grafted to protect it from drying out.

Cleft grafting. A scion (A) is sharpened into a wedge-shape point and inserted into a rootstock which is split (B). The cambium layers must be exactly lined up. All bare, exposed wood is covered with grafting wax, tree dressing, or rubber tape (C).

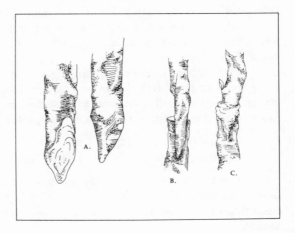

Sharpen the cut base end to a neat wedge shape (see drawings). Again, use a sharp knife so the edges will be smooth. Don't drop the scion or allow the cut edges to touch anything that could infect it, not even your fingers. Don't stick it in your mouth either; you don't want to get any bacteria into the incision.

Next, open the split part of the tree trunk with a knife and slide the wedge-shape scion down into it. Since your scion is not likely to be exactly the same diameter as your rootstock, take great care that the cambium layers of each are perfectly aligned on one side. This is where the sap is going to flow from one to the other. You will need a steady hand, but don't be nervous; the tree is not going to scream during the operation.

When the scion is solidly in place, the wound should be covered to keep the air from drying it out. Regular grafting wax is usually used for this purpose, but it's a bit messy since it has to be melted and brushed on. Various imported waxes, soft enough to ply in the fingers, are also available. I have had the best results by covering the graft with a tree wound sealer such as Tree Kote, or by wrapping it with strips of rubber electrical tape available in most hardware stores. Don't use plastic tape as that will constrict the tree as it grows. The rubber tape stretches and eventually weathers away.

GRAFTING TIPS

Some people like to gather the scions a couple of weeks before they are to be used and keep them sealed in a plastic bag in the refrigerator. By doing this the scions stay dormant while the rootstock is beginning to grow. Thus, after the graft is made the scions are less likely to dry out before the new sap gets to them.

Keep all sprouts below the graft rubbed or cut off so all growth energy can be directed into the new scion.

Stake the new tree if necessary. The graft union will be fragile for a few weeks. Staking may prevent its breaking off in a high wind.

Mark or keep a record of all grafts. It is easy to forget varieties, and when the tree begins to produce you'll want to know its kind and where it came from.

Remember not to be impatient. A new graft is unlikely to start growth for a week or two after all the other buds. Not all grafts will start at once, either. Give them all a chance. Even experienced grafters sometimes have failures, so don't expect 100 percent success. It is a precision operation.

BUDDING OR BUD GRAFTING

Cleft grafting requires considerable care in lining up the cambium layers perfectly. Bud grafting is less exacting and usually is easier for a beginner. I like it because it requires no wax and can be done over a longer season.

To bud graft you insert a single tiny bud, rather than a whole limb, into the tree to be grafted. Since budding is a mid- to late-summer operation, the bud is really the start of next season's leaf and branch. You'll see this little bud under the current year's leaf, right where the leaf stem comes out of the branch.

The time for successful budding varies year by year. You must wait until the next year's bud has grown large and is fat enough to use. All budding must be completed, however, before the sap stops moving or the bark will not slip well. So budding may be possible in June in parts of the South but may have to wait until mid-August in a late season in the North. Begin the budding operation as early as possible, though, so that if the first bud doesn't "take" there will still be time to put in another.

Collect your buds from wood that has grown during the current season. Cut a branch of the new wood a foot or more in length with 6 or more buds. The buds in the middle of the branch are usually the fattest and best to use. Cut these branches a day or so before using, and keep them in a cool place with the cut ends in a pail of water so that the buds can fill up with moisture.

When you're ready to begin you first cut a T-shape incision in the bark of the tree to be budded (see drawing C below). A tree slightly larger than the diameter of a pencil is a good size to bud. Next, pinch off the leaves on the branch (scion) that contains the buds, leaving about half an inch of the leaf stem to use later when handling the bud. Remove the bud from the scion by cutting a small shield-shape piece that includes the new bud, the leaf stem handle, and a thin sliver of the wood underneath the bud and bark (A and B). Make the cut with a sliding motion of a sharp knife so it will be smooth with no rough edges. Don't touch the cut edge. Here again, all operations should be sanitary to avoid possible infection.

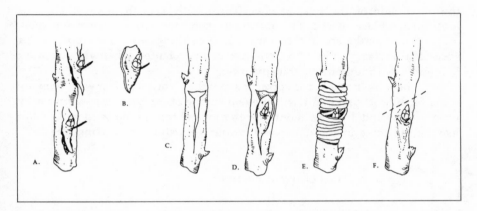

Budding is a fast, easy way to propagate fruit trees. Buds (B) are cut from a scion (A) in late summer. Note the leaf stem left as a handle for the buds. The buds are inserted into T-shape cuts made in the tree to be grafted (C and D) and are tied securely with rubber strips (E). Note that the buds themselves are not covered. The following spring, before growth starts, the top of the poor tree is cut off with a slanting cut (F) just above the new buds, which will then grow into the new tree.

Next, pull open the flaps of the T mark on the bark, and use the stem handle to insert the new shield-shape bud, making sure it is right side up. Line the top of the bud up tight against the top of the T (D). Let the flaps close back around it, and tie the bud in place (E). Tying used to be done with raffia or ordinary wool yarn, but rubber strips made especially for the purpose are much better and don't need to be removed later. By the time the bud has begun to grow, the rubber will have rotted away. Wrap the rubber budding strip bandage-style around the new bud, completely covering the whole incision but not the bud itself. You want it to hold the flaps tightly about the bud so that the sap will stay in and the air out.

If the bud looks fat and green after a week or two it has "taken" and all is well, even though the stem handle may snap off easily. If the bud shows no sign of life, there is probably still time to put in another in a different place.

Allow the tree to grow naturally the rest of the season while the bud just sits there doing nothing. Next spring, cut off the top of the tree with a slanting cut about a quarter of an inch above the new bud (see F, page 121). The bud should then grow into a completely new tree, the tree of your choice.

As in grafting, all the buds that grow naturally on the tree below the bud you're working with should be rubbed or pinched off to prevent competition from undesired growth of the rootstock.

Like cleft grafting, budding can also be done on limbs of larger trees if you want to change the limbs to new varieties.

Shading the new buds sometimes helps them succeed. Put the buds on the north side of the tree, or cover them with a small piece of cloth or loose-fitting black plastic. This may help them through a summer hot spell.

Some gardeners like to raise apple seedlings in 6-inch pots. After successful grafting or budding, the tree can be planted wherever you want it to grow without further transplanting.

The new sprout in the spring may tend to grow very fast with so many roots feeding it. Staking it will prevent undue strain on the new union by weight and wind. In a few months both root and top should become one, but leaving the stake in for a year will encourage a straight-growing tree.

SOURCES OF GRAFTING SUPPLIES

Grafting tape, waxes, tree dressing compounds, knives, and other tools can often be found in garden stores and many nursery catalogs. A list of firms selling these items is in the Appendix.

Sports or Mutations

For reasons that are a mystery to us ordinary gardeners, a limb may suddenly begin to produce a different kind of fruit than the rest of the tree. For instance, a tree that formerly produced all yellow apples with red stripes may sport a branch that has solid red fruit.

These mutations may produce fruit that is noticeably different in color, size, or quality. It may be better or worse than the fruit of the rest of the tree. Sports are not common, although they seem to happen more often in some varieties of trees than in others. They are mentioned here only so you'll be aware of them if and when they occur. Also, when you obtain grafting stock you want to be careful to get it from a limb that hasn't changed for the worse.

Not only limbs but occasionally whole trees may change. Some nurseries advertise "pedigree" trees, claiming that their grafts are selected from trees that produce better fruit than is usual with that variety.

If you notice a tree that's doing better than average, don't be too hasty in assuming it's a mutation. Sports are so rare that superior-appearing trees are more likely to be the result of good soil, climate, and care rather than any genetic difference in the trees. Don't be too surprised if you live out your life without ever encountering a sport. A lot of us have never seen one.

Is it necessary for you to be skilled at grafting to be able to grow good fruit? Not at all. Certainly you can live a long and useful life without ever acquiring this skill. Many good varieties are now on the market, and you can probably find just the ones you want by studying nursery catalogs. It is nice to know how trees are started, though, and grafting can be a fascinating and practical hobby. Besides, if you want to become known as Hortus the Great on your street, you will probably want to try grafting a few trees just to further your image.

14 / REVIVING AN OLD ORCHARD

If you buy property in the country, sometimes there will be a few fruit trees already growing there. The orchard may even have been a strong point in buying the place. An old fruit tree is beautiful, and everyone knows that the perfect country home always has a big spreading apple tree in the back yard.

The salesman probably knew this too: "And here is your orchard. Visualize those big crops of delicious plums, pears, apples, and peaches right on your own trees." He never lets you in on the probability that, come fall, there will likely be nothing on those beautiful old trees but a few small, hard, sour, wormy apples.

So now you own an orchard. Some of your friends are congratulating you on your good luck and others are recommending a weekend with a chain saw. You have to make a decision: Are those old trees really worth saving?

Perhaps your trees are quite old and suffering from the ravages of both animals and weather. If they are in really decrepit condition—old, badly broken, hollow inside, and falling apart to a sad degree, or if the fruit is quite small, hard, and unusually sour or bitter even when ripe—well, let's face it. The most practical thing to do is just turn the old trees into firewood and start over with young, healthy trees of good varieties.

On the other hand, if many of the trees appear to be in sound condition and the fruit is of good quality even though small, the orchard may actually be worth the considerable work of reviving it. Since it takes years for a newly planted orchard to get into worthwhile production, there's a definite advantage in renewing an old one, if it's at all practical.

Before you decide, examine your orchard carefully to see what is happening there. Most home orchards in the old days were planted with several varieties of trees in carefully laid out, well-spaced rows. They were nearly always grafted trees, and sometimes over the years grazing animals or rough weather killed the original tree. When this happened, often new sprouts came from below the graft, and these grew into relatively worthless trees producing wild-type fruit. If the trees in your old orchard have more than one trunk, or are growing in tight clumps, probably this is what has happened.

Seeds from fallen fruit often sprouted and grew into full-size trees. If the trees are growing much too close together and in a haphazard manner rather than in orderly rows, this has most likely occurred. Not all seedling trees are worthless, but very few of them are of good quality. You'd better take the saw to these, too, unless you're convinced that they are worthy of sauce or cider.

Both wild and domestic animals sometimes browse the lower branches of trees in abandoned orchards. This forces growth upward and makes the trees grow too high, often much higher than trees in a well-cared-for grove. Not only are tall trees difficult to prune and spray, but thinning and harvesting the fruit can be difficult and dangerous. If some of your trees are too tall to work with, you may not want to keep them either.

If you decide after inspecting your orchard that it is worth the time and trouble of saving, you can take certain steps to get the trees into peak production in the shortest possible time.

First, remove all worthless trees. This means taking out all the evergreens and hardwoods that definitely don't belong in an orchard, all fruit trees growing in clumps, and those so obviously decrepit that they would be hopeless to revive. Seedling trees and sprouts that have grown from the roots of good established trees should also be cut off, and all the branches and woods you remove should be burned for sanitary reasons.

Next, determine if the trees are spaced correctly. Fully grown trees should never quite touch each other. Many orchards have been planted with the trees growing too close together. In some you'll find dwarf trees that were set too deep and then grew roots above the graft, which allowed them to develop into full-size trees. In others, trees were just carelessly planted and not given the room they would need as mature trees; or perhaps filler trees were not removed when they should have been. If the trees appear crowded, sacrifice enough of them to allow the others plenty of room to grow into productive spreading trees with sufficient light, air, and soil.

Pruning the remaining good trees should be tackled next. Since fruit trees should be pruned annually, a tree that hasn't been touched in decades is in no way ready for the severe cutting that is essential to bring it back into shape. You'll have to resist the temptation to remake the whole tree too suddenly. The operation should take place gradually over a period of years, and the first pruning should always be a light one.

The reason for cautious pruning is that even a moderately heavy thinning of a mature tree that has been neglected for years may shock it enough to kill it outright; or at least it will stimulate a lot of new growth that may be too soft to stand the first frosts. It's especially important that you don't prune too heavily in northern latitudes or in orchards at high elevations where all late summer growth should be discouraged.

The first step in pruning an old tree is to remove broken limbs, dead or diseased branches, and all sucker growth at the base of the trunk. This can be done at any time of the year. Take care in cutting larger limbs so that no splitting back into good healthy wood occurs (see how to cut large limbs in Chapter 11), and always cover the cuts with a good tree paint to keep out infections and weather. Any branches that are growing crosswise or are rubbing against each other should be removed also. This operation, along with removal of broken, dead, or diseased branches and sucker growth, is about all the tree should be forced to withstand initially. Remember, *no heavy pruning of healthy limbs should be attempted the first year.*

The second year some light thinning of regular tree wood can begin. It is best to do this cutting only when the tree is dormant—that is, when the leaves are off. Late winter or early spring is most common. This pruning helps let in additional sunshine, which will improve the fruit color and add nutritive value. Removing part of the bearing wood also decreases the tree's production, thereby increasing fruit size and quality. And light pruning improves the shape of the tree, making it sturdier and more attractive.

By the third year you can prune more heavily, and in the years that follow it can be done in the usual way (see Chapter 11).

Feeding is also essential in restoring trees suffering from long-term neglect. Soils in old orchards are usually worn out and missing most of the elements necessary for good growth, especially nitrogen, which most fruit trees especially need. In abandoned orchards you'll also find that vigorous weeds, grass, and brush have been competing with the trees for what little fertility and moisture are available. Removal of all this competition is a good first step in restoring the fertility of the orchard soil.

You can start feeding the trees the first spring. Around each large standard-size mature tree apply 100 pounds of dried cow manure or 20 to 30 pounds of bloodmeal or the same amount of cottonseed meal, or soybean meal or a similar organic nitrogen fertilizer. The trees will absorb these plant foods slowly and as they need them for even, healthy growth. Nonorganic gardeners can use a complete chemical fertilizer, 5-10-10 for example, at the rate of 10 to 20 pounds per large tree.

Tree feeding should be in the area of the small feeding roots, so scatter the fertilizer in a circle with the outside rim just under the outside spread of branches and continue to about a foot away from the tree trunk (see page 36.)

Abundant nutrients are of little use if soil conditions or pH is not right for their release to the tree. If the soil is too acid, as is likely in an old orchard, the fertilizer will be "locked up" and unavailable to the trees. Apple and pear trees do best with a pH of from 6½ to 7. Plums, cherries, and peaches like a slightly more acid soil, about 5½ to 6. Some worn-out soil may test less than 5! To ensure that the nutrients are available to be absorbed and digested by the tree roots, it's wise to test your soil to see if lime is needed. Good orchardists, like all good gardeners, test their soil frequently since they know that climatic conditions, soil percolations, and other factors can change the acidity.

Mulch Helps Trees Get Going

Unless the area is to be mowed weekly throughout the growing months, I recommend using a mulch. By applying a heavy one the first year, you'll give the trees lots of encouragement. A mulch will smother grass and

weed competition, help keep the soil temperature constant, and hold moisture. It also allows roots to grow heavily in the upper soil layer where the
newly added fertilizers are and helps prevent winter injury. Last but not least,
by keeping the soil cool in spring, a mulch helps delay bloom on trees until
danger from late frost is past in northern climates. Those late frosts are a
hazard to delicate fruit blossoms and have been known to destroy an entire
fruit crop overnight.

The mulch, to be of real value, should be applied in the early spring
before the trees make their most vigorous growth. It should be thick enough
to effectively smother grass growth and should extend over the entire area
under the tree branches. (See Chapter 5 for the correct way to mulch.)

One of my favorite mulch methods for fruit trees is to apply a layer
of organic fertilizer followed by a layer of old newspapers, cardboard, and
magazines to smother grass and weed growth. Then cover the whole business
with a layer of old hay, shavings, or shredded bark 3 or 4 inches thick.

Earthworms and soil bacteria will soon get to work. If you pull away
the mulch in a few weeks to check on it, you will be able to see the soil
improvement. New tiny feeder roots are beginning to venture from the old
roots and are exploring the rich organic soil for new nourishment. The orchard is starting the trip back from its limbo, and you will feel the deep
satisfaction of being involved in Mother Nature's scheme of things.

Since pruning of the bearing wood is discouraged during the first year
of orchard renewal, one important way the fruit quality can be improved
immediately is to thin the fruit. Although many neglected trees bear only
every other year, if this is the year they are bearing you'll find that vigorous
thinning will do a great deal to conserve the tree's vigor.

In early summer when the fruits are very small—about the size of a
marble—thin them so that each fruit is at least 6 inches from any other.
Usually this means that in a productive year you pick and throw away about
80 percent of the crop. As I said earlier, the tree's energy is in this way
diverted into the remaining fruits, which will be of better quality. It's hard
to believe until you see it, but the remaining 20 percent grow so much larger
that they add up to more bushels of good fruit than if you'd kept them all.

Diseases and Insects

Diseases and insects may or may not be a serious problem in old and
neglected orchards. Chances are that some may be around, though, since bugs
and viruses thrive on broken limbs, exposed wood, loose bark, and weakened
trees. They also overwinter in decaying branches or in leaves and fruit on the
ground.

Careful orchard sanitation will help solve many bug and virus problems. Clean any tree wounds as soon as you spot them, then seal with a tree
paint to prevent development of insect and wind-spreading diseases such as
canker and fire blight. Pick up unused fruits from the ground each fall, or
allow animals to clean them up. Be sure to remove all tree prunings to a safe

area and burn them. Finally, diseased and insect-infested wild fruit trees that are near the orchard should be cut down for firewood.

After a few years of increasingly heavy annual pruning, the orchard will likely be in good shape and can be fed, mulched, pruned, and, if necessary, sprayed in the usual way.

New Trees Among the Old

Should new trees be planted among older kinds? Usually the presence of fruit trees indicates that growing conditions are good and new ones ought to do well there. Additional planting certainly may be considered, but you should be aware of the drawbacks.

Not only could years of misuse have made the soil far less fertile and more acid than it was in the original orchard, but the roots of living or dead trees quite possibly already fill the soil area. There is about as much of a tree below the ground as above, so in an old orchard there may already be a large amount of wood beneath the surface.

If good orchard space is scarce and you must plant new trees where old ones once stood, you'll need to use additional fertilizer to ensure good growth. Nitrogen is required for the bacterial action that helps the roots of trees decompose into the soil.

In most soils there is seldom enough nitrogen to take care of both the rotting of the old roots and the normal growth of the young ones. This is why new lawn trees usually do poorly when planted near the stump of the old ones they are to replace. By applying a larger than usual amount of nitrogen fertilizer you'll speed up the decomposition process of the old roots and encourage new growth on living trees.

Identifying Trees

If there are trees of merit in the old orchard you naturally want to know what varieties they are. Some kinds are readily identified by their fruit, such as the Yellow Transparent apple or the Green Gage plum. An old-timer can sometimes be helpful, but an honest face and a knowledgeable manner don't prove his memory is completely reliable.

The list of cultivated fruits is so huge, and some varieties resemble each other so closely, that finding the names of each kind can be a real chore and often not worth the effort. Of course there is always the exciting possibility of discovering a nearly forgotten but excellent old-time fruit, or even a chance seedling of a superior new kind on your lot—but the odds are slim. Just enjoy what you have, without worrying too much about their proper names.

Keep Orchard Size Within Reason

In reviving an old orchard, as in starting a new one, few are usually better than many. A small number of quality trees you take good care of will be more productive and much more satisfying than a large orchard of under-nourished and neglected trees. You naturally want beautiful and nutritious fruit, so it's important to limit your orchard to a size that fits in with the time you can spare for it. Save only the trees worthy of the expense and effort.

To sum up, bringing an old orchard back into good production requires time, hard work, and money. If the trees are vigorous and are good varieties, it is a rewarding and worthwhile venture. On the other hand, if their life expectancy appears limited or if their fruit seems of doubtful quality, your time and money will probably be better spent if you start a brand-new orchard in another area.

There are times, of course, when sentiment alone will rule. There is something majestic, nostalgic, and beautiful about a gnarled old apple tree. It exudes character. It may not matter in the least that its fruit is not the best. The flowers will be sweet, it may have a nest of robins in its hair, and the sour apples will furnish food for the deer, raccoons, and birds. Only a practical gardener would destroy a stately old tree. Alas, often practical we must be.

15 / THE APPLE *(Malus Sylvestris)*

When the wicked old witch selected an apple for poisoning beautiful Snow White, she knew exactly what she was doing. So did the serpent when he made his proposal in the Garden of Eden. There's no doubt that the apple is the most enticing and irresistible of fruits. No other fruit is available in so many varieties and flavors and can be eaten and drunk in so many delicious ways. We grow many different fruits, and I love them all, but every time a new nursery catalog comes, I automatically turn to the apple section first.

Customers at the nursery often ask what is the best apple. Over the years I've become pretty adept at wriggling out of a direct reply. Usually I hem and haw and end up saying, "That depends." If I attempted to make a list of the best-flavored, best-for-cooking, best-for-freezing, or best-growing varieties, there's no doubt I'd be drummed right out of the apple-growing world. Orchardists are very loyal to their favorites and would get "mighty het up," as we Yankees say, if their choices went unmentioned. So when an old-timer fondly remembers the Wolf River as the greatest fruit of all time, I'm not likely to compare its flavor with that of a wood chip. Likewise, I hope he won't shake his head too violently when I extol the virtues of the Northern Spy or the Cortland.

Several years ago on a trip to Maine we had lunch in a little seashore restaurant. The menu listed "Apple Pie—40¢ a slice" and "Duchess Apple Pie —45¢." There was no doubt about the favorite apple around those parts.

Some people like soft apples and some prefer hard. Some like a slightly sweet flavor while others claim they will eat only the very sour ones. Then there are those who hold out for juicy or dry or mealy or crisp or all sorts of other qualities they feel make the perfect apple. So don't pay much attention to other people's favorites. If it will do well in your climate, grow the kinds you like best.

Hardiness

One good reason for the apple's popularity among home fruit garden-ers is its ability to adapt so well to different soils and climates. One variety or another will grow in all fifty states. It is one of the hardiest of tree fruits and will grow where peaches, apricots, and pears haven't a chance. Crab apples have been developed that can be grown far up in the northern wind-swept prairies of Saskatchewan and Alberta, and the Russian apples brought by the early settlers are nearly as hardy. The Alexanders, Astrachans, Duchesses, Transparents, and many of their more recent hybrids are still being grown and enjoyed in the mountains of the northeastern and north-central states.

During the big freeze-up in the winter of 1917 when temperatures stayed below −40 degrees F. for days, many of the more tender apple varieties in the northern sections of the United States were knocked out. This paved the way for increased planting of the hardy, Canadian-originated, high-quality McIntosh and other members of its huge family. These apples are now being grown commercially and in home gardens all over Upper New England and New York State, southern Quebec, British Columbia, and the Maritime Provinces.

Further south and in the Pacific Northwest where the growing seasons are longer and winters are milder, many others can be grown, including the Baldwins, Delicious, Grimes Golden, Jonathans, Spies, Winesaps, and all their hybrids. So the home gardener, wherever he lives, has a good selection of apples from which to choose. See the list at the end of the chapter for suggestions for your area.

Rootstocks

After you've decided on the best kind of apple tree to plant and have located it in several nursery catalogs, you may be confused to find it available on several different kinds of rootstocks. The same variety of apple can be grown either as a big tree, medium-size tree, or small tree. It all depends upon which kind of rootstock is used.

Catalog A may state that the McIntosh can be purchased as a standard full-size tree growing perhaps 35 feet wide, or as a dwarf tree less than a quarter as wide. Catalog B may say it is available as a dwarf or semi-dwarf. You may also notice mysterious-sounding rootstock names with inexplicable numbers attached, such as Alnap 2, Robusta No. 5, Malling (or EM) IX. Don't let these descriptions throw you. Commercial buyers use these catalogs too, and sometimes nurseries forget to explain the details to beginning gardeners. Sometimes they tell which zones the trees are hardy in, but it will help you in making a good choice to know about rootstocks also.

Most dwarf apple trees for sale in this country are grafted on one of the Malling (pronounced Mauling) crab apple roots developed in England. There are many Malling variations, usually numbered with Roman numerals in true British fashion. The numeral indicates the tree's size, shape, or vigor. Malling IX roots produce the smallest trees, seldom over 6 or 7 feet high. The other Malling numbers produce trees from 8 to 12 feet high, which are usually sold as dwarf or semi-dwarf. Although the different Malling rootstocks are suitable for most parts of the country, they vary in hardiness. Nearly all are a bit tender for Zones 3 and 4.

Some semi-dwarf apples are grafted on Dolgo seedlings. These develop into hardy, vigorous, medium-size trees, about 15 to 18 feet high. They are widely planted in the north and north-central states and are often sold by nurseries in those areas.

Some places also offer semi-dwarf trees grafted on a Swedish apple root called Alnap 2 (A-2). These usually grow about 12 feet high and are very hardy, but since they are fairly new to this continent they haven't yet been thoroughly tested in all conditions of soils and climates.

Many Canadian and northern U.S. nurseries supply medium-size trees grafted on Robusta No. 5 crab apple rootstock. This produces a very fast-growing, extremely hardy, semi-dwarf tree about 14 feet high. This rootstock is much used in Quebec, northern New England, and Upper New York State. It is not recommended for warmer climates.

Standard trees—from 15 to 25 feet high—are usually grafted on apple seedlings that have been raised from seeds collected at processing plants such as cider mills. Trees grown on these seedlings are suitable for planting throughout most of the country. They vary in hardiness depending on the variety the seeds came from and the section of the country where they were grown. As you might expect, a tree grafted on a seedling grown from a Duchess apple in Minnesota would be more hardy than one grafted on a Delicious apple raised in Alabama. If possible, find out the point of origin of your rootstock.

Although full-size trees require more pruning and other care than their dwarf and semi-dwarf relatives, they produce much more fruit and, as a rule, tend to live considerably longer. If you have the room for a large tree, if you don't mind working on a ladder, and if you like the looks of an old-fashioned spreading tree, then apples growing on standard or full-size rootstocks are best for you.

To sum up: When choosing rootstocks, if you live in the colder climes of Zones 3 or 4, it's wise to avoid dwarf trees on Malling rootstock and standard trees on nonhardy seedling rootstock. You'd do better planting semi-dwarf varieties grafted on Robusta No. 5 or Dolgo seedlings, or standard trees grafted on hardy northern-grown seedlings, if you aim to have long-lasting, hardy trees that will supply apples for your grandchildren.

In the rest of the country, fruit growers have a better choice. Nearly all the dwarf and seedling rootstocks will thrive wherever apples grow well. The choice of rootstock then depends only on the tree size you want.

Culture

If you follow carefully the general directions for planting and growing fruit trees, you should be picking apples within a few years. Your tree will repay any extra care you give it while it's a youngster by bearing years earlier and producing heavier crops each successive year.

When you plant a tree you naturally wonder when you can expect your first crop. Again, "that depends" . . . on the variety, the weather conditions, and your tender loving care. Generally apples that ripen early in the season start to bear at a younger than average age, so a newly planted crab apple or Yellow Transparent may reward you with fruit within one or two years. A McIntosh or Winesap, on the other hand, may take four or five years, and some varieties such as the Baldwin and Northern Spy often take up to ten years before bearing their first apple. Luckily, though, unlike the earlier bearers their first crop is usually a big one.

Since you may have to wait a few years for your trees to produce, it's a good idea to keep a record and description of your plantings. We've heard of gardeners who lost a whole crop of luscious yellow apples because they were patiently waiting for them to turn red. Some other friends of ours picked their Delicious crop too early. They didn't realize that "winter" or late-ripening apples need to stay on the trees for a few weeks after they begin to color in order to bring out their best flavor. A few light frosts won't hurt the hard-fleshed apples a bit.

This brings up an important question. When is an apple ready to pick? Most fruit is ready when it separates easily from the tree. If you're uncertain, cut open an apple. If the seeds are still white, it is not yet ready. Apples are ripe and ready to harvest as soon as the seeds inside have turned dark brown.

Descriptions of various apple trees in catalogs usually indicate whether their ripening season is summer, fall, or winter. Summer apples usually ripen in July or August and are likely to stay in good condition only a few days or at best a few weeks after picking. Fall apples are ready for use in September and can be kept in good condition for a month or two. Winter apples should be picked in late fall and stored in a cool place where they can continue a slow ripening process. Depending on the variety, they can be kept from a few months to all winter in a well-made root cellar or similar storage place.

Some varieties ripen more or less all at once while other kinds need several pickings. Among those that have a very short harvest season are Baldwin, Black Twig, York Imperial, and Northern Spy. Those that ripen over a long season are especially good for home use since all the fruit doesn't need to be used at once. These include the Ben Davis, Gravenstein, Jonathan, Wealthy, Winesaps, and most summer-ripening apples.

All varieties of apples can be used successfully for cooking before the fruit is fully ripe. We often find we can't wait for pies and applesauce, and we've found that raccoons, birds, deer, and small boys can't wait either.

Crab Apples

Crab apples are often the neglected children in the apple family, which is too bad. The crab apple is an important addition to any home orchard, and there are a lot of good varieties from which to choose. Even many of the red-flowering ornamental crabs have usable fruit.

Our favorite is the Dolgo crab apple tree—often described as the perfect fruit tree. Not only is it beautifully shaped, vigorous, healthy, insect-

and disease-resistant, regular bearing, and likely to bear early in life, but it is also very hardy, the flowers are more frost-resistant than most fruits, and it is a prolific producer. It makes a good pollinator for other apples, too. If you have room, I strongly urge you to plant one. The large white blooms are so abundant that they hide the leaves, making the tree a mass of white beauty in the spring. In early fall it is red with ripening fruit. While the fruit is a bit sour to eat right off the tree, it makes the most beautiful jelly, spiced apples, and candied fruit; in addition the rich red juice can be safely used to color a lot of other foods.

Diseases

You'll discover that trees, like any other living thing, have their share of life's ills. The two most common diseases your apples are liable to encounter are apple scab and fire blight. Both can be quite troublesome, especially to the varieties that are most susceptible to them.

FIRE BLIGHT

Although the less common of the two, fire blight is by far the harder to control. If you are strolling through your orchard and see some sick-looking leaves hanging on branches that look as though someone had held them in a fire, you probably have it. The black scorched look means that disease-producing bacteria are at work in your tree.

It's important to remove at once any sign of the disease because it can spread rapidly and kill the tree. It can also be passed to other trees by bacteria blown around by warm spring winds and by insects, including pollinating bees.

The usual fungicides don't work on fire blight. The best remedy for the home orchardist is to cut out the infected parts and burn them. The tools used in cutting should be sterilized immediately after the operation (see Chapter 9, Disease and Insect Control) as contaminated tools are one way that fire blight sweeps through an orchard. After you've cut out all infected parts, I feel it's important to seal the wounds with tree paint. Because this disease spreads so quickly and easily, it's important to do this doctoring immediately after you find it.

APPLE SCAB

Few apple trees escape, throughout their entire lifetime, the far more common apple scab. In fact, some varieties seem to have it all the time. Unfortunately, the most susceptible are often the best kinds, like McIntosh and Prairie Spy.

There are few parts of the tree that scab doesn't attack. If your trees have it you'll find dark blotches discoloring the leaves, twigs, and fruits. Even trees that have just been planted will sometimes take on a sickly appearance since the disease spreads quickly by the wind, especially in cloudy, damp weather. Trees that have been overfertilized with chemical nitrogen are especially susceptible to scab.

Lime sulfur and bordeaux mixtures were once the common control. Now new fungicides like Captan make it much easier to keep the disease in check. (See list in Chapter 9.) Organic gardeners usually prefer a dormant oil spray (see page 87).

DISEASE RESISTANCE OF SOME APPLE VARIETIES

APPLE SCAB

Most Resistant	*Least Resistant*
Baldwin	Astrachan
Beacon	Cortland
Duchess	Delicious
Greening	McIntosh
Grimes Golden	Northern Spy
Jonathan	Prairie Spy
Nova Easy Gro	Quinte
Prima	Rome
Priscilla	Winter Banana
Starkspur Earliblaze	
Stayman	
Wealthy	
Yellow Delicious	
Yellow Transparent	

FIRE BLIGHT

Most Resistant	*Least Resistant*
Baldwin	Beacon
Delicious	Connell
Duchess	Cortland
McIntosh	Greening
Northern Spy	Grimes Golden
Stayman	Honeygold
Winter Banana	Jonathan
Yellow Delicious	Wealthy
	Yellow Transparent

In many years if weather conditions are excellent, scab will be no problem at all. When it does hit, however, you'll want to protect your crop because this disease not only weakens the tree and makes it look sick, but also causes the fruit to be unattractive and unusable.

Insects

As the apple advanced around the world it collected its share of insect pests, and you're sure to encounter at least a few of them sooner or later.

CODLING MOTH

This is one of the most common apple insects. Anyone who has ever found a big fat worm in an apple he was eating has encountered the larvae of the codling moth at work. You'll probably never see the culprit moth, for it usually flies at night as it goes about the dirty business of spoiling your fruit. The female lays her eggs inside the flowers. These later hatch into larvae, which grow inside the growing fruit where no spray can touch them.

The most effective way to control the moth, if this is your only orchard pest, is to spray an insecticide just after the petals are coming off the tree. Make sure the petals are off or you may accidentally kill the bees who are doing your pollinating. A follow-up spray in a week is a good idea, just in case you've missed any of the moths.

SAN JOSE SCALE

This small insect sucks nutrients from leaves, wood, and fruit. You'll recognize its activity by the minute scales that give the bark a rough appearance, and the hard bumps that appear on the fruit.

While scale was once viewed with a great deal of alarm, most orchardists have found that the insecticides to control codling moth and apple maggot also do a good job of controlling scales. Practically all the insecticides listed in Chapter 9 are effective against it. Since the pest may appear at any time, orchardists should keep a frequent lookout so that spraying may be done before any great amount of damage appears. Directions on the package should be followed carefully and, as with all chemicals, spraying should be completed a safe time before the fruit is harvested.

APPLE MAGGOT

This maggot, another pest you'll no doubt encounter in your apple-growing venture, is the small but familiar "railroad worm" that leaves its messy trail throughout the apple and often reduces it to a pulpy mess of brown worthlessness. The insect responsible for this destruction is about the same size and appearance as the common housefly. Sometime after the fruit is well developed, this fly punctures the apple and lays its eggs just under the skin. These hatch and the larvae tunnel their villainous way throughout the fruit.

The apple maggot larvae usually spend the winter in the orchard sleeping cozily in the ground under rotten apples that were never picked up. Often the best control is to clean up and dispose of all fallen fruit.

The same insecticides that help eliminate codling moths and San Jose scale will also control maggots. If spraying becomes necessary, you'll definitely want to begin as soon as the flies appear. If you wait until after the egg-laying is completed, it's too late—the hatching worms are already secure under the skin and will soon be at their mischief. Follow the orchard spray schedule in Chapter 9 for best control of all orchard insects and diseases.

Varieties

A century ago anyone wanting to buy apple trees had a tremendous selection from which to choose. There were a great many nurseries, and each

To most people fruit means apple. Off the tree, as cider, or in any of the countless ways they can be consumed, apples mean good eating, good health, good living (USDA).

listed all the local favorites. Unfortunately the customer didn't always get the variety he was promised in those free-for-all days. We've heard tales about one northern nursery where they used to write out a label for whatever variety was ordered, attach it to any fruit tree, and sell it to the unsuspecting customer. Luckily, in those days, there was usually a neighbor or local horticulturist who could regraft the tree.

Sometime after the turn of the century, home fruit growing went out of style. In fact, thirty years ago when I first went scouting for trees there was almost nothing available for the northern home gardener. Most catalogs listed only half a dozen apples, and these were mostly commercial varieties that needed a lot of spraying and a long growing season. Red and Yellow Delicious, Jonathan, Northern Spy, Baldwin, and Winesap were mentioned most often.

Now, due to increased demand, the selection is much better and the home gardener is being considered and even courted once again. Nurseries are rescuing formerly popular kinds, and experiment stations are developing new varieties especially suited for home culture. Happily, these days most nurseries are reputable so you don't have to regraft your trees.

So many new kinds are being introduced and old kinds rediscovered, it would be an impossible task to list them all. Catalog descriptions are so glowing one almost dreads making a choice for fear of missing out on something better. Some of the better-known varieties are listed here with brief descriptions. I hope it may help you make a better selection than throwing darts at the catalogs. The adjectives describing the varieties are common consensus, but you'll have to keep in mind that not everyone agrees when it comes to fruit flavor. See the list of nurseries in the Appendix for companies selling the apples described.

OLDER VARIETIES

These are listed alphabetically, with point of origin, when known, and with color, ripening season, and recommended planting zones. They are listed separately because only a few nurseries sell them.

ALEXANDER. Russia, red, fall. Used mostly for cooking. Zones 3–6.

AMERICAN BEAUTY STERLING. New England, dark red, winter. High-quality eating. Zones 4–6.

BALDWIN. New England, bright red, winter. Dessert and cooking. Zones 5–7.

BEN DAVIS. Upper South, red or striped, winter. Fragrant and good keeper, but poor quality. Zones 5–8.

BLUE PEARMAIN. Probably New England, red with blue blush, fall. Mildly aromatic and highly flavored. Zones 5–8.

CHENANGO STRAWBERRY. Northeast, yellowish with red stripes, summer. Very aromatic, high-quality cooking and dessert. Zones 5–8.

COX ORANGE. Europe, red and yellow, fall. Dessert, rich flavor, aromatic. Zones 5–8.

DUCHESS OF OLDENBURG. Russia, red striped, late summer. Excellent for cooking, pies, sauces, pickles; long-lived. Zones 3–6 and perhaps milder parts of Zone 2.

EARLY HARVEST. Unknown origin, yellow, winter. Excellent dessert and cooking. Zones 5–8.

FALL PIPPIN. Unknown origin, yellow, winter. Excellent cooking or dessert. Zones 5–8.

FAMEUSE (SNOW APPLE). Probably from France, red with blue blush, winter. Quality dessert fruit; aromatic. Zones 3–6.

GOLDEN RUSSET. Unknown origin, yellowish bronze, winter. Dessert and cooking; aromatic. Zones 5–8.

GRAVENSTEIN. Probably Germany, orange-yellow with red stripes, fall. Good cooking apple; aromatic. Zones 5–8.

GRIMES GOLDEN. West Virginia, yellow, early winter. Cooking and dessert; aromatic. Zones 6–8.

HUBBARDSTON. New England, yellow-green with red, early winter. Dessert quality. Zones 5–7.

JONATHAN. New York, red, winter. Dessert or cooking; aromatic. Zones 5–7.

LADY. France, red and yellow, winter. Very old and beautiful apple prized for dessert, especially at Christmas. Zones 5–7.

MAIDEN'S BLUSH. Unknown origin, light yellow with red blush, fall. Primarily for cooking. Zones 5–7.

MCINTOSH. Canada, red, fall-winter. Dessert and cooking; aromatic. Zones 4–7 and milder parts of Zone 3.

NORTHERN SPY. New York, red, winter. Aromatic; high-quality dessert, cooking; excellent keeper; hardy but too late for Zone 3. Zones 4–8.

PEACH. Russia, yellow, red blush, fall. Dessert. Zones 3–6.

PORTER. New England, yellow with red, fall. Dessert and cooking; aromatic. Zones 4–7.

POUND SWEET (PUMPKIN SWEET). New England, greenish white, early winter. Used for baking and canning; sweetish. Zones 4–8.

RED ASTRACHAN. Russia, red, summer. Cooking and dessert; aromatic. Zones 3–6.

RHODE ISLAND GREENING. New England, greenish yellow, early winter. Dessert and cooking; unusual flavor; good keeper. Zones 4–6.

ROXBURY RUSSET. New England, greenish-yellowish brown, winter. Very good home-type apple; one of the oldest American varieties. Zones 4–8.

ST. LAWRENCE. Canada, red, fall. Large and high quality. Zones 3–6.

SHEEPNOSE. New England, dark red, early winter. Baking and dessert. Zones 4–8.

SMOKEHOUSE. Pennsylvania, reddish yellow, fall. Dessert; aromatic. Zones 5–8.

SPITZENBURG. New York, orange-red, winter. Dessert; supposedly Thomas Jefferson's favorite apple. Zones 4–8.

SUMMER RAMBO. France, red striped, summer. Dessert and cooking; very disease-resistant; one of the oldest varieties. Zones 4–8.

THOMPKINS COUNTY KING. New Jersey, red with yellow, fall. Considered by some as the finest apple for dessert and cooking. Zones 5–8.

TOLMAN SWEET. New England, yellow, winter. Baking and cooking; sweet. Zones 3–6.

TWENTY OUNCE. New England, greenish yellow, fall. Cooking; large and coarse. Zones 4–8.

WEALTHY. Minnesota, red, fall. High-quality cooking and dessert; aromatic. Zones 3–6.

WESTFIELD (SEEK-NO-FURTHER). Massachusetts, yellow with red stripes, early winter. A favorite old-time eating apple; one of the best-flavored apples. Zones 4–6.

WINTER BANANA. Indiana, yellow with red blush, winter. Superb dessert quality; aromatic; regular bearer; excellent keeper. Zones 4–6.

WOLF RIVER. Wisconsin, red, fall. Cooking; very large but low quality. Zones 3–6.

YELLOW TRANSPARENT. Russia, yellow, summer. Excellent eating and cooking; juicy, soft; earliest apple; poor keeper. Zones 3–6.

NEWER VARIETIES

As with the older kinds, it is impossible to list all the newer varieties. Some are already outdated and are no longer being grafted in great numbers. Others are only now being evaluated as to how they do in various soils and climates. Rather than try to describe the fine differences among all the kinds, I am listing them in various categories that may help in determining your choice for a certain need, or for growing in a certain area.

Zones 2–3

These apples have been tested in Alberta and Saskatchewan and are among the hardiest apples grown. All should be hardy in Zone 3 and all but the most severe sections of Zone 2.

CRAB APPLES

DOLGO. Beautiful red fruit and one of the best-growing trees. Very hardy and a regular bearer. High quality but a bit sour to eat out of hand.

OSMAN. Very hardy, prolific bearer. Fairly good-size red fruit. Can be eaten out of hand.

RED SIBERIAN. Probably the hardiest of the group. Nearly frost-proof, regular bearer.

LARGE APPLES

HEYER NO. 12. Green, fair-to-good quality, regular bearer.

MIAMI. Good flavor, green with red blotches, may not be hardy in the far north.

REID. One of the hardiest of the group. Excellent for cooking.

Zones 3–4

These apples should be hardy in most of Zone 3 except very high elevations or in frost pockets.

ANOKA. Red, early fall. Bears when tree is very young. Rather uninteresting flavor but good for cider blends.

BEACON. Large red fruit, early fall or late summer. Excellent cooking apple, similar to Duchess in flavor. Vigorous grower, heavy bearer.

CONNELL. Hardy red winter apple with flavor somewhat like Delicious. Good quality. Bears young.

CORTLAND. Red with blue blush, winter. Excellent flavor. Large size. Ripens late but keeps well. White flesh of fruit doesn't brown quickly after cutting.

DUCHESS RED. The old Duchess in a redder color. Late summer. Excellent sauce and pies. Very hardy.

EARLY MCINTOSH. Red. McIntosh flavor in an early fall apple. Good bearing habits. Poor keeper.

FIRESIDE. Greenish red, winter. Another hardy Delicious type from Minnesota. Good flavor.

HARALSON. Red. Popular hardy winter apple in the Zone 3 parts of the north-central states. Good flavor and keeper.

HONEYGOLD. Yellow, winter. A Yellow Delicious and Haralson cross that gives northerners a chance to grow Delicious-type apples.

IMPERIAL OR MCINTOSH IMPERIAL. Red, winter. Improved McIntosh; better color and keeper.

JERSEY MAC. Red, winter. Good color. Flavor similar to McIntosh.

LOBO. Red, fall-winter. Good-flavored McIntosh type.

LODI. Yellow, summer. An early apple of the Transparent type. Firmer, better looking, but not as tasty.

MACOUN. Red with blue blush, winter. Good-flavored apple of the McIntosh type. Tends to be a biennial bearer.

MELBA. Red, early fall. Excellent flavor, good for eating, cooking, cider.

MILTON. Pinkish red, fall. Large, early, nice fragrance. Regular bearer.

NORTHWEST GREENING. Hardy yellow-green, winter. Good cooking, fair eating. Good keeper.

ORIOLE. Early-ripening, red summer apple. Large. Needs sheltered spot in Zone 3.

PRAIRIE SPY. Green with red blush, winter. Late-ripening. Fine flavor, large size. Good keeper.

PURITAN. Red, early fall. Red Astrachan-McIntosh cross. Like Macoun, may bear well only every other year.

QUINTE. Red, early fall. Attractive Canadian apple. Melba-Crimson Beauty cross. Good eating. Poor keeper. Susceptible to scab.

RED BARON. Red, fall. A Yellow Delicious-Duchess hybrid. Hardy, high quality. Keeps in ordinary storage until December.

REDWELL. One of the reddest hardy apples, winter. Keeps well.

REGENT. Red. High-quality winter apple. Cross between Duchess and Red Delicious. Hardy, but may not ripen fully in areas with early fall frosts. Good keeper.

SWEET MCINTOSH. Red, fall. Sweet apple with typical McIntosh tree characteristics. Good eating and baking.

Zones 5–8

Most of the apples in this list, if grafted on suitable rootstocks, can be grown in Zones 5–8. This means they are suitable for the major part of the Continental United States. Only the western mountains, north-central plains, Upper New England, and the Adirondacks of New York State, plus the warmest areas of the southern states and California, are off limits to this important apple group, although there are certainly many sections of Zone 4 where they will succeed.

ARKANSAS BLACK. Dark color, winter. Older variety. Popular in the southern states. Improved variety is Starkspur Arkansas Black.

BLACK TWIG. Dark red, winter. Formerly widely grown but now pretty much replaced by the Delicious and Winesaps.

DELICIOUS FAMILY. A chance seedling in an Iowa orchard began to change apple history about a century ago. Not only is the Delicious the most widely grown apple by far in the United States, but it probably has produced more sports and hybrids than any other apple. The red, unusually shaped apple with its distinctive five bumps on the blossom end is recognized by nearly everyone. The distinctive flavor is universally liked, although some object to the "mealiness" that the fruits often develop due to improper storage.

The Delicious family consists of so many different varieties that it is impossible to describe even a small part of them. Each section of the country has developed favorites that are liked best in that region —from the Vermont Spur Delicious to the Oregon Red. Home orchardists should study catalogs and check extension service recommendations for their area. When in doubt, stick with the old reliable Red Delicious.

Here are some other members of this large group: Double Red, Early Red One, Improved Ryan, Molly's Delicious, Red Bouquet, Red Gold, Red King, Redspur, Richard, Sharp Red, Skylene Supreme,

Skyspur, Star Crimson, Starking, Starkrimson, Starkspur, Topred, and Vance Double. When planting any of these apples, be sure to plant another variety that is not in the Delicious family for pollination.

EMPIRE. McIntosh-Delicious cross, considered one of the better new introductions. Ripens late and tends to color before it is fully ripe. Excellent red winter apple for eating. Not large.

GRANNY SMITH. Green-yellow, new, high-quality winter apple from New Zealand. Tart. Becoming very popular. Best in warmer zones.

JONATHAN FAMILY. Red winter apple. Another one that dates back at least a century and a half. Once regarded as one of the best eating apples but began to lose favor because of poor keeping qualities and somewhat small size of the fruit. Also susceptible to fire blight, scab, mildew, and rust. Certain hybrids have been developed that partially overcome some of these drawbacks, so many of them are a worthwhile addition to the home orchard. Some are sports and some, as the names suggest, are crosses between Jonathan and other popular apples.

Varieties most often for sale now include Anderson, Blackjon, Idared, Jonadel, Jonagold, Jonalicious, Jonared, Kingjon, Minjon, Nu-Red Jonathan, Valnur Red, Watson, and Webster.

PAULARED. New early red apple, late summer. High-quality dessert apple.

PRISCILLA. Red, fall ripening. Slight resemblance to its Red Delicious parent. Excellent quality. Very disease-resistant.

ROME. Originated in Ohio from a seedling planted as a grafted tree in 1816. The graft died, but a tree growing from the roots produced such good fruit it was named and soon widely planted. Popularity faded as it became apparent they were very susceptible to most apple diseases. Just as with the Jonathan, new hybrids have been developed to improve resistance and fruit size. The following are available in different catalogs and are suitable for many home plantings: Anderson, Barkley, Ben Hur, Gallia Beauty, Monroe, Red Rome Beauty, Ruby, and Warder.

SPIGOLD. Yellow-red winter apple, cross between Northern Spy and Yellow Delicious. Becoming quite popular. Good eating and good keeper. Very late ripening.

WINESAP FAMILY. Dates back to the early days of the Republic, probably starting in New Jersey before 1800. Best suited for the milder climates and longer seasons of Virginia, Washington State, and similar areas. Many hybrids and sports have been developed from it, including the famous Stayman. Regarded as an excellent cider apple, no small deal in the old days, and an exceptional keeper. Also enjoyed for its pink blossoms.

As with the others, there are hundreds of hybrids and sports, so only a few will be listed here. More detailed descriptions can be found in catalogs. Varieties being grown include Chesapeake, Double Red

Stayman, New Red Stayman, Nu Red Winesap, Starkspur Winesap, Staymared, and Turley Winesap.

YELLOW DELICIOUS. Next to the Red Delicious, the Yellow (or Golden) Delicious has been Stark Brothers' most famous apple. They paid West Virginia farmer Anderson Mullins $5000 for the original tree in 1914 —another chance seedling that made good. With Stark's tremendous capacity and know-how, the variety was an instant success and soon proved the public would buy an apple that wasn't red if it tasted good enough.

Like the Red Delicious, many hybrids and sports soon were developed from it. One, Honeygold, is now being planted in Zones 3 and 4 where the Yellow Delicious usually can't be grown. Some others are: Blushing Golden, Goldspur, Mutsu, Nugget, Prime Gold, Splendor, Stark Gala, Starkspur, Starkspur Golden, Virginia Gold.

Zone 9

For very warm climates such as Florida, Southern California, and others, these apples are worth trying: Beverly Hills, Brogden, Ein Shemer, Granny Smith, Morgan, Tropical Beauty, and Wiregrass.

16 / THE PLUM *(Prunus various)*

If you've never picked a fat, sweet plum off a tree in late summer and eaten it on the spot, you've missed one of the great adventures of gastronomy. One year I got impatient for ours to ripen and in a weak moment went out and bought a package of plastic-wrapped, commercially grown plums. They were much larger than ours and a beautiful deep burgundy color, but the taste was disappointingly flat. Plums picked before they are ripe and shipped hundreds of miles can never compare with those sun-ripened on the tree.

Every home fruit grower should include a few plum trees in his plantings. They are not difficult to grow. When I was growing up there were none in our family orchard, unfortunately, but our neighbors always had them. We children were always ready to help out at plum picking time, although I doubt if we were ever actually invited. We called them red, yellow, and blue plums, and because I never heard their real names I have no idea now what varieties they might have been. They got no care whatsoever but seemed to bear nearly every year. And how we missed them when they didn't!

Possibly because plums originated in so many different places, few fruits vary as widely in size, shape, color, and flavor. The range is even more varied than with apples—from the small native American types to the large European plum-prunes and the giant Japanese varieties. Yet despite their differences, each is recognizable as a plum, both by taste and appearance. Each variety is either a "freestone" with a pit that separates easily from the flesh, or a "clingstone" which doesn't.

Some people are not aware that prunes are a special kind of plum that contain less moisture and more sugar than is usual, so they dry better. They are delicious right off the tree, too, and this is the way most of us home orchardists choose to enjoy them. If you have lots of time and patience you can try drying them, but it's a rather involved process and perhaps better left to commercial growers.

If you're going to grow a few plum trees in your orchard, there are four main families you'll want to know about. Although the trees and fruits look similar, they are different enough so they usually won't even pollinate each other. This causes trouble for some growers who plant two plum trees thinking they will cross-pollinate, and they don't.

1. The European or Domestica is the most widely planted group.

These got their start in the southern regions of Europe and include many superior hybrids, including prunes.

2. The Damsons or Institia are closely related to the European species and are thought to have originated in the region that is now Syria. They might even have been one of the fruits that escaped from the Garden of Eden!

3. The Japanese very likely originated in China, but they were introduced into this country from Japan about a century ago. Although some varieties are fairly hardy, most are best suited for the warmer parts of the country; some can even be grown as far south as Florida.

4. Native American plums include the hybrids developed by crossing wild ones with the other three groups. Almost every section of the country has some type of wild plums growing in hedgerows that are completely neglected. They produce vast amounts of small fruits that wildlife quickly devour and people collect to make into tasty jams and jellies. These include:

Prunus nigra, the northeast variety that grows far into Canada

P. maritima, the Beach Plum that thrives along the sandy shores of the North Atlantic East Coast

P. hortulana, the wild plum of the Midwest

P. munsoniana, the wild plum that grows freely in the South

P. besseyi, the Sand Cherry of the Midwest

Many of these native plums have been crossed with the larger and better flavored imported varieties, creating completely new kinds. These hybrids are large, good-flavored, and sometimes better suited than the imports for growing in the soils and climates of the different regions of America, especially when they are grafted on native rootstocks. They can even be grown in soils that are too moist and heavy for apple trees, but like all fruit trees they should never be planted where water will sit on top of the roots even for a short time.

Hardiness

Since American hybrids are the hardiest of the plum groups, these are the trees to select if you garden in extremely cold parts of the U.S. European varieties are usually somewhat less hardy than the American, and the Japanese are least hardy of all, although varieties that have been developed within each group can stand considerably cold temperatures. Generally the non-American varieties are not very much hardier than the peach, and are suitable for planting only in Zone 5 and warmer climates.

The Damsons are more hardy than the Japanese and Europeans, but still are usually much less so than the native hybrids. Very few varieties of the Damsons have been introduced in this country compared to the other groups, and you'll probably find that many nurseries don't carry any Damson plums at all.

Frost Protection

If you're lucky to have enough land so that you can shop around for places to plant your plum trees, choose the high spot of a slope where spring frosts aren't as likely to strike the flowers. All varieties of plums bloom early, usually a week or two ahead of apples, which makes them a special target in the frost belt.

Once the trees are in bloom, if the temperature drops down into the mid-twenties (F.) there is little you can do to save them. We've even tried wrapping blankets and plastic sheets around a few limbs on cold spring nights, but with little success.

Heavy mulches help keep the roots cool, which may delay blooming for a few days. But in some cool climates this doesn't help because frost patterns are not predictable. Sometimes early blooming is even good; there have been years when our trees have bloomed during a warm spell and set little fruits before it turned colder. A few days later the temperature dropped to the low twenties but no damage was done to the crop since the tiny fruits are apparently more cold-resistant than the delicate flowers.

All in all, it's pretty much Mother Nature's decision that determines whether or not people in frost pockets get their annual crop of plums.

Rootstocks

Dwarf plums are not in as much demand or as easily available from nurseries as are dwarf apple trees. Since even the full-size plum trees never get very large, most orchardists prefer them. However, if you have a very limited area, if you like the novelty of growing miniature trees, or if your fruits are to be grown in large tubs, you can buy dwarf plum trees from many of the larger nurseries.

The dwarfs are usually grafted on *Prunus besseyi,* which grows into a very small tree. These rootstocks are hardy, so if hardy varieties are chosen too, this is one dwarf fruit tree that northerners can grow.

Almost all full-size plum trees that are sold are grafted on Myrobalan roots, which was quite satisfactory until it became infected with a virus. Now, unfortunately, a large number of trees being planted have this virus condition. The life of a plum tree was once nearly as long as that of humans—three score and ten—but is often shortened to fifteen or twenty years or sometimes less by this virus. Much research is being done to develop virus-free trees. Until they become widely available, all of us have to make do with what is presently on the market, buying only from reputable nurseries or grafting our own.

Pollination

Lots of gardeners plant a few plum trees without considering pollination at all, and they have wonderful crops every year. Many others have a terrible time, and we continually hear a lot of grumbling from people whose plums bloom heavily and set lots of tiny fruits, most of which then fall off.

There are numerous reasons for crop failure, including poor soil or frost damage, but lack of pollination is the most likely cause. If a gardener has only one tree, or several different trees that are each in a different family, he probably is being deprived of fruit because of poor family planning. Only a very few good plums produce well without cross-pollination, and even these do better with a partner. Stanley and Yellow Egg are two varieties that produce fairly well alone.

A confusing thing about drawing up rules for pollination is that the viability of the pollen of certain varieties may vary considerably depending upon where they are grown. In some areas plums in different families seem to interpollinate with no problems. In other areas, however, two varieties that should mate perfectly will not, either because the pollen of one is weak or because the trees do not bloom at the same time.

Don't be discouraged by the complexity of pollination. By being aware of what could go wrong you will be more likely to plant at least three different plum varieties of the same family for insurance. If you don't have room for a variety, maybe you can talk a neighbor into the many advantages of diversified fruit growing, and casually suggest just the right kinds of plums for him to plant.

If a plum is described as a good pollinizer in your nursery catalog, it may be well to include it in your orchard if it is suitable for your area. Compass, a fairly new cherry plum in the native American plum family, is becoming a widely planted variety because it produces so much vigorous pollen.

Another reason plum crops may be poor could be lack of proper pollination because there are few bees. Bee activity is, of course, necessary for pollination, and it is sometimes lacking when plums are blossoming. The bee population may be small in cold, late springs and their flying may be limited if days are rainy or cold. Chapter 7 on pollination suggests how you can lend the little stingers a helping hand when necessary.

Culture

If you start with the varieties best suited for your region, you will find plum trees are easy to grow. Their small size makes them easy to prune, spray if it's necessary, and harvest. They start producing early in life and seldom are subject to blights or other epidemics that sometimes wipe out large numbers of other fruit trees. Aphids, mice, and deer don't bother them nearly as much as they do apple trees.

Since the plum tree produces a large amount of fruit on a relatively small tree, fertilizer and moisture must be available all through the growing and ripening season. To help ensure this, I always place a thick mulch and a generous amount of organic fertilizer around the tree each year.

Because they bear big crops early in life, plums are often used as fillers in new orchards of full-size apple or pear trees. The trees are planted between the other varieties so use can be made of land that would otherwise be wasted for many years. Of course they have to be removed after a dozen years or so when the regular trees begin to crowd them.

Pruning

Several years ago in a garden magazine I found two articles in the same issue related to plum growing. One expert stated that plums needed little if any pruning. The other said that they were one fruit that should be pruned severely every year.

There's no doubt that certain small-fruited plums can produce well with no pruning at all, but I have found that most varieties greatly benefit from reasonably heavy pruning. As with the other tree fruits, you should prune to decrease the bearing wood (and thus cut down production), to let in more sunshine (for healthy and better colored fruit), and to shape the tree into a stronger and better looking unit. Just as with apples, proper pruning results in fewer but larger fruits, encourages annual bearing, and helps prevent breakage by eliminating bad crotches and weak limbs. Since plum trees bear their fruit on short stubby spurs, be careful not to cut off too many of these when pruning.

It is hard to grow a plum tree that has a central trunk with branches coming from it, like the apple or pear tree. Plums have a bushy habit of growth. Rather than try to change that, I let them go ahead and I adjust all pruning to their irregular style. Like apples, all plum trees don't grow in the same fashion, either. Certain kinds, such as La Crescent and Santa Rosa, tend to grow skyward—even the outside branches turn up. Other varieties spread so wide that the outer branches become weepy and soon hang on the ground.

Both kinds should be pruned so that the tree becomes nicely shaped, easy to work with, and productive. The tops of upright trees can be cut back occasionally to encourage a more spreading, lower growing tree, and branches spreading too wide should be cut back before they begin trailing.

A bit of light pruning to shape the young tree when it is still small will save a great deal of major corrective surgery later on and be less of a shock for the tree.

Diseases

Sooner or later you may find that one disease or another has appeared among your trees. Two in particular are quite likely: black knot, which attacks the limbs, and brown rot, which hits both tree and growing fruit.

BLACK KNOT

This disease is often seen in wild plum and cherry trees, especially in the winter when the leaves are off. The black excrescences along the limbs gave rise to the story often passed on that they are the feces of some small animals. Actually, the disease strikes in summer, opening wounds and causing the sap to develop into a dark sticky mess that can soon cover large portions of the branches. As the tree goes dormant in the fall, the goo turns hard and black.

Luckily the disease attacks only a few of the many varieties of plums. The European varieties are most susceptible; the Japanese are fairly immune to it. Even though native growing plums often seem to have the disease, many of the new hardy native hybrids appear quite resistant.

Cutting out and burning infected limbs as soon as the disease appears in the summer seems to be the only method of checking it. For the most part, chemicals are ineffective.

BROWN ROT

This is a fungus that can really break the home gardener's heart. After he has watched his tree become loaded down with growing fruit all summer, he suddenly finds that just as the crop is nearly ripe almost every fruit has become a mushy rot that's covered with evil-looking white flakes and is unfit to eat.

Like apple scab, brown rot spreads most rapidly during wet weather. The Japanese and native hybrid plums seem to be most susceptible; the European and Damson are least likely to be infected. Picking up all fallen fruit is the best method of combating the disease. For chemical control, Captan is excellent, especially when used as suggested in the spraying schedule in Chapter 9.

Insects

Plums are troubled by relatively few insects in most sections of the country. One of the pests that may find you sooner or later is the plum curculio, a tiny little insect from Europe. The female attacks the growing fruit much as the maggot does the apple. She pierces the fruit and lays eggs just under the skin, which then hatch into larvae and ruin the fruit.

Although the curculio can be effectively controlled by the use of any one of several low-toxicity sprays, if you want to avoid all spraying you can still control them quite well by hard work. Put several bed sheets under your trees on summer mornings when the air is quiet, and shake the insects onto them. Then collect and destroy them.

If you prefer the somewhat easier chemical approach, follow the spray schedule in Chapter 9. This is not only effective against the curculio but also takes care of scale and most other insects that might be wandering around looking for summer homesteading sites.

Harvesting

Plums are extremely productive. If all goes well they should bear two to three bushels per tree. The fruit is ripe when it is well colored and has a powdery "bloom." At this time it should come off the branch easily and be sweet and juicy to eat. Only the Japanese varieties may benefit from picking a short time before they are tree-ripe; allow them to ripen in a cool but not cold room for a few days before eating. Many varieties ripen over a fairly long season, making them an excellent home fruit. They will keep for a few weeks in a refrigerator or cool place but should be used before they begin to get mushy.

Besides eating them right off the tree, we have found that plums are delicious in lots of other ways. They make an excellent dessert sauce, pie, or coffeecake. We preserve rich plum conserve for winter treats, and also freeze them both raw and cooked. Sometimes we freeze the juice produced from cooking for a punch base—in fact, chilled and mixed with ginger ale it is our traditional Christmas cocktail.

Varieties

It would be a hopeless task to try to list all the thousands of plum varieties that can be grown. Many different kinds are available in various parts of the country, and new ones are introduced each year. Only a few are listed here as a guide for the beginner.

If you are a prospective plum grower, study catalogs suitable for your area and talk with other growers. You will probably want to contact your local extension service too. Plantings of new or completely unfamiliar varieties should be done as an experiment only, because new varieties are often introduced before all their growing characteristics have been discovered. Order virus-free trees if they are available and don't plant them within 300 feet of any plum tree that may be diseased.

EUROPEAN (*DOMESTICA*)

Zones 5–9 unless otherwise noted

FELLENBURG. Large, oval, purple, prune-type plum with red flesh. Productive, moderately hardy, late. Excellent quality.

GREEN GAGE. Old-time plum, still considered one of the best. Sweet, juicy. Fairly early.

MT. ROYAL. Prune type, blue, excellent flavor. Moderately hardy.

REINE CLAUDE. Green Gage type but ripens later. Clingstone, yellow, medium size, fine quality. Not very hardy.

STANLEY PRUNE. Sweet, large. Can be used fresh, preserved, or dried. Blue skin, yellow flesh, freestone, productive. Self-fertile, but good pollinizer for other European plums. Worth a trial in Zone 4.

YELLOW EGG. Yellow skin and flesh. Large, freestone, sweet, juicy, excellent quality.

JAPANESE

Zones 6–9 and warmer parts of Zone 5

ABUNDANCE. Medium size, red with yellow flesh, productive. Fruit should be thinned for best results.

BURBANK. Old-time favorite, red with yellow flesh. Good for home use where hardy. Ripens over a long season.

FORMOSA. One of the fine Japanese varieties. Yellow-red blush, clingstone, juicy.

REDHEART. New large plum. Early, needs thinning, high quality. Resistant to brown rot, canker.

SANTA ROSA. Reddish purple with red flesh. Clingstone, high quality.

SHIRO. Yellow, round, early, excellent quality. One of the hardier Japanese varieties.

STARKING DELICIOUS. Another of the hardier Japanese plums. Disease-resistant, heavy bearer, needs thinning. Red with blue blush.

DAMSON PLUMS

Zones 5–8

GIANT DAMSON. Heavy bearing, moderately hardy. Good-size fruit, offered by Stark Brothers.

SHROPSHIRE. Improved Blue Damson, large. Blooms late, bears early and regularly.

AMERICAN HYBRIDS

Zones 4–8 and most of Zone 3

EMBER. Hardy new Minnesota plum. Red, early, productive.

LA CRESCENT. Small but sugary sweet yellow plum. Small stone, fast growing, vigorous.

PIPESTONE. Fairly large, juicy, high quality. Red with dark blush. Early.

REDCOAT. Red, good size. Midseason, high quality.

UNDERWOOD. Red fruit with yellow flesh, large, good quality. Not too productive.

WANETA. Small red plum, very productive. Midseason. Fine eating.

AMERICAN CHERRY PLUM HYBRIDS

Zones 3–6

COMPASS. Dark color, productive, good for pollinizing many other kinds.

OKA. Dark purplish red, productive, early. Use fresh or for preserves.

SAPALTA. Purplish, sweeter than Oka, productive, extremely hardy. Replacing Sapa, an earlier variety.

17 / THE PEAR *(Pyrus communis)*

Two days after Christmas one year I found a partridge in a pear tree in our back yard. Even though three French hens and two turtledoves never did appear, it still seemed like a special holiday occasion. It was just another of those many unexpected delights of growing your own fruit.

The soft juicy pear is one of the nicest fruits. A ripe pear at a picnic or in a box lunch makes the whole meal something special. It is a perfect dessert fruit, and a fruit salad or fruit bowl without it always seems to be missing something. Not only is it delicious to eat raw, but it is also one of the few fruits that tastes nearly as good canned as it does fresh. In fact, it is one of the few that tastes better canned than frozen.

Pear trees came to America with the earliest settlers and were grown in Salem, Massachusetts, as early as 1635. Most pears grown in this country today are of southwestern European origin. One variety or another now grows over most of the temperate areas of the world, but they do their very best only in a few spots where climatic conditions are ideal for them. I always warn prospective pear growers that our region is not one of the great pear-producing areas of the country, but the fruit is so beloved that gardeners here keep planting pear trees even though they know a good crop every year is rare.

In addition to its being fussy about climates, it is also selective about soils and unfortunately is susceptible to fire blight. Much research is now going into developing new disease-resistant varieties, and the pear's popularity as a home-type fruit is spreading.

Hardiness

Will pears grow in a cool climate? Some varieties will. In general, the best-known pears are hardier than peaches but less hardy than the hardiest apples. Almost all pears need a period of low temperature during the winter, so only a few are suited for the nearly frost-free parts of Florida and California.

Some of the hardiest pears originated in the north-central states and in Canada. Andrew, Clark, Golden Spice, Luscious, Manning-Miller, Parker, and Patten are all worth trying in Zones 3 and 4.

Kieffer is widely planted because it grows so well and is quite hardy, having about the same hardiness as the Baldwin apple. It also grows over a wide range of soils and does well farther south than many of the common varieties. The quality leaves a lot to be desired, but it is productive and reliable.

Bartlett, which most of us would like to be able to grow for an eating pear because it is delicious and versatile, is the leading pear in this country as well as throughout most of the rest of the world (where it is known as the Williams). It is only a little hardier than the peach, though, so it can't stand the winters in cool climates.

Most pear varieties sold in nursery catalogs are suitable for Zones 5 through 8. The following are worthy of a trial in Zone 9 (Florida, Southern California, and the Gulf Coast): Apple, Magness, and Pineapple Pear.

In many sections of the country, pear growing should be treated as experimental and one should not expect a big crop every year. In places where they can be grown, though, the gardener is missing a good bet if he fails to take advantage of it.

Rootstocks

When you go shopping for pear trees you usually find that not only are several varieties listed but also, as with apples, some are available on either standard or dwarf roots. Both have certain advantages. Standard trees grow larger so therefore produce much more fruit per tree when they are full-grown. On the other hand, dwarf trees usually begin to bear earlier, take much less room, and are easier to look after. Usually dwarfs are grafted on quince roots while full-size pears are grafted on some kind of pear seedling rootstock.

Hardiness is generally about the same for both standard and dwarf trees, but the seedlings grown from the hardier varieties of pears will produce the hardiest rootstocks.

Pollination

It is usually safest to consider that all pears need cross-pollination for maximum yield, although some, such as Comice and Flemish Beauty, are somewhat self-fertile.

Pears, unlike plums, do not have family groups within which pollination takes place, so usually any two different varieties that bloom at the same time will cross effectively. An exception to this rule is the Bartlett and Seckel, which apparently are socially incompatible and need a third variety to pollinate them both if these two are planted together.

Because pears bloom early, pollination is sometimes difficult just as it is with plums. Some years I have had to resort to hand-pollination in order to save our crop when the bees failed to appear during bloom time because of cold, wet weather. In addition to weather interference, sometimes bees neglect the blooms for other reasons. Pear blossoms hang on the tree for only a very short time and are less fragrant and have less nectar than plums or cherries, so bees will sometimes visit the more inviting trees first. In fact, they sometimes neglect the pear blooms altogether. A good strong hive of bees in the neighborhood is an invaluable asset to any orchard and is especially beneficial to pears.

Culture and Soils

Pears seem to grow best in cool, moist, cloudy weather, and the trees thrive under heavy organic mulches. As a rule they do not care for sandy, light soil, although Bartlett and Seckel do fairly well in a variety of soils. Pears are usually regarded as delicate, but strangely, they can tolerate more moisture in the soil than either apple or peach trees.

Pruning is very similar to apple pruning and should be done each year. Thinning the small fruit is beneficial to some varieties of pears but

Pears, a choice fruit for the home orchard (USDA)

others seldom need it. Bartlett and Bosc should be thinned early in the season so that only one fruit remains in a cluster. Other large-fruited kinds should be thinned only when the tree sets an unusually large number of little fruits and you feel that if it matures them all it would likely strain the tree.

Many varieties of pears take a long time—sometimes up to six or eight years—to bear their first crop. Others may have a few fruits within two or three years. Golden Spice, Lincoln, and Duchess all tend to bear when quite young. Dwarf pear trees produce fruit at a much earlier age than standard-size trees.

Disease

By far the most serious trouble encountered by pear trees is fire blight. This disease strikes the flowers, limbs, and fruit, which all turn black as though they had been burned over a fire. One of the best controls is to cut off the branch well in back of where the disease is evident. Always disinfect the cutting tools and burn the infected wood. There is less danger of spreading disease if the tree is dormant, so all pruning should be done and all wounds sealed with a good tree compound before growth starts in the spring. After spring growth begins, the infection can be spread rapidly by the wind and by insects, including bees.

Agristrep, an agricultural form of streptomycin, is used commercially for control of fire blight in both pears and apples. It is expensive and must be handled with care, and is not usually recommended for home growers.

Insects

The insects that attack the pear are similar to those that bother other fruits. Most of them can be controlled by spraying with the all-purpose orchard spray during the growing season. Follow the spray schedule in Chapter 9.

SAN JOSE SCALE AND CODLING MOTH

These are two common insects. You can control them the same way you do on apple trees.

PEAR SLUGS

These sometimes attack the leaves, often riddling them over the entire tree. Following the spraying program suggested in Chapter 9 will control them.

PSYLLA

A less common but a bad pest where it is active, psylla is a tiny insect that secretes a sticky substance that turns black and covers limbs and leaves.

The pink spray and petal fall spray (see Chapter 9) are most important in controlling psylla, since this is when the eggs are laid and begin to hatch.

PEAR MITE

This mining insect attacks fruit and leaves. It is very tiny but can do a substantial amount of damage. For control use the regular spray schedule.

Harvesting

Beginning pear growers may be unsure of when to harvest their fruit. Unlike most other tree fruits, pears shouldn't be quite tree-ripened, even at home. They shouldn't be allowed to develop hard gritty cells in the flesh. If pears are left on the tree until they are perfectly ripe, they will begin to rot inside and will soon be completely spoiled. Many home crops are lost because people wait too long to pick them.

The fruit should be picked when it is well developed yet not quite ready to eat out of hand, and when it can be separated easily from the tree. You must pick extremely carefully so the delicate fruit will not be bruised, because even slightly damaged fruit spoils quickly.

Pears keep best in home storage if each is wrapped in soft paper and stored in a cool place free from odors. They will be ready to eat between a week and a couple of months, depending on the variety. For mellow, full flavor they should be allowed to complete their ripening process at room temperature.

Most people agree that a buttery pear is one of nature's most pleasurable treats, and certain varieties can also be preserved in a great many delicious ways. A typically southern use is pear "honey," which sometimes combines them with lemons, limes, ginger, or coconut. Then there are tasty pear conserves, chutneys, pickles, butters, and nectars. In Europe large amounts are pressed into a cider called . . . what else? Perry.

Varieties

Here are some standard old-time pears and some of the newer ones that may be available in different sections of the country. They are mostly suitable for growing in Zones 5–8.

ANJOU. Yellow-green, late, good for winter eating and for preserving. Must be picked quite green. Good trees but sometimes bear irregularly.

AYRES. Suitable for many areas of Zones 8 and 9 where pears are difficult. Takes quite a while to bear, but grows rapidly.

BARTLETT. Popular, large, beautiful pear for cooking or dessert. Productive. Good quality tree but subject to blight.

BEURRE BOSC. Winter ripening, dark brown. Dessert quality, aromatic. Subject to blight.

CLAPP FAVORITE. Large, beautiful, late summer. Excellent flavor but doesn't keep long. Subject to blight.

COLETTE. Large, excellent new pear that ripens over a long season and is well suited for home use. Good for preserves.

COMICE. Attractive pear of fine quality from France. Ripens midseason. Tree not the most rugged but widely grown in the West.

DUCHESS. Very large, good-quality dessert pear and good for preserves. Late, quite reliable.

EARLY SECKEL. Early-ripening Seckel (about three weeks earlier than its parent). Vigorous and healthy tree.

KIEFFER. Blight-resistant, fair quality, late ripening. Good North and South. Tree may live 100 years or more.

SECKEL. Small, sweet, high quality. Yellowish brown. Midseason. Vigorous and healthy tree. Moderately hardy. Worth a trial in Zone 4. Good for canning.

STARKCRIMSON. New all-red pear. Early, colorful, high quality.

TYSON. Early-ripening, sweet, juicy dessert pear. Good for canning. Tree is heavy bearer and long-lived. Fairly blight-resistant.

HARDIEST VARIETIES

These are worth trying in the cold regions of the country in Zones 3 and 4.

ANDREW. Very hardy but only fair quality. From the University of Saskatchewan.

GOLDEN SPICE. Small, juicy, attractive, tart. Good for sauce, spice pickling, general canning.

JUBILEE. Another very hardy Canadian pear suitable only for cooking.

PARKER. Good-size yellow fruits. Sweet, juicy, fine-grained. Ripens early September. Developed at the University of Minnesota.

PATTEN. Yellow, good quality and size, resembles Bartlett. September ripening. From the University of Minnesota.

Others worth a try in these zones are Clark, Luscious, Manning-Miller, and Mendell.

MOST DISEASE-RESISTANT VARIETIES

In recent years additional research has gone into developing pears more resistant to fire blight and scab. These are recommended for trial in Zones 5–8.

MAGNESS. High quality, keeps well, and is good for canning. Later than Bartlett. Blight-resistant. Developed by U.S. Department of Agriculture.

MOONGLOW. Blight-resistant early pear, regular bearer. Yellow with pink blush. Good for canning.

MORGAN. A fairly new variety developed at the Tennessee Experiment Station.

ORIENT. Round yellow fruit with red blush. Good canning pear. Vigorous and productive trees. Blight-resistant.

STARKING DELICIOUS. Stark Brothers says this is the most blight-resistant pear tree they sell. Also resists scab.

18 / THE PEACH AND THE NECTARINE
(Prunus persica)

When I was young I loved to eat fruit even more than maple sugar and ice cream, which certainly took second and third place. My love for fruits included all of them except peaches, which I thought didn't quite measure up. Then one day I ate my first peach that had been ripened right on the tree. Wow! From then on I liked *all* fruits.

What a different taste that tree-ripened peach had, compared to the small, hard, sour ones that had come from the store. And that difference is why most home fruit gardeners want very much to include some peach trees in their orchards. The peach is a challenge to grow, though. It seems to bring out the competitive spirit in gardeners, like growing the biggest and best tomatoes or the finest roses. Just as those plants are a step up from radishes and marigolds, so the peach is slightly more difficult to grow than apples and plums. But they're not much more difficult if the soil and climate are right.

The peach and the nectarine, like their close relative the apricot, are probably the most foreign of the temperate zone fruits. They are thought to have originated in China, and were brought to Europe by early traders. The Spaniards planted peach trees in Florida soon after their first settlement there, and from then on they were well established in the New World.

Although selection of outstanding seedlings and cross-breeding has developed a much hardier and better peach, the growing range is still much smaller than that of pears, plums, apples, and cherries. Peaches are grown in the Niagara peninsula of Ontario and even along coastal regions of British Columbia, but the main sections of Zones 3 and 4 and much of Zone 5 still remain off limits to them. Each year probably more little peach trees die in the northern parts of Minnesota, North Dakota, Wisconsin, Maine, Vermont, and New Hampshire than all the apple trees Johnny Chapman ever planted. Even in these areas where a peach cannot grow, gardeners just won't give up. If it's at all possible, everyone wants his own peach tree.

In addition to its aversion to cold temperatures, the peach also needs a long season to harden the growing wood and the fruit buds for the following year. This is the reason peaches can sometimes stand very low temperatures for a short time, but are unable to survive where the frost-free season is less than five months. Even in the North, newly planted trees may survive a winter or two, but seldom longer.

Even though they prefer a warm climate, like all of the temperate zone fruits, peaches need a certain amount of cold weather in order to survive. Gardeners in Zones 8 and 9 will want to plant only those varieties (see list) that require very little winter chilling.

The fussy peach tree is not only particular about temperature but also about soils. It is never completely happy in the cool, heavy soils that pears and plums enjoy. Commercial peach growers like to plant them on a well-drained slope with sandy soil just above a fairly large lake or river, so the temperature will stay more even. Home gardeners are not likely to have that ideal location, but many of us find that peaches do very nicely in ordinary garden soil, and most years the crop will be good. Peach trees respond to care and will quickly reward you handsomely if you do your part.

Rootstocks

Throughout most of the country peaches are budded or grafted on seedling peach tree roots. Peaches have been grafted on plums, almonds, or cherry stocks, too, in an attempt to get them to adapt to heavier soils, but the seedling peach is still the most commonly used.

Peach seedlings grow rapidly and vary widely in their growth habit. If possible, when you buy peach trees you should select them personally at a nursery and choose only the largest one-year-old vigorous trees. The smaller trees, according to the West Virginia Experiment Station, may have been stunted either by a virus disease, an incompatibility between rootstock and top, or some other difficulty that will later get worse.

The best insurance you could have in getting healthy, dependable trees is to bud graft your own by taking buds from healthy trees and grafting them on wild peach seedlings; or deal with a reliable nursery.

Dwarf Trees

Because of the demand for peach trees, many nurseries are supplying them grafted on dwarf roots. These make small trees only about 6 feet tall and 6 feet wide. They are easy to care for and bear at an early age, so they are often ideal for pot culture or for a home gardener with a small lot. As with all dwarfs, the trees are usually less vigorous than wild seedlings and, being shallow-rooted, often need staking to prevent leaning when loaded with fruit. Their crops are smaller than those of full-size trees, of course, but you can fit more trees in the same space.

Pollination

Most peaches do not need a partner to produce. A few varieties do, however, so it's well to follow the instructions given for the variety you purchase. The J. H. Hale, for example, should always be planted somewhere near a peach tree of a different variety for it to bear satisfactorily. Most catalogs give directions about the pollinating needs of each kind. When in doubt, it's always best to plant two different kinds, unless your neighbor has a peach orchard just over the fence.

Culture

Dry, sandy soils that warm up thoroughly are the best possible location for peach trees. Avoid planting them in frost pockets. If they are in the right place, your peaches will be in a hurry to grow up. In fact, they are often in too much of a hurry. Speedy growth should be discouraged because it usually causes a weak tree that breaks easily, gets winter injury, and is short-lived.

You can help slow down its growth by fertilizing it sparingly early in the spring, never overfeeding it. Another way to avoid overstimulating tree growth, if this is a problem, is to leave the area around it in sod and keep the grass mowed rather than mulching or cultivating it.

Because of its vigorous growth habit, the peach tree usually requires severe pruning. The forming fruit needs thinning, too, and by leaving a distance of 5 or 6 inches between fruits you'll help them develop to their best size and quality. Annual pruning and thinning will not only produce better fruit but will also aid in keeping the tree healthy.

A word of caution: Plant only the number of peach trees that you can care for easily. Of all the orchard fruits they are perhaps the most demanding, and even a partly neglected tree will be a great disappointment.

Harvesting

The home orchardist can revel in his harvest because not only can he grow better-flavored peaches than commercial growers, but he also has the added advantage of being able to pick them at the best possible time. Like the plum, it tastes best if it is tree-ripened, as I found out when I ate my first perfect peach.

When the fruit comes off the limb with a slight gentle twist, the peaches are ready. After a little experience with them you'll select each one like a connoisseur. They must be picked very carefully and never yanked from the tree, because tree-ripened peaches bruise extremely easily and damaged fruit rots very quickly. Although peaches are often picked slightly green for cooking, many people think that even cooking peaches should be picked only when they are fully ripe because they have more sugar and less acid then. If you plan to keep them for a while, store them in a cool place; in a warm room they keep right on ripening and will soon spoil. A refrigerator, cool basement, or root cellar is good.

Each of us has a favorite peach dish. Shortcake, pie, cobbler, and salads abound when they are in season, and I don't know of anyone who would refuse fresh peach ice cream, a sundae, or a milkshake. Nobody wants to be without peaches for long, so they are preserved in jams, conserves, butters, chutneys, pickles, brandied peaches, and are even dried. Most varieties can be frozen, but the flavor and consistency are usually better when they are canned.

Diseases

Although the spray program in Chapter 9 will control brown rot, the same disease that affects plums, and many other peach troubles, your tree may suffer a few additional ailments that need special care. Keep an eye out for the following.

POWDERY MILDEW

You can tell if this disease has hit if a gray-white, velvety, powderlike substance covers the leaves and twigs. Captan spray helps control it, and so do the sulfur sprays or dust. Benomyl gives excellent control for those who feel no hesitancy about using systemics.

LEAF CURL

This can strike the trees quite early in the season, causing their long narrow leaves to curl up, turn yellow, and finally fall off. A lime-sulfur spray has long been an effective control for this ailment. Ferbam, at the rate of two tablespoons per gallon of water, is now more widely used. It should be applied early in the spring before the leaf buds begin to open or swell.

Insects

Like apples, the peach trees have a host of insects that may visit them. It's a good thing that most of them are not a great threat because the delicate peach is less able to resist insects and disease than most other fruits.

SAN JOSE SCALE AND PLUM CURCULIO

These insects, which also affect other fruits, can be controlled easily through the spray program in Chapter 9.

TREE BORER

This is another serious pest. Check now and then to see that he isn't a tenant in your orchard. They have such a hearty appetite that even one of these large, fat grubs can quickly bore through the trunk at near-ground level or just below, eat out the wood, and cause the tree to die. You can tell if it is at work from the pile of jellylike excretion and sawdust at the base of the tree. DDT used to be a favorite weapon against this parasite, but use of it is now restricted. Home gardeners can cut the grub out with a knife or kill it by ramming it with a stiff wire. After you're sure of the worm's demise, seal the wound with a tree compound or dressing to prevent weather and rot from entering and further deteriorating the tree.

Varieties

Compared to the pear and apple, the peach is not a long-lived tree, so new plantings have to be made more frequently than with other fruits. The peach also hybridizes easier than most other fruits and a larger percentage of the seedlings are likely to be of good quality, so new varieties are constantly being developed and introduced.

Since experiment stations and nurseries develop so many new varieties every year, and old kinds are frequently being retired, it is hard to get a list

Peaches, where they can be grown, are an excellent choice for the home gardener (USDA).

that will satisfy everyone seeking information on peach varieties. You'll do well to check catalogs from nurseries that grow trees most suitable for your area. Also study the bulletins supplied by your local extension service (see the Appendix). The following lists may also be useful.

FOR CANNING. Golden Jubilee, Halehaven, June Elberta, Redhaven.

FOR FREEZING. Elberta, Fair Haven, Golden Jubilee, Halehaven, Redhaven.

TREES WITH MORE FROST-RESISTANT BUDS. Canadian Harmony, Candor, Harbelle, Harbinger, Harbrite, Harken, Madison, Redhaven, and also a series of Virginia developments called the Presidential Series, including Harrison, Monroe, Tyler, Zachary Taylor, and others.

FOR AREAS WITH WARM WINTERS (ZONES 8–9). Desert Gold, Florida Home, Jewell, Keystone, Redglobe, Redskin, Rio Grande, Sam Houston, Southland, and Suwanee.

Zones 5–8

The following are listed according to their season of ripening.

VERY EARLY

EARLI GLOW. Yellow flesh, one of the best quality early peaches. Vigorous tree and fairly hardy.

GOLDEN JUBILEE. Yellow with red blush. Freestone. Productive and vigorous tree.

MIKADO. Yellow, clingstone, fair quality. Good tree vigor, productive, needs cross-pollination.

REDHAVEN. High-quality, red with yellow flesh. Fairly hardy.

RELIANCE. Medium size, yellow flesh, good quality, early ripening. Probably one of the hardiest peaches.

STARK'S EARLY WHITE GIANT. White flesh. Early, disease-resistant tree.

VALIANT. Yellow with red blush. Freestone, round, good quality, productive.

MIDSEASON

CRESTHAVEN. High quality, yellow with red blush, nearly fuzzless. Vigorous tree, self-pollinating.

EARLY CRAWFORD. Yellow, medium size, freestone. Not very hardy, needs pollinator.

ELBERTA. Yellow, freestone, fair quality. Vigorous and productive tree but lacks hardiness.

HALEHAVEN. Yellow with blush, fine quality, freestone. Attractive, vigorous, fairly hardy tree.

J. H. HALE. Good size and quality, nearly fuzzless, clingstone. Good for all peach uses. Tree needs pollinator.

LATE

AFTERGLOW. Large fruit, good quality. Tree is vigorous and productive.

Nectarines

If you noticed that the scientific name for the nectarine is the same as that of the peach, you might have thought there was a mistake somewhere. Actually, botanists can't find any real differences between the two trees. Only the fruit is different. The nectarine is simply a peach without the fuzz. It is somewhat juicier and has a sweeter taste and, like the peach, can have either white or yellow flesh.

Nectarine seeds will often grow into peach trees and peach pits into nectarine trees. The two are so alike that culture, insect and disease control, pruning, and harvesting are the same for both.

Most nurseries don't offer much variety of nectarines, and most of the ones they list are hardy only where the more tender peaches do well. Formerly nectarines were seldom recommended for the home gardener, but many of the new varieties are ideal for that purpose and no doubt more will be forthcoming.

These varieties are most often grown on the West Coast in Zones 7–8, although some might be worth a trial in Zones 5–6: Dixie, Gold Mine, John Rivers, Mabel Pioneer, and Silver Lode.

The following are hardier and are suggested for planting in the East, Zones 5–8: Flaming Gold, Hunter, Stark Delicious, Stark Early Flame, Stark Red Gold, Sun Glo (this one seems to be the most frost-resistant), and Sure Crop.

19 / THE APRICOT *(Prunus armeniaca)*

In my early days as a young boy on a Vermont farm, I thought apricots only came in white paper boxes. They were one of the few foods we bought at the store and, like raisins, salmon, and cornflakes, were treats and a change from our home-grown diet.

Not everyone likes the slightly different taste of the apricot. Many people, in fact, have never eaten a fresh tree-ripened one so they may not be sure whether they like them or not, since most of the commercially grown apricots are raised on the West Coast and are canned or dried before being shipped to the rest of the country.

The apricot got its start in China many centuries ago. It had apparently reached Rome by the first century; by the early 1700s it was growing and thriving in Virginia. At the present time the Soviet Union is the world's leading producer. Several hardy varieties that have come from there have extended apricot growing into colder areas where it had never before been possible to grow them. In fact, it is only in recent years that the apricot has become popular as a home fruit. The noted horticulturist U. P. Hedrick, in his famous book *Fruits for the Home Garden* (1944), scarcely mentions apricots. Now that their growing range is so greatly enlarged, home gardeners are finding this fruit a fine addition to their orchards.

Much about it, including its flavor, resembles the peach. The trees tend to bloom early in the spring, and they are ornamental and well shaped. Pruning and spraying are the same for both fruits. Culture and harvesting are also similar, and the fruit of the apricot, like that of the peach, is often dried and sold commercially.

Apricots grow easily from seed, and many of the seedlings produce very good fruit. Moorpark, one of the most popular varieties, has spawned so many seedlings that closely resemble it that nowadays it's difficult to be certain what is a true Moorpark. You'll have to be patient if you plan to grow any fruit from seed. A small grafted tree may have a few fruits in only a couple of years, but a seedling may take many additional years and quite likely will be a big tree before it produces a single fruit.

Apricots are usually grafted on peach, nectarine, or apricot seedlings, but sometimes plum seedlings are used to make them more suited for cool northern soils. Like the peach, they tend to grow very fast and usually live only a few decades. They are not large trees. Most nurseries offer only standard-size varieties, although a few have dwarf varieties that are grafted on *Prunus besseyi,* the same dwarfing stock used for plums and peaches.

Because apricot trees grow very fast, care must be taken not to over-feed them. As with peaches, too much growth stimulation will result in a weak tree that can be easily damaged by disease, insects, and sudden temperature changes. Because apricots bloom very early, the blooms are often hurt by late frost, however.

Harvesting

Allow apricots to ripen on the tree; once they are picked their sugar content does not increase. When they are ready they will have a beautiful blush and still be firm to the touch. Although they're not quite as tender as their peach cousins, they do bruise, so be careful not to poke them or throw them around.

Apricots are delicious right off the tree and also cooked in any number of ways—from marmalade to mousse. They are sometimes frozen, but the skin toughens in freezing so you should peel them first. More often they are canned in syrup or dried. They are one of the best fruits for drying and are good for winter snacks or to use in granola, breads, or "leathers," the paper-thin confections. Last but not least, they make wonderful preserves. One of the best spreads we've ever had on toast is homemade apricot jam.

Diseases and Insects

The problems that beset the apricot are very much like those affecting the peach, and the controls listed in Chapter 9 are usually adequate. Ordinarily, apricots are slightly more resistant than peaches to insects and diseases, and if good sanitation methods are followed they may not need spraying at all. Some varieties are slightly hardier than peaches, too, so they are also less troubled by frost damage to the fruit buds in late winter.

Varieties

Apricot varieties do not vary tremendously except in their hardiness. Most varieties are suitable for planting only where summer seasons are long and winters are relatively mild—Zones 6–8. Any plantings in Zones 3, 4, and the colder parts of Zone 5 should be considered experimental.

Many varieties are at least partly self-fertile, but most nurseries advise planting two or more kinds for better fruit crops. Moongold and Sungold, two of the hardier new ones, do best when planted together.

USUALLY PLANTED ON THE WEST COAST. These are good for Zones 6–8: Royal and Blenheim (much alike), Hungarian Rose, Moorpark, Perfection, Tilton, and Wenatchee.

USUALLY PLANTED IN THE EAST. All of the following are worth a trial in

Zones 5–8: Golden Grant, Henderson, Hungarian Rose, South Haven, and Stark Earli-Orange.

HARDIEST OF ALL. Moongold and Sungold from Minnesota, Scout and Andy's Delight from Canada, and Manchu from South Dakota are all being grown in Zone 5 and sheltered parts of Zone 4, which were once considered too cold for apricots.

20 / THE QUINCE *(Cydonia oblonga)*

When the word quince is mentioned it usually doesn't create much enthusiasm among home gardeners. Few claim it for their favorite fruit or describe it in the superlatives used for the apple, plum, peach, pear, or cherry. Some even maintain it shouldn't be dignified by calling it a fruit. Yet it is widely grown and has admirers who praise it highly. If you want to have a complete orchard and add variety to your fruit diet, and if the quince will grow in your climate, you'll probably want to plant a quince tree. Like many other fruits, the quince was grown by the Greeks and Romans, who regarded it as a health food and gave it much more respect than it generally gets nowadays.

The quince fruit is hard with a slight fuzz, and has both an unusual flavor and smell. The odor is so pronounced, in fact, that it's wise never to put it in the refrigerator or leave it near other fruits, which will soon take on the smell. Perhaps that is why it is little grown commercially and rarely found in stores or fruit markets.

Some people plant the tree for its attractive appearance rather than for its fruit. The well-behaved trees are small—usually not over 15 feet tall—and have a rather twisted habit of growth. They bloom late in the season, after the apples, so there's not much danger of frost damage.

Culture

Usually quince trees are budded or grafted on quince seedlings or a special Angus-Quince rootstock. It is also possible to layer them or even start them from cuttings if you are patient.

You grow them much as you would pears, but since quinces are not as hardy as most pears, first be sure they will grow in your location. They thrive in similar soils and unfortunately have the same susceptibility to fire blight. Although they are slow-growing trees, it is wise not to fertilize them too much, since this makes them even more likely to get fire blight.

Unlike most other fruit trees, they can grow and produce well year after year with very little pruning, although you should remove crossed limbs, dead wood, or any irregularities. Quinces are bothered by practically all the same diseases and insects that strike pear trees, so it's a good idea to follow the suggestions in Chapter 9 for pest control, which should protect them nicely.

Two different varieties are not necessary since quinces are one of the few tree fruits that are self-pollinating. This is probably just as well because quince trees are so productive that one tree usually supplies all of the average family's needs.

Harvesting

Even if they were hardy everywhere, quinces ripen so late that most northern gardeners could never grow them. Fruits should stay on the tree until they turn deep yellow, have developed their strong odor, and snap off easily. This can be as early as mid-October in some areas, but is more often well into November.

The fruits must be handled with great care because they bruise easily. They will keep in home storage for a month or more in a cool place and are best stored in shallow trays where there will be little weight on them.

The fruit is seldom eaten raw as you would eat most other fruits, even though the Pineapple variety was especially developed for that purpose. Most are cooked into jellies, preserves, marmalades, or a sauce that is mixed with applesauce. Some people are devotees of the quince custard pie they remember from childhood, or quince ginger, quince honey, or quinces baked and served with whipped cream. The fruit can also be canned or spiced. Because of their high pectin content, they are often combined in jellies with berries or grapes that have low pectin.

Varieties

Orange is the variety most likely to be listed in nursery catalogs. Pineapple has the most agreeable flavor when raw but is seldom available in nurseries, except on the West Coast. Both of these kinds are best suited for Zones 6–8.

Champion, Jumbo, Meech, and Van Deman are all offered by various nurseries and are also suitable for Zones 6–8, although these might also be worth a trial in those favored sections of Zone 5 that have a relatively long growing season.

Flowering Quinces

Some gardeners confuse the flowering quinces (*Chaenomeles japonica* or *Chaenomeles speciosa*) with the eating quinces (*Cydonia oblonga*). The flowering quinces are small trees or shrubs used as ornamentals and hedges. They grow up to 6 feet tall and have beautiful flowers ranging from white to bright red.

Because the orchard quinces and the flowering quinces are closely related, both can be used for preserves. The fruits of the ornamental varieties are small, often stay green, and are of an inferior quality. The bush is subject to most of the diseases that trouble the *Cydonia,* with San Jose scale being one of the most troublesome.

Flowering quinces are usually much hardier than their orchard-type cousins, although in the colder areas they may grow to be only 1 or 2 feet high and the fruits usually do not ripen properly.

21 / THE CHERRY—
SWEET *(Prunus avium)*
AND SOUR *(Prunus cerasus)*

In grade school one year we read a book about some English children who had a great many adventures and most of them, I'm sure, were exciting. But the only thing I remember about the whole book was that on summer mornings the boys would climb out the upstairs window of their big house into a monstrous cherry tree and eat the giant sweet cherries. That made a big impression on me, and I decided that someday I would have a tree just like that.

Over the years I've planted lots of cherry trees, but most never got over 8 feet tall and only a few reached 12 feet. Even a small child couldn't climb to the second story in one of them, so we've had to pick most of our cherries right from the ground.

The cherry trees in which the English children climbed to such great heights were sweet cherries, probably grafted on Mazzard roots. I was growing sour cherries, which are naturally smaller trees anyway, and they were grafted on an even more dwarfing rootstock, the Mahaleb.

So I never did climb in my trees and now I've quite lost interest in doing so anyway, but I do love the cherries. Not only are they one of the most beautiful fruits, but they bear early in the season and regularly, and when fully ripe they are scrumptious. Now, thanks to experiment station research, there are varieties that can grow in almost every fruit garden.

All of us are familiar with some sort of cherry since nearly every region has wild cherries. The black cherry, chokecherry, sand cherry, and bird cherry are all used for jelly and are also eaten raw by birds and kids in different sections of the country. They're valued, too, for their blossoms, because in many areas they are one of the first wild trees to bloom in the spring.

The cultivated cherries that are grown in orchards and gardens are mostly European in origin. Thousands of varieties of these have been developed and named, although only a few are now being offered by nurseries.

There are two main groups of cultivated cherries and one lesser group. The sour or tart cherries—often called pie cherries because that's where so many of them are destined—have the widest growing range. Most are as hardy as the Baldwin or Delicious apple. The sweet cherries, which have many varieties, have about the same growing range as the peach. They are either firm-fleshed or soft-fleshed. A smaller group, the Dukes, are thought to be crosses between the two; they are somewhat hardier than the sweets but not nearly as hardy as the pie cherries.

Still another group, the cherry plums and bush cherries, are quite different from the orchard cherries, even though the fruit somewhat resembles them. The flavor is often more like that of a plum, and they are described under plum varieties. These are very hardy and can be grown even in the coldest parts of the country.

The sour cherry group is the most widely grown in the home orchards of the eastern U.S., and even commercially they have a slight edge over the sweet cherries in total production. Although called "sour," most varieties can be eaten raw when they are fully ripe—and thoroughly enjoyed. Only the English Morellos are used almost entirely for cooking.

Rootstocks

Cherries, like the other stone fruits, can be grafted upon other cherry, plum, peach, or apricot roots. I have even bud-grafted them on various wild cherries, which worked well except that the fast-growing roots suckered so badly it was well-nigh impossible to keep the vigorous undergrowth from crowding out the good top.

Nursery-grown trees are usually budded on a semi-dwarf native European wild sour cherry called Mahaleb. Although inferior to the wild European sweet cherry, the Mazzard, nurseries like both the ease of budding the Mahaleb and the way uniform, saleable-size trees develop quickly from it.

Some nurseries offer dwarf cherries on *Prunus besseyi* stocks, the same roots that are used for dwarf plums and peaches. They make attractive little trees for small lots, and are ideal for planting in pots or tubs to be used on terraces.

Pollination

Sour cherries are self-fruitful and only one variety is needed in order to get fruit. Sweet cherries always require two different kinds, and sometimes three, for best results. For example, Napoleon and Emperor Francis cannot pollinate each other (probably royal rivalry), so a third kind is needed. Sweet and sour cherries cannot be counted on to pollinate each other, partly because they bloom at slightly different times. Nor can the other stone fruits, such as cherry plums, satisfactorily pollinate cherries.

The Dukes should be regarded as sweet cherries when you are choosing varieties for proper pollination. That is, they will cross-pollinate either with another Duke or any of the sweet cherries.

Culture

Sweet cherry trees do best when planted in light sandy soils similar to those preferred by the peach. Sour cherries can stand heavier and cooler soils, and more extremes in weather. In fact, they thrive under thick, cool mulches. Because none of the cherries are deep-rooted, they don't stand droughts well, particularly when planted in the lighter soils. All fruit trees need careful planting, but cherries require special care because their roots dry out so easily. *Never* let the roots get dry during the planting process, and keep them well watered until they begin to grow well.

Cherries need less pruning than most fruit trees. Removing the broken, crossed, and dead limbs may be all that's necessary for the first seven or eight years. Later on some thinning of the bearing wood will be beneficial and, of course, corrective pruning any time the tree is growing out of shape. Cherry tree limbs seldom break from weight of fruit as do apple limbs, but trees that grow too wide or lopsided are not attractive or easy to care for.

Cherries, like plums and apricots, bear their fruit on short blunt spurs. When pruning the tree these spurs should not be removed unless they are very old or too numerous.

Cherry trees don't need much fertilizer, and if the soil is really good they may not need any. Overfeeding will produce a tree that grows too fast, doesn't bear well, and is more susceptible to disease.

Unlike plums, cherry trees should never be used as "fillers" between the regular trees in an apple or peach orchard, because cherries begin to ripen during the summer while spraying may still be necessary on the other fruits. It's always best to keep cherries a safe distance away from all other fruit trees for this reason.

Probably birds are the cherry grower's biggest problem, unless you're growing your cherries only to attract birds, which few of us are. Growers have worked out many ingenious methods to thwart these same feathered friends we value so highly when they're eating bugs. It may help somewhat to plant the trees near the house where you can watch them. Noisemakers are sometimes useful, too, if family and neighbors can stand them, and people have used scarecrows, stuffed owls, plastic snakes, and other contraptions. Some desperate growers use netting; others have even built large chicken-wire cages around their cherry trees. It sometimes helps to plant mulberry trees nearby, because the birds often prefer to eat those berries. Some orchardists have tried to outwit the birds by planting yellow cherries, thinking the birds will wait for them to ripen and turn red. But birds are no fools, at least not for long.

Diseases

Many home orchardists never spray their cherry trees and have no problems at all. It is possible, however, for cherries to get most of the diseases that bother the plum, including black knot and brown rot. Brown rot can be especially troublesome during wet years.

The treatment is the same as for plums. The chemical Captan has proven to be a great boon for cherry growers because it controls so many diseases yet can be safely used right up until time of harvest.

Just as plum trees are bothered with a virus, many of the cherry trees now being produced are grafted on roots that are also infected. This virus spreads later throughout the tree. By the time the tree has produced for a number of years a few limbs have begun to wilt and die, and often within two or three years the tree is dead. This problem has been particularly bad in the Northeast in recent years. Either make sure you are buying virus-free trees from a reliable nursery or bud-graft your own scions from "clean" trees.

Insects

There's always the possibility that insects may attack your cherries, although we've never had any trouble on ours except tent caterpillars, which are apt to appear on almost anything. We simply cut these off and burn them as soon as the huge webbed clusters appear.

The same insects that bother the plum can also strike the cherry, although there may possibly be some additional ones, too. The cherry maggot, for example, operates in much the same way as the apple maggot, laying eggs inside the fruit which soon hatch and cause wormy cherries.

Control of most cherry pests is possible by following the sanitary methods described in Chapter 9, but when necessary you should follow the suggested spray program in the same chapter. Be sure to read the directions on the spray package and stop all spraying the specified number of days before harvest. While newer sprays are not as toxic as the old arsenics and DDT's, instructions should still be followed carefully, especially when you use them on ripening fruits such as cherries.

Frost Damage

Frost damage is often mistaken for a disease on cherries. The damage may have been done during the winter but you may not notice the splitting and eventual loosening of the bark until spring or early summer. Avoid overstimulating the tree's growth by fertilizing it sparingly, and be sure to choose tree varieties suitable for your climate. If an unusually early cold spell or extra-low winter temperatures damage the tree, seal any loose bark with tree paint and rubber electrical tape immediately, to prevent bark loss and to keep out the weather and bacterial infection.

Like many other fruits, cherries need a cooling period of several weeks in the winter in order to grow satisfactorily. If you garden in the frost-free or nearly frost-free parts of the country, you are likely to have trouble growing either the sweet or sour varieties.

Harvesting

There's no question about the fact that the birds who steal cherries have good taste. Cherries are superb, and among human aficionados there are not many leftovers after they become ripe.

Their size, color, taste, and ease of "pull" from the tree will tell you when they are ready to pick. The longer you leave sour cherries on the tree, the sweeter they'll become—but be careful that you pick them before the skins crack, and of course watch out that the birds don't get there first.

Picking cherries is easy and fun. You can pile them in a container without harming them at all. They should be used soon after picking because they keep only a short time. (In a refrigerator the firm sweet cherries should keep from two to three weeks, but the soft sweet ones and the sour ones will keep only about a week.) If you have a surplus there are 101 different ways to use them. There are few people whose mouths don't water at the mention of fresh-baked homemade cherry pie. And they can be frozen, canned, dried, or made into relish, juice, and preserves. And you're likely to find one even on top of your ice cream sundae—the Maraschino. The Maraschino is simply a sour cherry that has been specially processed in brine, with artificial color and preservatives added. Many gardeners will probably prefer a less colorful but equally tasty home-processed one.

Varieties

Although new cherry varieties do not appear as fast as some other fruits, there are still many kinds being grown. Here are a few that are readily available:

SWEET CHERRIES

Zones 5–8

BING. Dark red, firm, aromatic. Ripens midseason, needs a pollinator.
BLACK TARTARIAN. Good home cherry. Medium-size fruit, best quality, productive tree.
EMPEROR FRANCIS. Red, firm, superior flavor, good home cherry. Ripens late. Tree disease-resistant, productive, more tolerant of soils than most sweet cherries.
NAPOLEON (ROYAL ANN). Yellow with red blush, large, high quality. Tree productive but not very hardy.
SCHMIDT'S BIGARREAU. Fancy, firm-fleshed, crack-resistant. Good productive tree.
STARK GOLD. Rot-resistant. Vigorous tree and one of the hardiest sweet cherries.
STARK LAMBERT. An improved Lambert. Huge size but cracks in wet weather. One of the hardier varieties.
VENUS. Excellent home cherry. Red inside and out, crack-resistant. Tree very productive.
VISTA. Early, high-quality home-type cherry. Tree not so productive.
WINDSOR. Late, black-fleshed. Needs less spraying and is hardier than most sweet cherries.

There are so many kinds of cherries that one variety or another can be grown almost anywhere (USDA).

DUKE CHERRIES

Zones 5–8

OLIVET. Dark red. Good tree growth and productivity.

REINE HORTENSE. Pale red, large, showy, fine flavor. Tree irregular bearer.

ROYAL DUKE. Large dark fruit, midseason. Good tree habits, productive.

LATE DUKE AND MAY DUKE. Later and earlier versions of the Royal Duke.

SOUR CHERRIES

Zones 4–7 unless otherwise noted

EARLY RICHMOND. One of the hardiest old-time pie cherries, fair quality. Not good in warm climates.

ENGLISH MORELLO. Very dark red, late, good quality. Good for home use, mostly for cooking and preserving.

METEOR. New, extra-hardy dwarf red. Especially good for northern home gardens. Worth a trial in milder sections of Zone 3.

MONTMORENCY. The most commonly planted, best-known red sour cherry. Excellent for home use.

NORTH STAR. New dwarf cherry, very hardy, red. Worth a trial in Zone 3.

SUDA HARDY. Morello-type, new, late, dark red. Good for home use.

Bush Cherries and Cherry Plums are described in the plum varieties listed in Chapter 16.

22 / THE SMALL FRUITS

One wintry evening we sat around the fire making our spring gardening plans and decided to check over the list of what we'd put into the freezer the previous season. We were surprised to find what a large percentage of our frozen food crop was small fruits.

We begin freezing them in the spring with rhubarb, which isn't technically a fruit but tastes like one and has much the same makeup. Then in early summer we put up strawberries, and after that the gooseberries, currants, raspberries, blueberries, and elderberries. There is one or another going into the freezer nearly all summer, or into our favorite foods: pies, shortcakes, sauces, puddings, ice cream, milkshakes, juices, jams, jellies, conserves, butters, and on and on.

If we were to buy them all they would cost hundreds of dollars. As it is, they cost us very little money and take less work than our vegetable garden. We feel that the convenience of having them in our own back yard more than offsets the work of growing them, anyway. Of course, there is no way to buy them if we wanted to. Where could we get ripe yellow or purple raspberries, or red gooseberries or elderberries? Even red raspberries and strawberries are hard to find in our area, and if the stores have them they are usually in less than perfect condition.

Hopefully you won't have to make a choice between growing tree fruits and small fruits, but the latter do have certain advantages. For one, they take only a little room. Besides that, they need little care and fertilizer, and the initial cost is small. Once planted they bear quickly and abundantly, and most will go on producing for decades. They make a good cash crop for a bit of extra income, too. But above all, for your own eating pleasure small fruits are something you won't want to miss.

You may sometimes be tempted to accept gift plants from a neighbor rather than buy them. Strawberries, blackberries, and raspberries are frequently offered since they create new plants at a fast rate. You could reason that besides saving money and getting freshly dug plants, there is the additional advantage of getting locally grown plants which, if they grow well for your neighbor, should do likewise for you.

The trouble with gift berry plants—in fact, with all gift plants—is that you may be acquiring diseases and insects that will give you a peck of trouble ever after. Nurseries are now going to a great deal of trouble to grow disease-free plants, and we should all take advantage of them. Starting with a bug-free, disease-free fruit garden is a tremendous advantage, and will facilitate keeping it that way.

Equally important as starting with disease-free stock is getting plants well suited for your climate. Kinds that were developed especially for one area often do poorly in another, even if climatic differences seem slight. Luckily, experimenters in each section of the United States and Canada have been introducing new varieties of fruits and berries for many years, so there's something for each of us. Experimenting is fun, but if you're counting on a crop it's best to plant varieties you know are especially suited for your corner of the world.

Preparing the soil thoroughly for your small fruit bed is an important step you won't want to neglect. Make sure that the soil is rich, loose, and deeply prepared so that the roots can start growing as soon as they are planted. The soil should be in as good shape as it would be if you had prepared it for a fine vegetable garden. Add lots of manure (15 pounds dried or 10 bushels fresh per 100 square feet), work it in well, and get rid of all grass and weeds.

When you plant small fruits be careful not to crowd them. The bush

Though a fairly new fruit in cultivation, blueberries are becoming more popular with gardeners each year (USDA).

fruits—currants, gooseberries, and blueberries—are all treated like little trees. They should be planted 4 to 6 feet apart, and if they are mulched and fertilized each year they should produce abundantly and live practically forever. Berry bushes need lots of room because they are heavy feeders with large root systems.

You'll find that the brambles—raspberries and blackberries—sucker badly. Because little plants are always coming up all around them, you won't want to plant them near a vegetable garden, strawberry bed, or flower patch. The best location for them is a place where you can mow around the bed or have some other certain way to keep the suckers under control.

Keep in mind, too, when you are planting any small fruits, that they should be placed away from fruit and shade trees that might need spraying during the summer when the berries are ripening.

Most berries that fail probably do so because the plant was merely stuck in the ground and forgotten. Subsequent care of your small fruits is as important as good planting. Many books say that a good raspberry patch can produce for ten years, but we are still picking bushels of fruit each year from a patch set twenty years ago, and there is no sign of its retirement. Some people report that their berry patches have gone on for half a century. It's care that makes the difference.

How Many?

How many plants you grow will depend on the preferences of your family, whether fruit is to be preserved or not, and how much room you have available. Here is a suggested berry garden for a family of four who will freeze some fruit. It is only a suggestion, of course, and whatever you choose could be quite different.

NUMBER OF PLANTS	FEET APART IN ROW	FEET BETWEEN ROWS	APPROX. YIELD
8 blackberry	3	7–8	16 pints
4 blueberry	5–6	6–8	50 pints
4 currant	5	—	10 pints
4 elderberry	5	—	10 pints
4 gooseberry	5	—	12 pints
10 black or purple raspberry	3	6	50 pints
40 red raspberry	2–3	6	70–80 pints
10 yellow raspberry or everbearing	2–3	6	20 pints
25–40 strawberry	2	3–4	25–40 quarts

23 / THE RASPBERRY AND THE BLACKBERRY – BRAMBLE FRUITS *(Rubus various)*

We're lucky to have enough land to grow lots of fruits, but I'm sure that if we had room for only one kind, we would choose the red raspberry. The years that the porcupines cut off our canes and ate them we were most unhappy because the loss of a whole row of raspberries meant a sharp cut in our winter fruit diet. Now we keep a close watch for the prickly pillagers, even going so far as to camp out in the berry patch when invasion seems imminent.

Not only do we love raspberries, we've found that nearly everyone else does too. Luckily, raspberries are one of the easiest fruits to grow. Usually you can get a big crop the third year after planting and after that be certain of continuous crops year after year—sometimes for nearly a lifetime. They produce abundantly; we figure that a foot of row produces about a pint of berries during the season.

Raspberries have lots of other good points too. They blossom so late that the frosts never bother them, and so many varieties have been developed that there is one that's suitable for nearly every section of the country. Diseases and insects are easy to control if you grow the new virus-free plants. Raspberries take little care and are easy to pick without bending over. And they're inexpensive! In my opinion, the raspberry is a near-perfect fruit.

Someone else might choose the rich-tasting blackberries as a favorite. Equally prolific, reliable, and useful, they also can be counted on to live for many years. Almost every section of the country has them growing wild, and a wild blackberry is every bit as delicious as the garden variety.

You might think that the rank-growing blackberry would thrive anywhere, but when a friend of ours put in a dozen plants a few years ago, he was surprised and disappointed at the results. The plants barely grew at all on his side of the fence, but the roots slithered into the adjoining yard and soon his neighbor, with no work or expense whatever, had a blackberry patch that was the envy of the neighborhood. Particularly envious was the man who had bought the plants and done the planting. It was one of those mysteries in the plant-grower's world.

Unlike almost every other fruit, blackberries have a slight constipating effect, so they are a good supplement to the more laxative fruits and vegetables that are ready at the same time. Even the leaves have this effect, and a tea made from them is an old-time remedy for dysentery.

Because they bear heavily, are little trouble, and because the fruit is so tasty, red raspberries are a favorite with home fruit growers (USDA).

Classes of Raspberries

Red raspberries are by far the most familiar bramble, and there are still people who refuse to eat a raspberry of any other color. The reds come in both one-crop and two-crop varieties. The one-crop variety matures in midsummer in most areas, on canes grown the previous season. Two-crop raspberries are often called "everbearers," which they are not, or "fall-bearers," which they are. They bear a crop during the regular season on canes grown the year before and another one in the fall on canes grown the current year.

Yellow raspberries are closely related to the reds and vary in color from yellow to pale pink. These are so fragile they are seldom seen in stores, but they're ideally suited for home gardens. Many fruit lovers regard the yellow raspberry as the finest fruit in the world. A handful of them tossed together with the bright red variety makes an elegant dessert.

Black raspberries are dark in color, with an unusual flavor and odor. Some people like them very much, while others don't care for the slightly musky aroma and taste. Besides being eaten fresh, they are much used in flavoring drinks, ice cream, and other desserts.

Purple raspberries are closely related to the blacks, with a similar flavor and similar growth habits and uses.

Classes of Blackberries

Blackberries come in three types: the *upright*, the *trailing kinds* called dewberries, and the *semi-upright*. The growth habit of the upright is very similar to that of the red raspberry. The canes of dewberries grow very long and vinelike, trailing on the ground unless supported. The third group has some of the growth characteristics of both.

Hardiness

Many varieties of red and yellow raspberries can be grown far up in Canada. Black and purple raspberries are nearly as hardy as the reds, with some varieties being suitable for Zone 3. Other varieties have been developed for milder climates. As with all other fruits, you should buy whichever plants are suitable for your area and those that are grown as nearby as possible. Here again it is wise to check with your local extension service for their recommendations, and study those listed at the end of this chapter.

Many fall-bearing red and yellow raspberries are winter-hardy, but if you decide to plant them in Zones 3 and 4, make sure the variety you choose will mature before early frosts destroy the berries.

Most cultivated upright blackberries are not as hardy as raspberries, although some have been developed that do very well in Zone 3. Because very few nurseries carry these, growers in cold areas may have trouble locating a blackberry worthy of growing. Snyder is one of the hardiest, but unfortunately its size and quality are much inferior to other kinds.

Trailing blackberries are even more tender, and most can be grown only in Zone 6 and warmer. Lucretia, one of the hardier varieties, is sometimes successful farther north and might be worth a trial in Zones 4 and 5. Like the other dewberries, it needs a long growing season to properly harden the wood before the first fall frost.

Planting

First prepare the ground thoroughly as described in Chapter 22. It is important that grass and weeds be eradicated as completely as possible to get the brambles off to a good start. Since red raspberries and blackberries sucker so badly, remember to locate the planting where "volunteer" plants springing from the long roots can be kept under control. Plant in rows that can be easily pruned, mulched, and harvested.

Mail-order plants are likely to be shipped bare-rooted and may be dry when they arrive. Unwrap them and soak their roots for several hours in a tub of water as soon as possible to help them recover from their trip.

If you purchase the plants from a local nursery or garden center, the plants may be bare-rooted or in small pots. The potted ones, although more expensive, will probably get off to a better start because of their established root system and be well worth the extra money.

Plant raspberries and blackberries 2 feet apart, setting each plant to the same depth as it grew in the ground or pot. Water heavily so that each plant sits in a muddy mixture and is therefore free of any air pockets around the roots. Continue to water the newly set plants thoroughly every two or three days for two weeks unless it rains heavily. Water is cheap fruit insurance.

If potted plants are used, no pruning at planting time is necessary. With bare-rooted plants, however, you should cut back the canes to 2 inches above the ground to encourage new root growth. If the canes are not cut back enough, the tops will grow too rapidly with not enough corresponding root growth to support them. A weak plant will result that will most likely give up or take years to get going.

Mulching

Grass and weeds can be one of the worst enemies of your brambles. They compete with the plants for nutrients, limit their growth, and reduce berry production, to say nothing of giving the garden a messy appearance. Since rototilling or hoeing can easily damage the shallow bramble roots, heavy mulching is a better way to control grass and nourish your plants at the same time.

Thick layers of shredded bark, maple leaves, shavings, or wood chips are all excellent mulches. Paper and hay can also be used. Sawdust is not a good mulch for berries because it packs too tightly and has a bad habit of taking much nitrogen from the soil as it rots. If the mulch around the plants is several inches thick, enough shade will be provided to suffocate new weed and grass seedlings, which are always desperately trying to get started, yet the new berry canes will push through easily.

Sometimes black plastic or sheets of old metal roofing are laid between the rows to keep berry plants as well as weeds from growing there. Never use asphalt or roofing paper, for asphalt is not good for plants.

Support

Probably you'll have to provide some means of support to keep your bramble fruits from falling over. Some berry growers like to tie the canes to stakes or posts placed every 2 or 3 feet along the row (see drawing A, below). Others put up a fence consisting of strands of smooth wire on each side of the row (B). Still others never support the plants at all but simply cut all the canes back to a height of 4 or 5 feet in late fall, making them stiff enough so that they're less likely to fall over.

Whether you give any support to your plants or not may depend partly on the variety you grow. The short-growing Newburgh raspberry is less likely to need staking than the taller-growing Viking and Latham. Trailing blackberries (dewberries) always need some kind of fence or trellis to keep them off the ground, and upright blackberries and black raspberries are apt to fall over when they get loaded with fruit unless they're supported in some way.

Pruning

If pruning is neglected when you grow the bramble fruits, the planting will deteriorate rapidly. The brambles, both raspberries and blackberries, are

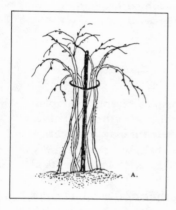

Brambles supported by a stake (A) and by a fence (B)

unusual in that while their roots are perennial, their canes are biennia
while the roots of these plants often live for many years, each cane sprouts
and grows to its full height in one year, bears fruit the following year, then
dies. Because of this, after a few years wild raspberries and blackberries
become a jungle of dead canes, and soon the entire patch dies off. Cultivated
canes that are neglected will do the same.

This is fairly simple to avoid: Simply cut off each dead cane to ground
level after it has finished bearing in late summer. You'll recognize the dead
ones by their pallid color and brittle appearance. Hand-held clippers are ideal
tools for this job, and you'll probably want to wear thick gloves to handle
the thorny canes. Because insects and disease enjoy wintering over in the old
canes, it's a good idea to remove them to the local landfill or to burn them
as soon as possible.

I've found that as the berry patch ages, more pruning becomes necessary. Usually too many new canes are produced each year, so all the weak
ones should be cut off at the same time the old dead ones are removed. Berries
will be larger if all the weak canes are removed and even the strong, healthy
canes are thinned sufficiently so they are at least 6 inches apart.

I have noticed that black and purple raspberries do better with even
more room than the red ones. I would space their canes even farther apart,
probably 8 to 10 inches. Also, while the rows of red or yellow raspberries or
upright blackberries may be permitted to become 2 or 3 feet wide, those of
black or purple raspberries or of trailing blackberries should be kept to a
width of no more than a foot or a foot and a half. The extra room between
plants and between rows allows air circulation, which will reduce the plants'
likeliness to contract spur blight, mildew, and other diseases. It also will help
increase berry size and add to your ease in pruning and picking.

Harvesting

Both raspberries and blackberries taste so good and have so many uses
it is hard to get an oversupply of them. Furthermore, since they ripen over
two or three weeks, you can enjoy the berries daily over a relatively long
season.

Fruit picked on sunny days has the best vitamin content, but no matter
what the weather, the berries should be picked when they are ripe. Usually
this means picking at least every other day during raspberry season. Early,
midseason, and late varieties can be planted if you want to extend the season
even more.

Be sure to handle the tender berries with care so that you don't bruise
them. Use only small picking dishes because too many berries in the same
container will crush the bottom ones badly. Avoid handling them any more
than necessary, and move your freshly picked berries out of the sun as soon
as possible.

All kinds of raspberries and blackberries are delicious right off the
bush. Eating them like candy with no extras is one of the best and most

healthful ways to enjoy them. Some people prefer them with cream and sugar, and of course there are the traditional pies and shortcakes, jellies, jams, and juice. Some of our friends swear their own homemade raspberry-rhubarb wine is the best there is.

Steps for Success in the Raspberry and Blackberry Patch

FIRST YEAR

Prepare the soil carefully and plant the berries 2 feet apart. If bare-rooted plants are used, cut the tops back to 2 inches above the ground after planting. Mulch heavily.

SECOND YEAR

Spring. Cut back all plants to 2 inches above ground level in early spring. This encourages maximum cane growth for big crops.

Fall. Cut tops of plants back so canes are about 4 feet tall. This makes a stiff plant that doesn't fall over in winter's snow and wind.

THIRD YEAR AND EACH YEAR THEREAFTER

Summer. Mulch, cultivate, mow or pull out tips or sucker plants that grow in the wrong places and make the row too wide. Keep each row only 2 feet wide for ease of picking, weeding, and pruning. Cut off and burn wilted tops as soon as they appear. Dig or pull out any sick-looking plants and destroy them (far away).

Late Summer. Cut to ground level the canes that bore fruit and now look sick. Remove and destroy them. Thin the new canes to 6 inches apart. Cut out any weak canes that won't produce.

Fall. Cut back canes to 4 feet in height for winter. Put up wire for support if necessary. Add mulch and manure. Spray with Ferbam if spur blight is a problem.

To Get the Biggest Fall Crop from Everbearers

If two-crop raspberries (everbearers) are grown and you want a large fall crop, follow all of the preceding procedures *except* under "Third Year and Thereafter" insert the following:

Spring. Cut *all* canes off to ground level. This means there will be no summer crop, but the fall crop will be larger and earlier. It won't be necessary, of course, to do any pruning in late summer, because there will be no old canes.

Diseases

These are some diseases you should be on the lookout for in your berry patch:

VIRUS DISEASES

These are especially serious since there is, as yet, no apparent cure. Both plant and fruit get smaller and sicker-looking each year until the bushes finally die. These are the most common:

Leaf curl. New leaves curl down and inward.

Mosaic. If you find that the leaves on your new canes are marbled green or have a greenish-yellow mottled look, mosaic might be the cause.

Orange rust. This one is especially bad on blackberries. Look for bright orange spores during the summer on the undersides of leaves and on the canes. This is a fairly common disease and one of the reasons so many blackberry plantings have failed. Some nurseries still sell infected plants, and many wild blackberries have it.

OTHER DISEASES

Anthracnose. This blight shows as gray blotches with purple edges on the bark. Black raspberries are most susceptible. Captan sprays control it.

Root (crown) gall. Fleshy growth on roots. Plant only certified plants in soil not previously infected with diseased plants.

Verticillium wilt. This is the same disease that strikes tomato plants, maple trees, and many others. There's not much you can do about it, unfortunately. The canes wilt suddenly, usually in midsummer. It's best to plant the brambles away from potatoes, peppers, and tomatoes if you've noticed that these plants have ever shown signs of this disease.

Insects

When you consider how many pests bother the tree fruits, it is surprising that so few insects attack the brambles. The cane borer is one of the most troublesome, and rare is the bramble grower who doesn't encounter this one sooner or later. Happily, it is easy to control without poisons. The sudden wilting of the tops of the new canes is evidence that this critter is at hand. Inspection will reveal two complete circles near the top of the cane. If you open it at this point, the larva will be found sitting quietly here as though it had every intention of making this plant its own. If undisturbed, the borer will go down the cane, killing it and continuing on to infect other canes with increasing damage to your patch in future years. Control is easy. As soon as the wilted, infected ends appear, simply cut them off below the bottom ring and burn them. Exit borers.

Tree crickets, crown borers, sawflies, and raspberry beetles may attack the plants in certain areas of the country and may be especially troublesome at times to commercial growers. All-purpose orchard spray can be used to control these pests if necessary, but luckily large bug colonies seldom show much interest in us small-time berry growers.

Transplanting Wild Plants

Because the flavor of wild berry plants is so good, sometimes gardeners ask if it is practical to transplant these wild brambles to the garden and improve them. Usually the answer is no. Even in a garden, wild berry plants are apt to be short-lived, mainly because they are likely to be infected with some of the virus diseases.

Even if they weren't infected, most gardeners wouldn't want to pass up a century of fruit progress. It would be a shame not to take advantage of the wonderful new cultivated berries. They are large, easy to grow and pick, and the flavor of most of them is superb. If you occasionally have a hankering for the wild ones, you can usually find plenty in the woods.

Varieties

Here is a partial list of the most used and most available plants:

RED RASPBERRIES

CHIEF. Early variety, fairly good quality, small fruit. Recommended for the Midwest.
CUTHBERT. Old variety. Good quality but not a heavy producer.
LATHAM. Fairly good quality. Susceptible to disease, so be sure to buy virus-free plants.
NEWBURGH. Good quality and producer, disease-resistant. Plants are short so need little staking.
TAYLOR. Large, good-quality berries, good producer.
VIKING. Fair quality, very tall-growing, good producer.

New kinds worth trying: Anelma, Polaris.

For Zones 8 and 9: Dormanred, Ranere, Surprise.

FALL-BEARING RED RASPBERRIES

DURHAM. Medium early.
FALL RED. One of the earliest, so are good for areas with short growing seasons.
HERITAGE. Promising new variety. Especially good for home gardens.
INDIAN SUMMER. Fair quality, late.

SEPTEMBER. Medium early.

SOUTHLAND. High quality, productive. Developed in North Carolina.

YELLOW RASPBERRIES

AMBER. Pink-yellow, excellent flavor, good producer.

FALL GOLD. Fall-bearing. Good for home use where frosts are not early.

GOLDENWEST. Recommended for the Pacific Northwest. Developed by the Washington State Experiment Station.

BLACK RASPBERRIES

ALLEN. Sweet, high quality, good for home use.

BLACK HAWK. Early ripening, drought-resistant, productive, large berries. Good for freezing.

BRISTOL. Good quality and producer. Tall-growing plants, fairly resistant to mosaic. Good home-type berry.

CUMBERLAND. One of the hardier old-timers. Subject to mosaic and anthracnose.

JOHN ROBERTSON. New introduction. Supposed to be one of the hardiest.

For Zones 8 and 9: Ceylon, Mysore.

PURPLE RASPBERRIES

CLYDE. New, fairly hardy, vigorous and disease-resistant. From the New York Experiment Station.

SODUS. Good quality, good producer. Tall-growing plants, moderately hardy.

UPRIGHT BLACKBERRIES

COMANCHE. Good quality, large fruit. Good for home gardens. Midseason, from Arkansas.

DARROW. Large and tall, good quality, heavy producer. Long season.

EARLY HARVEST. Good size and quality. An old-time variety. Popular in the Midwest.

EBONY KING. Purplish black. One of the hardier new varieties.

ELDORADO. Another old-timer still widely grown but being replaced by Darrow.

RANGER. Sweet, large, good quality, early, productive. Used for wines as well as eating.

SNYDER. Fruit small and of poor quality. Probably one of the hardiest.

Early Harvest, Flint, Humble, and Lawton are grown in the more southern regions; Himalaya is widely grown in California.

TRAILING BLACKBERRIES (DEWBERRIES)

BOYSEN. Rich full flavor. One of the largest dewberries. Grown commercially in the West.

LUCRETIA. Large, black, good quality, early. Hardiest of the dewberries.

MARION. Black, large berries, heavy yielder. Vigorous, yet fewer canes make it easier to train.

THORNFREE. Medium-size fruit, tart flavor, late. Semi-upright blackberry from U.S. Department of Agriculture.

THORNLESS. Huge purplish-maroon berries, almost seedless. Like boysenberry, but with no thorns. Vigorous grower.

YOUNG. High quality. Heavy yielder. One of the older varieties.

24 / THE STRAWBERRY *(Fragaria)*

During one of the Sunday services in our little church when I was a child, a visiting minister remarked that he was thoroughly sick of hearing about Heaven's pearly gates and golden streets. Heaven, he said, was a personal reward that he visualized as a land where, among other pleasant happenings, juicy red strawberries ripened eternally. It was one of the best sermons I'd ever heard. Probably lots of other people would agree, for it's hard to find anyone who doesn't like strawberries, even though there are those unfortunate folks who are allergic to them.

Like many gardeners I have often risen in the dead of a late spring night, looked at the thermometer with half-opened eyes, and suddenly awakened in shock. Soon we were grabbing blankets, quilts, tablecloths, boxes, and anything else we could find to cover up the tender blossoms that had foolishly opened just before the moon turned full and the temperature plunged.

Is it worth fighting the frost, the bugs, the disease, the weeds, and the witchgrass? Every strawberry lover will answer a booming "YES!" The reward comes when you gaze at the reddening row in hungry anticipation and then pick those luscious big crimson berries on a bright summer morning. I find it's hard to break the childhood habit of one for the pail and one for the mouth.

The strawberry we grow in our gardens today is unique because it is one of the few fruits that actually originated in the United States. These large berries were all developed in fairly recent years by European and American breeders from the wild strawberries the early explorers found growing in the New World.

While few claim that the beautiful easy-to-pick hybrids can compare in flavor to the wild ones picked among the thistles and garter snakes on youthful expeditions, the gardeners who choose the best flavored varieties and grow them in rich organic soil maintain they come mighty close.

Buying Plants

Because of the popularity of the strawberry, a great many new varieties have been developed during the short time it has been in cultivation.

There are now kinds that grow well all over the United States as well as in parts of Alaska, Canada, and even in the really warm parts of Florida. Because of the wide range of varieties, be careful to choose the right ones for your region. And try to locate some that are grown nearby and are freshly dug.

Like the brambles, both wild and cultivated strawberries are troubled by a host of diseases and insects, and for a few years it looked like commercial berry growing might be a thing of the past. Vigorous work in developing disease-free and disease-resistant strains has saved it, however, and you should be sure to buy only those plants that are certified virus-free. By doing so you are likely to save yourself a great deal of distress later on.

Preparing the Soil

Since your strawberry plants will be growing in the same spot for at least two years, it is extremely important to have the ground very well prepared. The plants are small and shallow-rooted compared to all other fruit plants, so they get all their moisture and nourishment from the top few inches of soil.

This soil should be light, rich, slightly acid (pH of 5 to 6), and full of

Strawberries are nearly everybody's favorite. Not only is it a good home fruit, but it is also a good berry to grow if one wishes to raise a few fruits to sell (USDA).

rich humus (manure, compost, or peat) that will hold moisture even during the driest weather. Generally, soil that will grow a good crop of potatoes is also good for strawberries. In fact, it is always important to plant strawberries on land that has been used first for cultivated crops for a year or more previously in order to get rid of the grass, weeds, and white grubs. These are the worst enemies of the strawberry, and well-prepared soil helps eliminate all three. White grubs live mostly in grass-covered soils, and one of their favorite foods is strawberry roots. Grass and weeds compete with the shallow-rooted berry plants for nutrients and moisture, and they crowd and shade the plants as well. You can wage war on weed competition by frequent cultivation, hoeing, and hand-weeding or a heavy mulch.

Planting

How many plants do you need? Gardeners usually plant from 25 to 100 plants in their first strawberry bed. Later on you will better know whether to plant more or less. The number you choose will depend on your yield and how many berries you eat, freeze, preserve, and give away.

When should you plant? Spring is usually regarded as the best time, the earlier the better. There doesn't seem to be much gained by fall planting, even if the plants survive—and many don't. I have always felt that if you plant anything in the fall you just have to weed that much longer.

Now your plants have come. The soil is tilled to a depth of nearly a foot and is loose, crumbly, and rich. You're ready to plant and have two planting methods to choose from: the matted row or the less-used hill system.

THE MATTED ROW

In the matted row method, set the plants about 18 inches apart in the row at the proper depth as shown on page 199. Water them well. If you plant more than one row, keep the rows at least 3 feet apart or even wider if you plan to use a power tiller for cultivation. In this method the plants are allowed to produce runners freely (runners produce new little plants). You'll have to steer them so they will grow toward their adjoining plants, take root, and fill in to make a row matted with strawberry plants (see page 198, A).

In this system the crop is treated like a biennial and is planted one year, harvested the next, then plowed under. If kept for a third year, so many new plants are produced that the bed becomes overcrowded, the fruit crop is small, and the berries are usually small and hard.

THE HILL SYSTEM

The hill system takes more plants and usually more attention, but it saves annual replanting and is ideally suited for home gardeners with little growing space. Those who like raising plants organically with a deep mulch also prefer it.

The plants are set 12 inches apart in three rows, which are also 12 inches apart. The plants are mulched. If you want more than three rows, leave 3 or 4 feet of walking space between the beds.

After setting, keep the plants well watered. Unlike the matted row system in which you let the runners grow freely, in this system you cut off all runners as soon as they form and permit no new plants to grow (see below, B).

In other words, the strawberry plant is treated as a perennial, which it is. When grown this way it will keep producing for six years or more. Since none of the plant's energy goes into setting runners and making new plants, both plant and fruit get quite large.

Whichever method you choose, be sure to set your plants at the correct depth (see page 199). If the crowns are planted under the soil, the plant will smother and die. If the crowns are set too high above the soil, they will dry out. If you cultivate or hoe the bed, it is important never to hoe soil up around strawberry crowns as you would around corn or beans. They need the breathing space.

ROTATE YOUR CROPS

Although the hill method of growing strawberries has much to recommend it, most home growers I know use the more familiar runner method.

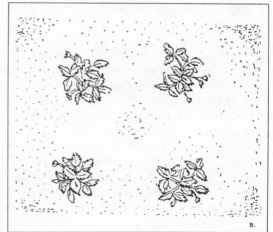

(A) *The matted row method of growing strawberries and* (B) *the less common hill method*

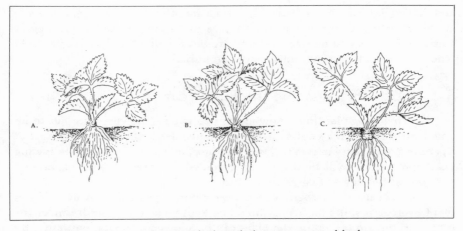

Plant strawberries at the proper depth, with the crown at ground level.
A *is too shallow,* B *just right,* C *too deep.*

In the spring they set their plants alongside the vegetable garden and cultivate them as they do the other plants. The next spring they plant another bed on the other side of the garden. Berries are picked in the second year from the first bed planted. After bearing, it is plowed under and the bed is planted with winter rye or oats; or if you don't want to plant it, instead it can be heavily fertilized and covered with mulch or black plastic to keep it weed-free.

The next spring strawberries are again planted for the following year in another spot in the garden. The quick plowing under of the old plants and continual change in location of the new plants aids greatly in disease and insect control. The annual planting of virus-free plants means a good crop of large fruit from brand-new plants each year.

You may wonder why you shouldn't save money and dig extra plants out of your own patch for planting. Of course you can, but unless you are absolutely sure they are disease- and insect-free it's a lot smarter to get them each year from a certified virus-free nursery.

Weed Control

Even more than with the brambles, weeds and grass are a real problem in growing strawberries. Yankee gardeners say that a man should never plant a bigger patch than his wife can look after.

To keep out those wily weeds, hand-weeding, hoeing, cultivation, or mulching with organic material or black plastic are all used. Some growers use chemical weed killers such as Dacthal or Dymid. Others allow geese to run in their berry beds to eat the grass and dandelions.

For home growers, hand-hoeing, cultivation, or mulching are safest and do less damage to the plant. Chemicals are often tricky to use, and geese are very dirty and not always selective as to what they eat. If you hoe or cultivate be sure you do not "hill up" around the plant and suffocate it. As when planting, the crown must never be buried.

Pick Off Blossoms the First Year

Whichever planting arrangement you choose, be very sure not to let any fruit develop on your strawberry plants the first year. Growing and ripening even a berry or two will weaken the plant so much that the following year's production will be drastically curtailed. To prevent fruiting, simply pick off all blooms as fast as they form.

Everbearing strawberries are an exception to this rule, however. If you plant everbearers, the blossoms should be kept picked until midsummer the first year, but from then on the plant can be allowed to flower naturally. By that time it is well-enough established to support its fall crop.

Everbearing Strawberries

Everbearing strawberries bear a light crop in early summer, a few more fruits off and on throughout the summer, and another heavier crop in late summer or fall. They're ideal for summer home gardeners who preserve very little fruit but like to pick a few berries now and then all season. They are the best kinds to plant in pots, jars, barrels, and pyramids, as described in Chapter 3. They begin to bear quickly and look nice all season. Another advantage, as I mentioned before, is that with everbearers it is possible to get a small crop the first year.

We preserve lots of fruit and berries, so the heavier bearing regular varieties appeal to us more. Everbearers are a bit tricky to grow in some areas, too. Most kinds don't do well in southern sections and they're usually not recommended where growing seasons are unusually short. That leaves Zones 5–8 as their ideal growing spots.

Climbing Strawberries

Glowing ads in recent years have hailed this fruit as a major break-through in the gardening world. With all the superlatives we old-time gardeners have learned to expect, we are told that climbing strawberries will produce wonderful large berries on long-climbing vines that will amaze and astonish all who survey them.

According to most people we've talked with who have tried them, the best they have gotten is a limited number of small fruits resembling wild strawberries. The plant must be taken off the trellis and covered up for the winter, too, in all but the warmer sections of the country. The climbing strawberry may be an interesting novelty and even produce some good fruit, but you'd better not expect to see amazed tourists creating traffic jams as they gaze at it, nor should you start making elaborate plans on how to dispose of your abundant surplus.

Winter and Frost Protection

In almost every spot north of the Mason-Dixon line—and in some to the south—some sort of winter protection is necessary for best strawberry production. The prominence of the word "straw" in the name strawberry suggests that the two have long been connected. While the strawberry was still in its early development, growers realized that the fruit buds, even before they began to show in the spring, could be easily hurt by below-freezing temperatures. Straw was cheap and plentiful, so the plants were thoroughly covered before winter with thick layers to protect the buds and increase the size of the crop.

Straw is still the preferred winter cover, although it is harder to find nowadays. It doesn't mat hard or contain lots of weed seeds like so many other covers. Also, when the plants are uncovered in the spring the straw makes a nice mulch that both conserves moisture and keeps the ripening fruit clean and away from the soil.

You should cover the plants about the time the hard frosts start (15 to 18 degrees F. above zero) and the ground is beginning to freeze slightly. The covering should be left on all winter and not removed until all medium-hard frosts (25 degrees F. above zero or under) have finished. When you remove the covering, it's best to do it on a cloudy or rainy day, or at least late in the afternoon, so the bright sun won't hit the tender shaded shoots before they have had a chance to toughen up a bit.

Besides needing protection from winter's cold, the plants will probably need to be protected from late spring frosts that sometimes hit when strawberries are blossoming. This is the time you quickly rip the quilts off the bed to cover them up, or set out kerosene flares. Small patches of strawberries can be protected by running lawn sprinklers over them all night. It may also help to cover them with plastic sheets, newspapers, or cardboard cartons or to move the straw mulch back over the blooms.

We frequently hear of ingenious new ways our gardening friends have found to lick spring frost damage. Some have used Christmas tree lights laid along the rows and covered with a plastic tent; others have experimented with large fans to keep the air moving. Whatever method you use, you've got to be tuned in to the spring weather. Be sure to watch the thermometer closely at blooming time, especially on clear nights. It can be a balmy 60 degrees at dusk and plunge to well below 30 degrees by 2 a.m. You won't want to work all year and then lose your crop a few weeks before it's ready to eat.

Harvesting

Strawberries should always be picked on the day they ripen, which usually means daily picking during the harvest season. Overripe fruit spoils quickly, on the vines or off. Early morning is the best time to pick; gathering the fruit while the air is still cool and rushing it to a cool place will help keep the berries fresh longer. But even in a refrigerator it's hard to keep strawberries more than a few days. Wash them just before you use them, because when they are wet they spoil faster.

Nobody needs to be reminded of the delightful taste of ripe strawberries and cream or strawberry shortcake, milkshakes, ice cream, or parfaits. Furthermore, they're good for you, with a healthy amount of Vitamin C in the fruit and in the leaves, which are used for making strawberry tea. The berries freeze very well either whole or squashed with sugar, and a great many of them in our house go into jam.

Insects and Diseases

Some manuals on growing strawberries list dozens of bugs and diseases that bother them. If we read those bulletins first, most of us would never have the courage to plant at all. Most of these pests are no serious problem to the home gardener, fortunately, and only when large plantings are grown on the same lot for years do they sometimes become a serious threat.

By all means, don't give up growing strawberries because you're afraid hosts of evil fungi are lurking behind a tree waiting to pounce. Buying virus-free plants is the best insurance against disease. Leaf spot, leaf scorch, verticillium wilt, red stele, and other virus diseases are most common, but you may never encounter any of them.

Captan, Ferbam, and other fungicides can be used to control many of the berry diseases if they become real problems. Fungicides are expensive, though, and ordinarily they shouldn't be necessary for home growers.

As for insects, you very likely will encounter at least a few. Many garden insects also attack strawberries, and the Japanese beetles, aphids, thrips, leafhoppers, slugs, grasshoppers, spittlebugs, and leaf rollers that sometimes bother garden and flower plants often lunch on strawberries as well.

WHITE GRUBS

These root-eating pests are more likely to be a problem on new ground that was only recently in sod. The grubs develop into those big May (or June) beetles that bang on the windows and buzz around lights on early summer nights.

CYCLAMEN MITES

These small, hard-to-see insects also bother delphiniums, house plants, and other ornamentals, causing leaves and buds to curl tightly. It's hard to find safe sprays to use for control of this pest; natural parasitic insects often control them best.

WEEVILS

Weevils are one of the most serious problems for many growers. They lay their eggs in the bud cluster, causing it to be partly severed from the plant. If an insecticide has to be sprayed to control these weevils, care must be taken to use it before the blooms open so it won't also kill the pollinating bees.

If spraying becomes necessary for these insects, the general-purpose orchard spray mix described in Chapter 9 can be applied at intervals of ten to fourteen days from the time the leaves begin growing in the spring until a week before the flowers open. This will control most strawberry diseases and insects.

Some strawberry growers plant a marigold between every plant to help repel certain insects. Since these are annuals, they never become weedy and they do dress up the patch.

Varieties for Special Regions or Purposes

FOR AREAS WITH LITTLE FROST. Fresno, Headliner, Pocahontas, Tioga.

FOR THE NORTHWEST. Fresno, Goldsmith, Shasta.

HARDIEST. Catskill, Dunlap, Empire, Fairfax, Premier (same as Howard 17), Sparkle.

EVERBEARERS. Gem, Mastodon, Ozark Beauty, Rockhill.

EXCELLENT FLAVOR. Albritton, Dunlap, Empire, Fletcher, Midland, Sparkle, Suwanee.

BEST FOR HOME FREEZING. Earlibelle, Earlidawn, Marshall, Midland, Midway, Pocahontas, Redglow, Sparkle.

LARGEST FRUIT. Atlas, Catskill, Guardian, Jersey Belle, Sequoia, Tioga.

MOST RESISTANT TO LATE SPRING FROSTS. Catskill, Earlidawn, Midway, Premier (same as Howard 17).

EARLIEST. Atlas, Blakemore, Dunlap, Earlibelle, Midland, Premier, Sequoia, Sunrise, Surecrop.

MIDSEASON. Apollo, Catskill, Empire, Fairfax, Fresno, Guardian, Marshall, Midway, Raritan, Redchief, Robinson.

LATEST. Albritton, Armore, Badgerbelle, Columbia, Garnet, Hood, Jersey Belle, Ozark Beauty, Redstar (very late), Sparkle, Tennessee Beauty, Torrey, Totem, Vesper.

25 / THE BUSH FRUITS

For many years we had a large gooseberry bush in our front yard that "belonged" to the boys in my 4-H club who frequently visited us. It was mutually agreed that they could eat freely from that one if they would ignore those in the back garden. The bush produced so lavishly year after year that it always supplied more than their needs, even though several boys sitting around it eating with both hands was not unusual. I'm sure nearly every berry on that bush got squeezed at least twice each year as the impatient 4-H'ers waited for them to ripen.

Like the brambles, the bush fruits furnish a tremendous amount of good eating for the amount of time and money spent on them. They bear at an early age and regularly, and add exciting variety to the home grower's fruit collection. You'll certainly want to include in your plantings all the bush fruit varieties that climate, space, time, and government regulations will permit.

Every section of the country has its own native bush fruits. Some are delicious eaten right off the plant, some are all right if they're cooked with lots of sugar, others are favored only by wildlife or those who have grown up with them and learned to like their unusual taste. Beach plums, buffalo berries, bearberries, chokecherries, sand cherries, highbush cranberries, huckleberries, and Juneberries are some of the fruits that can be gathered in their wild state or transplanted to be cultivated in the garden if you wish, although few have been "tamed" or improved with any great success.

Several other bush fruits have been domesticated and developed into outstanding specimens that are worthy additions to any home garden. They are the blueberries, currants, elderberries, and gooseberries. You'll find at least a few varieties of each in most nursery catalogs. Even though their appearance and flavors are quite different, they are all grouped together in this chapter since their culture is so similar.

Currants, gooseberries, and elderberries are among the hardiest of fruits and are grown in Zones 2 and 3, far into northern Canada. Cultivated blueberries vary widely in hardiness; since some kinds are even less hardy than the peach, growers in Zones 3 and 4 should buy only the hardiest and plant them in sheltered spots.

Blueberries grow much more slowly than the other bush fruits and often take as long as ten years to come into full production.

Getting Started

If you are just starting out with small fruits you will probably want to buy your plants from a nursery to be sure of getting healthy plants and the best varieties. If you should decide to mooch a plant or two from a neighbor who you are sure grows only disease-free plants, you can often sever a small sprout from a large bush with a quick thrust of a sharp spade. Make sure the fledgling plant is well rooted, leave the soil about it intact, and plant it quickly. The best time to separate plants in this way is in the spring before new growth starts.

Often it is hard to find a well-rooted sucker plant of blueberries because they start much less easily than the other small fruits. It will probably be necessary to buy blueberry bushes, because even your best gardening friends are not likely to let you hack away at theirs. You may find that blueberries cost more than the other bush fruits because they are so much more difficult to propagate.

As with the brambles, if you buy bare-rooted stock it is best to plant them in early spring. Nursery-grown plants that are already established in pots may be set anytime the ground isn't frozen.

Culture

Except for the special soil requirements of blueberries, culture of all the bush fruits is much the same. Set the plants 5 or more feet apart unless you want a tight hedge, in which case make a slightly closer planting. In the North full sun is recommended, but farther south they all will tolerate light shade.

Growth habits of the bush fruits differ considerably. While blueberry plants will stay within bounds for years, the currants and gooseberries are likely to spread somewhat. Elderberries, unless controlled, often become very rank and spread all over the lot; in fact, if you plant elderberries it is wise to banish them to a spot by themselves and keep them in it by regularly mowing off all the persistent suckers.

Since all the bush fruits are really small trees, you don't have to prepare the soil for them as carefully as for strawberries or the brambles. They can be planted by digging a large hole, adding lots of fertile organic matter and water, and set just as you would a fruit tree. You'll want to keep grass and weeds from choking them, and water them heavily two or three times a week for a few weeks.

All the bush fruits are heavy feeders and thrive on soil rich in nutrients and humus. Manure is an ideal way to provide both. If a mulch will fit into your mowing plans and esthetic sense, it will be of great benefit to the plants. Bark or wood chips make an ideal mulch. Although the bush fruits are often found growing well on abandoned farms where they're choked with grass and receive no fertilizer, mulch, or pruning, they still do their very best with at least a little attention.

Besides annual additions of fertilizer and mulch, you'll help ensure their success if you give them a light pruning to get rid of excess wood every few years (see below), and keep a lookout for insects and disease.

Pollination

Currants and gooseberries seem to have no problems with pollination, and one bush usually produces abundantly with no trouble. Blueberries, however, benefit greatly by having two or more different varieties planted near each other, and hybrid elderberries also bear much better if two different kinds are close by. If only one variety of hybrid elderberry is used, a few wild ones planted nearby or growing naturally in the neighborhood will provide adequate pollination. Make sure they aren't growing close enough so the plants will spread together, though, or the wild ones will likely crowd out the hybrids.

Diseases and Insects

Although there are numerous diseases and insects that bother bush fruits, most cause no serious worry. Currant or gooseberry worms can strike the plants in early spring and strip off all the leaves within a few days. Quick dusting with Rotenone garden dust or spraying with all-purpose orchard spray (see Chapter 9) will knock out these pests easily. The first spraying is important and must be done immediately, because if they're left unchecked the insects will keep breeding and eating all summer, eventually killing the plant.

Bush fruits require less pruning than most other fruits and berries, but need to be thinned every few years. A *is before pruning;* B *is after.*

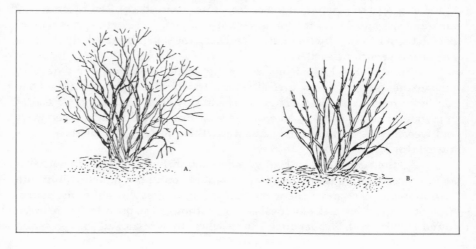

Mildew may strike the bush fruits, particularly currants. You can help prevent it by leaving plenty of room around each plant to allow better air circulation. Powdered sulfur has long been a standard but only partially effective remedy for mildew. Benomyl, a new systemic fungicide, can be used in extreme cases (see page 85).

While other diseases and insects may strike, birds are likely to be the home grower's worst problem, just as they often are for commercial growers. If neighborhood birds are persistent, you'll need a lot of ingenuity to save your crop. Nets, scarecrows, cats, plastic snakes, and frequent visits to the garden are all used to thwart these persistent purloiners who often strike very early in the morning while the orchardist sleeps.

Harvesting

Few instructions are needed for picking the bush fruits. You harvest them when they are ripe—that is, when they are soft and juicy and have developed their full color and taste. Although gooseberries are sometimes picked for cooking purposes before they are soft, it's much better to pick even these when they are in their prime.

None of the bush fruits bruise as easily as raspberries, but they are perishable and should be eaten or processed within a few days. All can be eaten fresh, canned, or frozen, and they make delicious pies, tarts, jams, jellies, juice, and wine. Elderberry wine is famous in fact and fiction.

Currants and blueberries dry well and will keep for years that way . . . a good substitute for raisins. If you live where it is difficult to grow grapes, the bush fruits are a satisfactory substitute. On the other hand, if you're lucky enough to be able to grow nearly everything, the bush fruits will complete your fruit cornucopia.

Blueberries *(Vaccinium)*

Only in recent years has the highbush blueberry been widely grown in home gardens. Although each section of the country had its wild varieties, very few plants had been developed for cultivated use. Progress in originating large-fruited, tall-growing varieties has been so rapid that practically every section of the country except possibly the tropical tip of Florida can now grow the highbush kinds.

Unlike most of the other tree and bush fruits, blueberries are extremely fussy about the soil they live in, and this is the most limiting factor in their use as a home-grown fruit. They do best at a pH of from 4.5 to 5, which is very sour soil; so sour, in fact, that usually only azaleas, rhododendrons, laurels, and certain wild flowers will grow well in it.

If you decide to invest in blueberry plants it's a good idea to take a soil test, because your plantings are likely to fail if the soil is much more or less acid than that. Sometimes the wild vegetation near you will give you a clue about your soil type. If you have lots of wild blueberries nearby, you'll probably be able to grow them, but it's no sure sign. In areas where glaciers flung deposits at random, the acid and alkaline soils often lie side by side.

If you have ordinary garden soil but still want to grow blueberries, you no doubt wonder how you can go about getting and maintaining a soil *that* acid. I'd begin by finding the most acid soil you have that is still deep enough and gets enough light for growing things. Make sure it's a spot where lime or wood ashes haven't been used in recent years. Mix bushels of peat moss and pine needles with the soil and add some cottonseed meal and rotted oak leaves, too, if you have them. Even some old rotten sawdust from a sawmill is good; don't use fresh sawdust, though, because it could rob the nitrogen in the soil. Mix all these acid-inducing materials with the soil and let it set a year. Then test it. If it passes at 4.5 to 5, you're ready to plant.

You'll still have to continue working with the soil after you've planted, because you must maintain that acidity. If all the surrounding soil is alkaline, lime will constantly be leaching into your bed. Rain, percolation, and melting snows can all move material from nearby lime deposits into your blueberry bed, so each year you'll need to add more cottonseed, oak leaves, peat moss, and pine needles to the mulch.

If you aren't an organic gardener you may prefer a quicker way to make your soil acid by applying fertilizer from a garden store that is made especially for azaleas and blueberries. Or you can sprinkle on some aluminum sulphate, also available in garden stores. Follow the directions and soon you'll have a soil that only a blueberry could feel comfortable in.

Because many varieties of cultivated highbush blueberries are not very hardy, be sure that you choose the kinds best suited for your plant zone. If you live in the northern areas, choose only the hardiest plants. Even then it's a good idea to plant them where evergreens, buildings, or walls shelter them from the north and west winds. Highbush blueberries vary in height from 5 to 15 feet, so this may also be a consideration when you're looking for a good location.

Is it practical for you to grow blueberries? If your climate is especially severe or your soil above pH 6.5, it may not be worth all the trouble. It will depend mostly on how much you want to grow them. One gardening friend showed me several beautiful giant-size plants one day, all of them heavy with ripening fruit. "Do you like them?" she asked. "I'm sure each one of those berries has cost me at least a dollar." But she was enjoying them very much —both the fruit and the acclaim.

VARIETIES

Would-be blueberry growers should seek the advice of their gardening neighbors and the extension service in choosing the varieties best suited to their region. Recommendations from nursery salesmen and catalogs are not always the most reliable choices for home gardeners. Jersey is probably the most widely grown variety in the U.S. Others that are grown in various sections include:

UPPER NEW ENGLAND, UPPER MICHIGAN, MINNESOTA. *Early:* Earliblue. *Midseason:* Berkeley, Bluecrop, Blueray, Rancocas. *Late:* Coville, Darrow, Herbert, Jersey.

SOUTHERN NEW ENGLAND, NEW JERSEY, NEW YORK, PENNSYLVANIA. *Early:* Blueray, Earliblue, Ivanhoe. *Midseason:* Berkeley, Bluecrop, Collins. *Late:* Darrow, Herbert, Jersey.

NORTH CAROLINA, MARYLAND, VIRGINIA, AND SIMILAR. *Early:* Angola, Morrow. *Midseason:* Croatan, Scammell, Wolcott. *Late:* Jersey, Murphy.

FLORIDA AND OTHER SEMITROPICAL AREAS. Bluebelle, Briteblue, Florablue, Sharpblue, Tifblue.

PACIFIC NORTHWEST. Dixi and Stanley are widely planted. Those recommended for the East are worth a trial, too, in most of this area.

Varieties no longer recommended are the Cabot, Concord, Pioneer, and Weymouth. They've fallen from favor in recent years because of their susceptibility to disease, low quality, or small berry size. Although they were once old-time favorites, they've now been replaced by better varieties.

Currants and Gooseberries (*Ribes*)

One time when I was in New York City some of us were discussing our favorite pies. I voted for gooseberry and a hush fell over the group. The city folk had finally met an honest-to-goodness country hick. Poor souls! Even though acid fruits have gained favor as health foods in recent years, lots of Americans still regard rhubarb and gooseberries as hayseed foods, suitable only for low country humor rather than the healthful delicacies they really are. In fact, in Europe gooseberries are a most respectable food and emigrants from there are responsible for most of the fruit's successful development in this country.

In addition to their poor public image, the gooseberry and its cousin, the currant, have another major obstacle to being more widely grown. Just as blueberry growing is restricted by its fussiness about soils, and peach growing by its insistence on a mild climate and light soil, the *Ribes* group are denied admittance in some areas because they can't always get along with their neighbors. This has long given them a black eye. The plants carry a disease that may infect and kill the native white pine (*Pinus strobus*). They are, in fact, one of the Typhoid Marys of the plant world.

The disease they host, blister rust, does no harm whatsoever to the *Ribes* plants. But spores carried to the white pines will infect them; first a few limbs will die and finally the whole tree. Curiously, the disease does not spread from one pine tree to another, but must always come from one of the host plants. While blister rust is inherent in most of the currant-gooseberry clan, the most danger comes from the black currant and the native wild gooseberry. Laws in most states require that all *Ribes* be planted at least 900 feet from any of the white pine family, and even farther from a nursery where white pine seedlings are grown. No restrictions or danger is involved with planting them near mugho (dwarf) pine, Austrian pine, jack pine, Japanese pine, or Norway (red) pine. You can identify the white pine easily—it is light green and has five needles in each clump.

Be sure to inspect your area well before ordering plants. In some states you may have to sign a witnessed document swearing you're going to obey the rules before you can buy them, so do a bit of measuring and looking around before you write out your check. Otherwise you may find yourself at odds with the local constabulary and an unhappy group of neighbors who have carved their deceased white pines into war clubs.

Gooseberries can be a bit tricky to pick if the bushes are very thorny. I like to wear a leather glove on the left hand to hold up the limbs while I pick the fruit with the right. Currants bruise less if they are picked by the bunch like grapes, but this is not necessary. Both fruits get sweeter as they stay on the bush, so don't pick either one too early. Both are wonderful eating right off the plant or made into delicious desserts, jams, or drinks.

Gooseberries are a dependable fruit, ripen early, and are an excellent source of juice. Unfortunately they are a "forbidden fruit" in many areas (USDA).

VARIETIES

Both currants and gooseberries are cold-weather plants and aren't likely to grow well in the warmer parts of the country. The kinds listed are suitable for most of Zones 3 through 5, but one variety of gooseberry, Glenndale, is widely planted in Virginia and Arkansas. Our favorites are the Welcome, a beautiful, sweet, good-tasting, large red gooseberry with a nearly thorn-free bush, and the Red Lake Currant, an old-timer that is still hard to beat.

CURRANTS

RED CURRANTS. Cherry, Perfection, Red Cross, Red Lake, Stephens No. 9.

WHITE CURRANTS. White Grape and White Imperial are two good ones.

BLACK CURRANTS. I'd avoid these, even if you can smuggle them in. Besides being disease carriers, their musky flavor and taste are not universally loved. In Canada the variety Consort is grown outside the white pine areas.

GOOSEBERRIES

RED OR PINK. Pixwell, Poorman and Welcome are three good ones. We feel Welcome is the best flavored and easiest to pick.

GREEN OR YELLOW. Downing and Green Mountain are two other favorites. The latter is one of the largest-fruiting kinds, but few nurseries carry them.

EUROPEAN. The delicious flavor and plum-size fruits of these plants make lots of gardeners want to try them. They are so susceptible to mildew and other troubles that they are seldom found in catalogs. Chautauqua and Fredonia are two that are grown in a limited way.

Elderberries (*Sambucus*)

The elderberry is extremely hardy, gets on well with pine trees, grows in almost any soil, and is easy to grow. So what's wrong with it? It is perhaps a bit too easy to grow and can spread rapidly, both by seed and root suckers. Nevertheless, we like elderberries very much. Fortunately we have lots of room, and by keeping the grass mowed all around the elderberries we keep them well under control. Furthermore, we like them because they grow well in a place which, although not swampy, is much too wet for most other fruits. The elderberries really thrive in it. Our row of 6- or 7-foot-high bushes is about 20 feet long and 2 feet wide, and it produces gallons of highly flavored fruit each year.

The flavor is something like blackberries but richer. The bushes have no thorns, and there's no bending over to pick them. The hybrids are especially a joy to pick because they're so much larger than the wild ones. We simply scoop the berries off the plant when they're dead ripe.

I'm not including any cultural directions because I don't know any. They take the least work of any of the fruits and seem to make it on their own with very little attention, although we do cut out the dead branches as they appear. Bugs and disease apparently never bother them.

As with most of the berries, our biggest problem with the elderberry plantings is that birds love them so much. Every year they try to grab all the fruit, usually by picking it a day or two before I think it is ready. We put strips of recycled aluminum foil all over the branches just before they're ripe, which helps somewhat. Birds were an even worse problem when we were growing early-ripening varieties. It was nice to find that many of the new hybrids ripen so late that many berry-eating birds have already gone South before the fruit turns color.

Since elderberries are ready when we're up to our necks in apples, cider, plums, and vegetables, we've found it works well to pick them and freeze them immediately without processing. Later in the season or in the winter, when time isn't quite so precious, we make them into jellies, wine, or pies, or cook them into syrups that are bottled for delicious drinks and toppings, all rich in Vitamin C.

The tiny white elderberry blossoms can also be eaten in many ways and made into wine, vinegar, or flavorings. Some people fry them in batter. We make them into a delightful soft drink called elderberry blow by putting a few bunches of the freshly picked flowers into a gallon jar containing a little sugar, lemon juice, and enough water to fill the jar. The mixture, tightly

Elderberry blooms have nearly as many tasty uses as the fruit.

capped, is allowed to stand in the sun for a day and is then strained, bottled, and chilled for use right away.

Although the flowers and fruit are delicious, the woody part of the elderberry plant is not. Don't let anyone use the hollow stemmed branches for blowguns. There are numerous stories of children being poisoned in this fashion and, while probably some are exaggerated, it's best to be on the careful side and forbid it.

Elderberry leaves have a distinctive shape. One night while we were transporting some husky potted elderberry plants in our car, we were stopped by a county sheriff who took an unusual interest in our load. It took nearly half an hour before he was completely convinced that the plants were not marijuana and he finally let us on our way. Naturally we got lots of kidding later about our potted "pot." While the leaves could only be confused in a dim light, it is possible that, if you grow elderberries, sometime you may get some undeserved attention for your horticultural abilities.

VARIETIES

Some of the recently developed hybrids include:

ADAMS. Early ripening, best for areas that have early fall frost. Large, very productive plant.

JOHNS. Large berries. Later and not as productive as Adams.

NEW YORK 21. Considered one of the best of the new hybrids. Large berries, medium-size bush. Ripens midseason, productive.

NOVA. Large bush, probably the heaviest bearer of all. Fairly early.

YORK. Large productive bushes, good-size fruit. Ripens late.

26 / THE GRAPE *(Vitis)*

According to an ancient fable, a fox once found a beautiful bunch of grapes growing on a vine just out of his reach. He leaped at it a couple of times and then backed up and took several running jumps, all to no avail. He just couldn't reach the grapes. Finally he gave up and trotted off muttering, "They're probably too sour to eat anyway." Aesop not only gave us the worthwhile and oft-used expression "sour grapes," but he probably helped name the wild North American Fox grape as well. This is only one of thousands of stories about the grape, one of the most romantic fruits. Almost everyone wants to grow them. Maybe they are moved by the old legends, or they dream of the day when each man will sit under his own fig tree and vine as the Bible promises. But more likely, they just love grapes.

Grapes are one of the world's oldest cultivated fruits. When civilization started in the Fertile Crescent of the Mediterranean, the grape was there. Tables were piled high with the fresh fruit, and wine making and selling were important industries. Ruins of ancient cities and ships sunk ages ago always contain wine jars in vast numbers.

Much of later European history is also involved with the grape. The wine-producing areas of Italy, France, Spain, and Germany became world famous, and naturally when the early settlers came to America they brought the European vines with them. Most of their plantings were doomed to failure, however, because the highly developed Old World grapes could not adapt to the cool climate, diseases, and insects of eastern North America.

America did have two native grapes, though: the Fox, or wild grape, of the Northeast—which the Vikings found when they named the country Vinland—and the Muscadine grape of the southern United States. Some persistent horticulturists kept a few of the imported Old World grapes alive long enough to make some crosses with the native Fox and Muscadine.

The Concord, developed at Concord, Massachusetts, in the mid-1800s, was the most famous of the new varieties. Ephraim Bull, a gold beater by trade, became interested in grapes and abandoned his trade to devote full time to experimental grape growing. His discovery of the Concord was not an accident or a simple stroke of luck. It's said that he planted and grew over 22,000 seedlings before he developed the vine that ushered in the exciting future of the American grape industry.

A mature grape vine can produce 15 or more pounds of fruit annually, and in a small space (USDA).

Today the Concord is still the leading grape in most of the northern and eastern United States, not only for commercial production but also for home gardeners. It adapts easily to many different soils and produces an abundance of quality fruit for eating, juice, and wine. Furthermore, it is vigorous, quite hardy, and propagates easily from cuttings.

The European grapes, on the other hand, found a home to their liking in California where, thanks to a good climate, irrigation, and careful culture, nearly every year is a "vintage" year.

Other crosses of the Fox, Muscadine, and European varieties and their hybrids have provided a host of new red, white, and blue grapes, some of them seedless. Where growing conditions are right, many of these new kinds are well suited for home culture, too, but climate is sometimes a limiting factor in growing them. Commercial growers would never plant grapes in regions where there are fewer than 150 continuous frost-free days during the growing season, and they would rather have more. This rules out Zones 3, 4, and part of Zone 5 as true grape country.

Luckily for the home gardener in the cooler zones, horticulturists have developed a good number of grape varieties that require far fewer hot days to grow and to ripen. These are rarely grown commercially but are ideal for the small home orchard. The Beta, for instance, can be grown successfully even in the short seasons of the Dakotas, Minnesota, and Upper New England.

Grapes are one of the easiest fruits to start. Hardwood cuttings taken in early spring (see Chapter 13) will root easily and make a husky, well-developed plant by fall. The following spring the cuttings should be carefully transplanted to their permanent home. Grapes can also be started by layering and by softwood cuttings.

When you buy them, select the heaviest grade one-year-old vines. In most of the country, spring planting is best.

Culture

Grapes need an abundance of heat and sun to grow and to produce well. Because of this they are one of the last fruit plants to start growth in the spring, and they bloom much later than any of the tree fruits. If you live in one of the cool northern states, you will want to plant them in heat pockets whenever possible. Places where buildings, walls, or hills form corners that face and trap the southern and eastern sun are best, especially when they are protected from the cooling north and westerly winds. Grapes prefer light, sandy soils that warm up fast, too.

In the cold regions of northern Vermont where the climate is often compared with the Arctic, we know of a steep southerly slope dropping sharply to a small lake. It is protected by woods and hills and gets all the morning and midafternoon sun. Here, year after year, the late-ripening Concord produces beautifully. The summer sun, protection from the cold winds, and the gentle warming currents from the lake at night all combine to give the grape just what it needs.

In some areas you may have to create your own heat trap. Fiberglass fences, plastic tents, and other artificial structures have all been used to increase and hold the heat for the sun-worshipping grape. It can also be beneficial to mulch with black plastic or crushed rock, which attract and hold heat better than organic mulches.

If you are a gardener in a warm area, you'll probably have little trouble growing grapes, and most certainly you will want to take advantage of this healthful and delicious fruit. If grape culture sounds a bit involved, don't worry. It actually is little more complicated than staking peas.

Pruning is probably the most important part of grape culture. Because of the grape's tendency to grow so vigorously, a lot of wood must be cut away each year. Grape vines that are overgrown become so dense that the sun cannot reach into the areas where fruit should form (see page 217). Those grown on latticework and trellises are particularly hard to prune, but it can be done. Usually grapes grown in this way are more ornamental than productive.

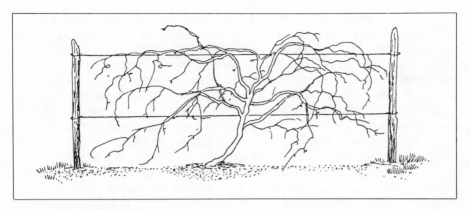

Grape vine in need of pruning

The best and easiest way to grow grapes for fruit is on a two-wire fence in a method called the Kniffin System.

FIRST YEAR

Vines should be planted about 8 feet apart, with a post midway between each plant and one on each end. String two strands of smooth 10-gauge wire on the posts, the first 2 feet above the ground and the second about 3 feet higher.

After planting, cut back the new vine so it is only 5 or 6 inches long and contains two or three fat buds. This encourages additional root growth. Allow the vines to grow freely the first year.

SECOND YEAR

Very early in the spring, before the buds swell, cut them back to a single stem with no branches. This will encourage more vigor.

During the year allow four side branches to grow (two in each direction) and train them along the wires. Pinch off all other buds that are inclined to grow in other directions.

By the end of the second year if growth has been good, the space along both wires should be filled. These vines should then bloom and produce a few grapes the third year.

THIRD YEAR

During the year four more canes (only) should be allowed to grow from buds along the main stem. These should parallel and eventually replace the first four.

In late winter following the third year, cut out the old canes that produced and tie the new ones to the wires to replace them. Trim off all excess growth except the four new canes (see below).

Treated in this way, each mature vine should produce from 12 to 15 pounds of grapes or 30 to 60 bunches per year. If more bunches than that are produced, remove them before the grapes develop, to avoid overbearing and thus weakening the plant. With this renewing process, your vines should go on producing for fifty years, and often they last even longer.

Vines can be either cultivated or mulched, but whatever you do, don't allow weeds and grass to choke them.

Like peaches, even the hardy varieties sometimes have trouble terminating their rapid growth in time to harden up before the first frost. Because of this, all fertilizing should be done early in the season. And be careful never to overfeed the vines, especially with nitrogen fertilizers.

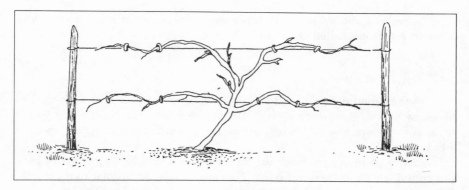

A well-pruned grape vine trained to the Kniffin System

Pollination

Almost all kinds of grapes are self-fruitful, so pollination is seldom a problem. If there is any question about pollination, check your nursery catalogs. Brighton is one of the few varieties that is not self-pollinating, so it will need another grape for a partner in order to bear well.

Harvesting

It is a mistake to pick grapes too early because, unlike most other fruits, grapes don't continue to ripen after they are picked. Ripe grapes separate easily and the seeds are brown. If they are to be used for jelly they can be picked before they are completely ripe, but if you want them for eating or for juice, they should be left until fully ripe. Don't let them freeze, though.

Like berries, you will want to pick them on a dry day, because wet grapes don't keep well. It's a good idea to clip the bunches from the vine rather than break them, so there will be less chance of damage.

Grapes must be refrigerated to keep for any length of time. A temperature of just above freezing is best. They're a treat eaten fresh or preserved in jelly, juice, or wine. Of course, grapes can be dried, too. Raisins are usually made from certain sweet seedless varieties of grapes but, as with making prunes out of plums, it is an exacting process and a bit difficult for most home growers.

Diseases

When you are growing grapes in an isolated home garden you usually don't have many problems with either insects or disease. Life is never simple, though, and sooner or later one of the following diseases is likely to show up:

ANTHRACNOSE

Anthracnose, or bird's eye rot, will appear as spots on the fruit. It also affects leaves and the new sprouts. Captan is a good form of control.

BLACK ROT

This disease affects the fruit and turns it black, rotten, and shriveled. Leaves are covered with brown spots and black pimples. Spraying with Captan gives good control.

DEAD ARM

A fungus is the cause of this disease; it gradually kills the plant. Cutting and burning the infected parts is about the only cure, although Captan and Ferbam applied early in the season may help control it.

DOWNY MILDEW

Another serious disease, especially in the East. Leaves and new shoots as well as the fruit become covered with a gray down. Bordeaux mix or powdered sulfur were often used to control mildew in times past. Benomyl (see page 85), Karathane, or Ferbam are now being used.

Insects

Hundreds of insects attack grapes in different parts of the world, and even isolated vines may be visited by some of them. Many, such as the

Japanese beetle, are familiar names to growers of other fruits. Others bother only the grape.

Curculio attacks the grapes the way its relatives attack other fruits.

Cutworms feed on opening buds at night.

Flea beetles are similar to other flea beetles. Attack the vine and leaves.

Grape berry moths are the main source of wormy grapes. Their larvae eat the pulp of the grape.

Phylloxera are small sucking insects, similar to aphids, that attack European grapes mostly.

Rootworms are small, grayish-brown beetles that attack leaves. Their larvae eat the grape vine roots.

Rose chafers eat blossoms, buds, newly formed fruit, and leaves. Usually they are most troublesome to vines grown on sandy soil.

Thrips are sucking insects that also attack other small fruits.

All grape insects can be controlled by good sanitation and, when necessary, careful spraying. Sevin, Rotenone, Imidan, and Methoxychlor are all chemicals that give good control and are safe for the beginning orchardist if directions are carefully followed. If chemical means seem the best solution, follow the grape spraying schedule in Chapter 9. Isolation, sanitation, and encouraging birds are better than spraying, however, and should be used whenever possible for insect control.

Varieties

Every nursery wants to introduce a few new varieties of fruit every year so they won't be branded old-fashioned, but newer doesn't always mean better—at least for the home gardener. Why not start out with the old reliable Concord if your season is long enough, and Beta if you live where it's cold. Then add others one by one. Later on, if your skill and climate are right, who knows? You may one day become the Bacchus on your block.

Probably even the apple has fewer named varieties than the grape. In millenniums of culture, thousands of kinds have appeared and disappeared. Varieties that are usually easily available and suitable for home gardeners are the only ones mentioned in this list:

DESSERT AND WHITE TABLE GRAPES. Golden Muscat, Himrod, Interlaken, Niagara, Seedless.

BLUE GRAPES. Beta, Buffalo, Concord, Fredonia, Moore's Early, Schuyler, Stark Blue Boy, Steuben, Van Buren, Worden.

RED GRAPES. Brighton, Catawba, Delaware.

WINE GRAPES. Aurora, Baco-Noir, Cascade, Catawba, De Chaunac, Delaware, Dunkirk, Foch, Moore's Diamond, Seyval Blanc, Siebel (No. 1000, No. 5279, No. 5898, No. 9549), Steuben.

EARLIEST. Alpha, Beta, Moore's Early, Ontario, Seneca, Van Buren.

NEXT EARLIEST. Brighton, Buffalo, Fredonia, Schuyler, Worden.

HARDIEST. Alpha and Beta, two of the hardiest early grapes, are both more suitable for processing than eating fresh. Concord is a high-quality, easy-to-grow, very hardy grape, but it ripens too late for most northern areas. Others are Delaware, Hungarian, Jonesville, Moore's Early, Van Buren, Worden.

SEEDLESS. Concord Seedless (blue), Himrod (yellow), Interlaken (pink-yellow).

FOR THE WARMEST CLIMATES. Black Spanish, Blue Lake, Chapanell, and the Muscadine grapes—Cowart, Magoon, Roanoke, and Sugargate.

27 / NUTS FOR THE HOME GARDEN

Nearly every region in America once had an abundance of wild nut trees. You could easily locate a winter's supply of the tasty treats by taking a trip into nearly any forest or along back roads in early fall. It used to be an annual event for country folks to take empty burlap bags into the woods on a crisp fall day and race the squirrels to the crop hidden among the newly fallen leaves. They'd bring home whole bags full, then dump out the sticky treasure on the attic floor to dry for winter cracking. But heavy cutting, blights, and weather have all taken their toll, and nutting, as it was called, is almost a thing of the past. But not quite.

With the renewed interest in do-it-yourself growing, nut trees are coming back, and more and more of them are being planted in home gardens. Varieties are now being developed that are hardier, bear younger, and best of all, produce nuts that are larger, tastier, and crack more easily. If you have the right climate and enough room, you may want to plant a tree or perhaps even an acre of them.

Nuts are logical companions to fruits. Like fruits, they offered early man a welcome change in his monotonous meat diet, but unlike fruits and most other foods, many nuts could be stored for months or even years with no special care. Today we realize that they are an excellent source of protein and other nutrients and value them for that as well as for their fine flavor.

While eating nuts is one of the most enjoyable ways to use them, they also have other uses. The shells are sometimes made into ornaments and jewelry, burned to make a fragrant smoke used for smoking meat and to make activated charcoal, the main ingredient in many filters and gas masks.

Lumber from nut trees is among the most prized in the world. Windmill propellers used to be made from butternut, which is one of the strongest lightweight woods. Gun stocks, fine furniture, and many other wood products are made from black walnut. Even before the blight struck, most of the great chestnut forests of the East had already been cut for their fine lumber.

Improved Varieties

Nut breeding has progressed less rapidly than fruit and berry development because there has been little interest in improving them and because they take such a long time to bear. The most progress has been made with almonds, filberts, pecans, and Persian walnuts, which have been grown commercially in large numbers for many years. Only recently has there also been interest and activity in improved strains of butternuts, black walnuts, chestnuts, and hickories. Some excellent new varieties of these nuts are now being offered by a limited number of nurseries.

Most nut trees being sold by nurseries are actually seedlings from ordinary wild trees. However, a few offer improved grafted varieties that are usually from specially selected superior wild trees.

Your Tree in a Nutshell

Since most of the nut trees being sold are seedlings, if you're not in a great hurry you might as well grow your own. It's easy. Just imitate Mother Nature. Practically all the great nut forests of this country were planted by squirrels, who always stashed away more food than they could possibly use and then forgot where they hid it. Like them, all you need do is dig a small hole and bury your nut an inch or so deep. You can plant it where you want the tree to grow permanently, or you can plant a lot of them together in a bed for transplanting later, after they have become well started.

Fall is when the squirrels do their planting and it's the best time for us too. Most nuts sprout better if they freeze a few times, so if you forget to plant them in the fall you can freeze each nut for a few days inside a teacup of water in your freezer and plant them anytime.

Whenever you plant, it's a good idea to protect the nuts with a wire screen or in some other way if you have squirrels or chipmunks around. They may forget where they've hid their own, but they are likely to delight in digging up yours and hauling them away.

Don't worry if your new little tree doesn't appear at the same time as the dandelions or even with the first sprouts of corn. It may be midsummer before it finally bursts through. As soon as it does pop up, it will grow rapidly and sometimes become 2 or 3 feet tall within six or eight weeks. The nut itself carries nutrients enough to get the tree off to a good start, so you don't need to feed fledgling trees. In fact, you shouldn't feed them because you won't want them to grow too late in the season.

A word of warning: If you grow nuts in a seedbed don't wait too long before transplanting them. Most nuts, except for the filberts, grow tremendous taproots that head speedily toward the center of the earth. So transplant them within a year or two or before they get 3 or 4 feet tall. This taproot shouldn't be broken or bent when transplanting. Transplanting is best done in early spring.

Planting

Planting nut trees is very much the same as planting fruit trees, but when choosing their location you must be sure to keep in mind their eventual size. While the filbert may remain within fruit tree dimensions, all the others are likely to get very large—50 feet high or more—and nearly as wide, so be careful to give them plenty of room, and don't plant beneath overhead wires. It is also a good idea not to put them where the falling nuts will create a nuisance. Better keep them away from streets and house roofs, and any part of the lawn that has to be mowed late in the fall. Nuts are hard on lawn mowers.

Culture

Because they are still wild, most nut trees need little care. You will get a much stronger tree, however, if you prune them to have one central trunk rather than a lot of tops in their early years.

Diseases and insects are not usually great problems to the home nut grower, luckily, because nut trees can grow as large as many shade trees, and spraying trees that size is not easy.

Most nut trees like well-drained, deep soil. After the first year they will benefit from yearly applications of fertilizer. Mulches help them along, especially when the trees are still young, probably making them think they're living back in the forest floor. As with fruit trees, the nut seedlings usually take much longer to produce their first crop than grafted trees. Plan on eight years or more for most nut seedlings to bear.

Pollination

Although some nut trees seem to produce nuts if they live alone—the black walnut and butternut, for example—many growers think that even they benefit from having a companion. Most nut trees definitely do need a partner, which must be of the same species and be fairly close by for good pollination, because most are pollinated by wind instead of bees.

If you're planting grafted trees, it is a good idea to plant two different hybrids or a few seedling trees of the same family to pollinate them. In other words, if you plant a Royal Filbert, another filbert hybrid such as Graham or Skinner could pollinate it; or some wild filberts could do the same thing. Two Royal Filberts would not pollinate each other.

Each seedling tree is different, of course, so they will pollinate any other seedling or hybrid as long as they are in the same species.

Harvesting

When the nuts begin to fall off the tree they are mature and ready to pick. Squirrels don't always wait for them to fall, and it's usually safe for you to begin picking as soon as the squirrels begin harvesting. If you're careful not to damage the limbs, you can shake some kinds of nuts from the trees. In fact, walnuts are often harvested commercially in this fashion by mechanical shakers. The whole crop of most nuts can usually be gathered at one time, although some kinds, like walnuts, may need several pickings. As soon as the nuts fall from the trees they should be gathered, not only to get them away from the squirrels but because they deteriorate if they stay on the wet ground for long.

Most nuts aren't good to eat until they have been thoroughly dried and the meats have ripened. They may be spread out on raised screens—never more than one layer deep—so air can circulate all around them, or on greenhouse or garage benches or attic floors. If you dry them on the floor or bench rather than on screens, they should be turned occasionally. In our attic the playful kittens used to do that.

After several weeks of drying, the nuts can then be stored in bags, boxes, or barrels in a cool place. Of course, both the drying room and storage should be squirrel-proof. We use an old washing machine for storage.

If you can locate improved nut varieties that are hardy in your area, they'll be much more satisfying than the native ones. Some of the new developments are as superior to wild nuts as named varieties of apples are to the sour green wild ones.

It would be unfair not to mention some of the bad habits of nut trees after I have praised them so loftily. Some kinds are not the best trees to plant as close neighbors for other plantings. Both black walnut and butternut roots give off a mysterious toxic substance that kills many other plants growing in their root area. It's wise not to have either of these trees growing where the roots could touch those of fruit trees, vegetable gardens, flower beds, hedges, ornamentals, or berry plants. They don't seem to have this toxic effect on grass, however, or on many other plants.

Only the nut trees that are most often grown by home gardeners are discussed here in more detail. The zones listed indicate areas where the trees seem to do best and are most widely grown, although it is possible for them to succeed in other zones if given the right growing conditions.

The Chestnut Family (*Castanea*)

Zones 5–9

The American chestnut (*Castanea dentata*) was an important part of North America during its developing days. Not only was the lumber valued for home use and for trade abroad, but all winter the nuts popped in many a Colonial fireplace, and holidays were never complete without chestnut dressing for the turkey or goose. In New England there's still a rumored tradition that blacksmith shops must stand "under a spreading chestnut tree."

When the tragic blight of the early 1900s wiped out nearly every chestnut tree, the search for resistant varieties began. Trees were introduced from Spain, Japan, and China, and crossed with the few remaining American trees. Many of the resulting new hybrids are now producing quality nuts in American back yards.

One of the imports, the Chinese chestnut (*Castanea mollissima*), is offered by many nurseries. Unfortunately they are somewhat difficult to grow in many areas because they're less hardy than most peaches. Like the peach, too, fertilizing has to be done very carefully when the trees are young because they shouldn't grow too rapidly.

Southern nurseries offer several named varieties including Abundance, Crane, Kuling, and Meiling. The grafted Chinese chestnuts haven't done well in the North, and in Zones 5 and 6 the seedling varieties usually do better.

American chestnuts and their hybrids are slowly coming back. New varieties now being offered for sale are Central Square, Eaton, Sodus Point, Sweet Home, and Watertown I, II, and III. Central Square is probably one of the hardiest.

Very few nurseries carry chestnut trees. Two sources are the St. Lawrence Nurseries, Route 2, Heuvelton, New York 13654, and Lundy's Nursery, Route 3, Box 35, Live Oak, Florida 32060.

The Filbert and Hazelnut (*Corylus*)

Zones 5–9

The round filbert (*Corylus avellana*) is familiar to everyone because it is usually part of the holiday nut mixtures, although it isn't often found grow-

Nearly wiped out by the blight, chestnuts have made a big comeback (USDA).

ing in home gardens. Most of the commercial production is in the Pacific Northwest, and the varieties grown there seldom do well in the rest of the country. Barcelona, Daviana, and Du Chilly are three of the leading filberts for that area.

The filbert is a native of southern Europe, probably originating in Italy, but its American cousin, the hazelnut (*Corylus americana*), grows wild in hedgerows all over the northern U. S. and southern Canada. The small nuts are a favorite collector's item of the chipmunks and squirrels, and we used to gather them too, but it always seemed to me that taking off the prickly burrs, and drying and cracking the nuts to get the tiny sweet meat, was hardly worth the effort.

Filberts grow to a size that is ideal for the home garden. The tree is about the size of a semi-dwarf apple tree, and they should be planted about 20 feet apart. The fact that they don't have a taproot like the other nut trees makes them easy to transplant. The filbert should be fertilized carefully, if at all. Soils suitable for fruit trees usually suit the filbert too.

Even the named hybrids are seldom grafted because they root easily from layers and are often started from suckers that come from the roots. You may want to start one of your own trees in this way.

Zones 6–8

Besides Barcelona and Daviana, which are best suited for the Northwest, the following European filberts are worth a trial in these zones: Bixby, Buchanan, Cosford, Graham, Italian Red, Purple Aveline, Reed, Royal, and Skinner.

Zones 4–8

Many catalogs also list the American hazelnut which, although it does have much smaller nuts, is hardy in Zones 4–8. Rush and Winkler are two improved selections of this strain that some nurseries offer for sale.

Some crosses have been made between the European filbert and the hardy wild American hazelnut. One of the hybrids produced from these crosses is Potomac, which is reputed to have catkins (buds) that are hardy to −15 degrees F.

The Hickory and Pecan (*Carya*)

Zones 5–8

Hickory nuts will grow over a wide area. Although they are seldom offered commercially, they are enjoyed mightily by those lucky enough to live near their habitat. Few hybrids have been made of the wild hickories. The shagbark hickory, best of dozens of native hickories, has the disadvantage of a very tough shell and a small meat that usually breaks in cracking. The hardiness of the new kinds isn't always known and few are offered by nurseries; however, seeking out outstanding wild trees and grafting them is showing some promise. Named varieties include Davis, Glover, Mann, Nielson, Porter, and Wilcox.

Zones 7–9

If you don't live in these zones, talk it over with your extension office before deciding if there should be a pecan in your plans. Pecans need such a long season to develop their nuts that the trees do well only in certain areas. They belong to the same family as hickories and grow natively in southeastern United States as far south as Mexico. Unlike most North American nuts, the pecan has been cultivated commercially for some time, and many improved varieties are now in production. Most of the pecan groves are south of the Mason-Dixon line, although the trees are sometimes grown in home gardens farther north.

Pecans are a little harder to store than most nuts but can be kept for a year or more after picking if stored at a temperature of 32 degrees F. or less. In ordinary storage they will keep only a few months.

Some of the named varieties being grown are Apache, Barto, Cherokee, Comanche, Major, Mohawk, Schley, Sioux, and Stuart.

Hybrids have been made of the pecan and the shagbark hickory. Burton and Gerardi are two of these hybrids.

The Walnut and Butternut (*Juglans*)

Zones 5–8

The black walnut (*Juglans nigra*) can be grown over most parts of Zones 5 through 8, and new hybrids are being developed that are extending the growing area into Zones 3 and 4. The grafted nuts are larger and better flavored than the wild kinds. Not everyone cares for the black walnut's unusual flavor, but they do have their champions. They may be eaten raw, and are also used for flavoring cakes, ice cream, and other desserts.

In addition to the many different strains of seedlings that vary widely across the country, the following are some of the improved varieties that have been recently introduced and are now being sold by some nurseries: Burns, Cochrane, Elmer Meyers, Huber, Michigan, Ohio, Patten, Patterson, Rohiver, Snyder, Sparrow, Stabler, Stambaugh, Thomas, and Weschcke. Weschcke and Patterson are among the most hardy.

Zones 3–7

The butternut (*Juglans cinerea*), like dried corn, beans, and smoked meat, was one of the foods that helped the Iroquois Indians live well through the hard northern winters. The early settlers liked them too, and they have been a favorite ever since. There's no evidence that the Indians ever mixed butternuts with maple sugar to make what I consider one of the most delicious confections in the world—maple butternut fudge. But since they used both products and were very smart, they probably made and enjoyed it. (See Treats from Nancy's Winter Kitchen, page 250.)

Butternuts are one of the hardiest nut trees and certainly one of the most flavorful. New hybrids and selections are larger and easier to crack, but even the wild ones crack easily if you pour boiling water over them, let them stand for fifteen minutes, and then drain. With one easy hammer blow the halves pop apart easily and intact.

Butternut blooms are often damaged in late spring frosts in the North, and even if they are not the trees can seldom be counted on to produce a crop every year. They seem content to bear abundantly once in a while, then often take a few years off. It's lucky for us butternut lovers that the nuts store so well that we can save our surplus for the off years.

Some of the improved varieties now being sold are Ayres, Beckwith, Chamberlin, Craxeasy, George Elmer, Johnson, Thill, Van Syckle, and Weschcke. Ayres has very large nuts; Chamberlin and George Elmer may be the most hardy of the list.

Zones 5–9

Persian walnuts (*Juglans regia*) are the so-called English walnuts, which were grown mostly in the warm regions of the West Coast until a missionary, Reverend Paul Crath, discovered a hardy strain growing wild in Poland. Bringing in several thousand seeds in the 1930s and growing them in Ontario, he found they succeeded so well that in only a few years the walnut-growing area was completely changed. The Carpathian strain he introduced has been dispersed so widely that now walnuts can be grown throughout Zones 5 through 9. Experimenters are now at work developing strains that will probably be hardy in Zones 3 and 4 too.

Walnuts are without doubt the most popular of all the tree nuts and are a favorite to eat out of the shell or enjoy in a countless number of appetizing desserts. Unfortunately those few people who get canker sores in their mouths from eating walnuts have to sacrifice a real delicacy. Perhaps a variety without this unpleasant side effect will be developed, but until it is, we've found that eating raisins helps to counteract the walnuts' sore-producing effect.

The California walnut industry has spawned so many new kinds that most of the trees being grown there are named varieties. The Carpathian walnut is still so new that not many named kinds have been introduced as yet. Ashworth is one Carpathian variety, however, that appears to be fairly hardy. Colby, Deming, Hansen, Jacobs, Morris, and Shafer are others. Some of these trees are now for sale, but as yet most nursery catalogs offer only Carpathian seedling trees for sale.

Introduction to the Carpathian walnut has increased the walnut-growing area of the United States and Canada by many times (USDA).

In California, Hartley is one of the leading commercial varieties. Mayette and Franquette are two of the hardiest of the California strains, and they are even occasionally grown in the eastern United States.

If you want more information about nut growing, new varieties, sources, and so forth, investigate what the Northern Nut Growers organization has to offer, and perhaps try a trial membership. They began as a northern organization but have expanded to include the entire country. In addition to current information they also offer an excellent book: *Handbook of North American Nut Trees.* For prices and information, write Northern Nut Growers Association, 4518 Holston Hills Road, Knoxville, Tennessee 37914.

A list of extension services that can usually supply information on nut growing for your locality, and a list of nurseries supplying nut tree seedlings and hybrids, may be found in the Appendix.

28 / EXPERIMENTING WITH FRUITS

In addition to growing the best fruit in the world and saving money while doing it, home orchardists can have a lot of fun with their trees. If you like to experiment you will enjoy searching for a superior new fruit or dwarfing your own fruit trees. You may get a kick out of multiple grafting, too, or want to help your trees bear fruit at an earlier age. For some of us fruit addicts, fooling around with fruits is almost as much fun as eating them.

Searching for Superior Fruit

The perfect apple, peach, plum, pear, cherry, berry, grape, and nut has yet to be developed, so you still have a chance. Don't assume that you can't compete with the big experiment stations, because most of the best fruits have been accidentally discovered by small orchardists. In fact, of all the leading apple varieties being grown today, only one, the Cortland, was developed by scientific methods.

If you would like to be a local Luther Burbank, there are any number of improvements to be made on existing varieties of fruits. For instance, we could use a great many better flavored and better colored fruits that are suitable for home growing. We need ones that will keep longer in home storage, and are more disease-resistant. Wouldn't it be nice to have plums that need no cross-pollination; grapes, nectarines, peaches, and sweet cherries that are hardy and less fussy about soils; hardier walnuts, pecans, and chestnuts? How about some blueberries that don't need an acid soil, thornless gooseberries and bramble fruits, seedless raspberries for denture wearers, blackberries with smaller cores, and strawberries with frost-proof buds and blooms? And you can probably think of many more.

Among the many ways you can begin to search for unusual and superior fruit characteristics in your home orchard are by searching out accidental seedlings or sports and by hybridizing.

ACCIDENTAL SEEDLINGS

The search for superior seedlings can be a fascinating hobby like hunting for intact bottles in old dumps, or panning for gold in mountain streams. When fruit is ripening you search around old farms where seedlings are likely to be growing—in old orchards, back yards, and even farther out in the wilds where birds, picnickers, or hunters may have dropped seeds. Be on the lookout for fruit with especially fine appearance and taste, or any other superior characteristic. Finding a good fruit is not enough because there are already lots of good fruits.

If you are young enough and have the time you can plant your own seedlings and see what happens. Choosing seeds from good kinds should put the odds for finding a superior tree in your favor, but as Mendel's famous law of heredity proved, certain desirable characteristics may not show up until the second generation.

Although it takes time to grow seedlings, it always surprises me how fast a small seed can grow into a sizeable tree; but it can also be frustrating to see how long seedlings often take to bear fruit. Probably lots of good trees have been cut down because the experimenters thought there was no merit in a tree that took eight or nine years to produce its first crop. This is not unusual for seedlings and is called the youthful factor of the tree. After it does begin bearing, it can be propagated by grafting or other asexual means and the resulting new tree will bear in a normal length of time (two to four years for grafted trees).

Since seedling trees take so long to bear, any means that will speed up the process is useful. One method commonly used is to graft limbs from dozens of different seedlings onto a large tree. Bearing will often take place in two or three years, and the quality of the fruit can be easily compared by having so many kinds in a small area.

HYBRIDIZING

Hunting down superior kinds or planting seeds from good apples leaves a lot to chance. Hybridizers want to increase the odds and also want to develop certain characteristics more than others, so they bring about a cross between two fruits, each of which has some of the qualities they are seeking.

Rather than leaving pollination up to the bees who may bring in pollen they've collected at random from any old tree, you can do it yourself. Simply put a bag over a blossom bud cluster on each tree before the blooms open to keep out any ambitious bee that might beat you to the job. Then, after the blooms open, remove the bag and transfer the pollen from the blossom of another tree you wish to cross with this one, as described in Chapter 7. It is better to leave only one pollinated bloom in a cluster, so that the fruit will be large and stay on the tree until it is ripe. Pick off all blossoms except that one, and mark the limb spot carefully so that the fruit won't be lost.

When the fruit is ripe or slightly overripe, pick it and plant the seeds. Then await the results. Hopefully your selected seedling will be something special. Although it's like playing the Irish Sweepstakes, your chances of getting a choice seedling are better this way than if you plant a seed at random from just any fruit.

When you're hybridizing keep careful records of the parent trees because if an exciting worthy new variety is developed, the horticulturists will want to know all about its ancestors.

SPORTS

Another way to achieve fame and fortune in the fruit world is to find some superior sport or mutation growing on a fruit tree. When a limb suddenly begins bearing fruit noticeably different from the rest of the tree, you may have a sport on your hands. Naturally the fruit can be either better or worse, but you're keeping an eye out for the better ones, of course. The great sports of fruit history have usually been hailed as having superior color, size, better ripening habits, or a better shape. In your search for quality, look for good flavor too. Since most sports have been introduced for commercial purposes, flavor is seldom mentioned, and many fruit lovers maintain that the improved varieties are not always as tasty as the original. Sports are exciting to find, and can be very profitable to the finder.

In 1963 the famous Stark Brothers Nursery paid Elon Gilbert of Yakima, Washington, the sum of $51,000 for the rights to the Starkspur Golden Delicious apple, a sport that appeared in his orchard.

True sport hunters roam large and small orchards every harvest time looking for the magic limb that big nurseries will buy for thousands of dollars. Isn't it fun to know that there is always a chance it could sprout in yours or mine?

Berry Improvement

If fruit trees seem to take too long to bear and you want faster results, small fruits such as grapes and berries will often bear within two or three years from seed. Use the same careful hand-pollination procedure you would for fruit trees. Since there are so many wild berry plants around, the bees are likely to bring pollen from them if you don't keep your blooms covered until you pollinate them. Berry seeds should be planted quite shallow, mulched if possible, and kept moist. You may discover something of great local value, even if you don't make a big splash nationally. Horticulturist George Aiken, who later became a prominent Senator from Vermont, developed the Green Mountain strawberry, which was a popular variety for many years in the Northeast.

Nut Selection

There is a constant search for better varieties of nuts as well as tree fruits and berries. Not only would we enjoy nuts of larger size, better quality, and those that can be cracked easier, but also nut trees that bear heavier and more regularly and at a younger age. Professionals and hobbyists alike search the wilds for better nuts, and some hybridizing is being done both commercially and in back-yard nut orchards. The process is the same as it is for fruit trees.

Ordinary nuts aren't the only ones getting attention, either. Among the new discoveries listed by the St. Lawrence Nurseries in Heuvelton, New York, is a Jenner Beechnut with much larger nuts than the ordinary beechnut, and an Ashworth Burr Oak that produces acorns that are not bitter.

Your Own Multiple Grafts

Although I don't usually advise buying the 3-in-1 or 5-in-1 trees, you can have a lot of fun creating your own combinations by following the grafting instructions in Chapter 13. Not only can you graft different kinds of apples for a tasty mini-orchard on the same tree, but you can also try for attractive combinations. Imagine one limb of a beautiful red flowering crab amidst all the white blooms on one of your apple trees.

If stone fruits grow well in your region, you might try grafting plums, cherries, peaches, apricots, and nectarines all on the same tree. There may not be much reason for it, but it will certainly be a delicious curiosity.

Dwarfing Fruit Trees by Surgery

Fruit trees that have been grafted on ordinary standard-size seedlings can be dwarfed by surgery, which makes it possible for home fruit growers to have true dwarf trees even if they live where the usual Malling rootstocks are not hardy.

In early spring when the bark slips easily, completely remove a strip of bark about one inch wide from around the young tree. This is done by cutting two circles through the bark but not into the wood—about a foot from the ground. Make a vertical cut to separate the circle so it can be removed. Then turn the bark upside down and put it back on the tree, with the same side out, of course. Cover the whole thing with grafting wax, Tree Kote, or rubber electrical tape (not plastic). Since the bark should fit tight, you can see why it should be cut exactly the same width all the way around. You'll need a sharp knife for the operation, to make your cuts exact; be careful not to cut yourself with it.

The inverted bark will slow down the tree growth for many years. Not only does it keep the tree small, but it forces it to produce fruit at a much earlier age. Eventually all the cells will readjust and the tree will grow large, and if you sell your property in the meantime, this will puzzle the future owner no end.

Making Trees Bear

Sometimes fruit trees, even the grafted ones, go on year after year without blooming at all, to say nothing about producing. Sometimes this happens because the soil is too rich and the tree is growing too fast. It could be a slowpoke because it is missing a necessary nutrient, or possibly it's just that a fruit like the Baldwin apple takes a long time to bear.

Orchardists have long known that a tree can be made to bloom by slowing down activity in the sap movement. This is done in early summer by cutting a slit through the bark on two or three limbs where they come out of the trunk. The slit can go nearly all around the limb (but not totally around), and often forces fruit buds to set the same season. These buds should produce fruit the following years. Don't be too eager to try this out on all your trees, though. Ringing, as it is called, is rather hard on a tree and should be done only if necessary.

What's Ahead?

For the first time in half a century we home orchardists are so numerous that we are regarded as important persons in the fruit-growing world. We're already beginning to see more berries, fruit and nut trees, equipment, and supplies designed especially for us.

We can also expect to find more virus-free trees, more disease- and insect-resistant varieties, and more trees developed especially for small areas. Trees will be available that need less pruning and fruit that needs less thinning. The growing range of many fruits will be extended so that gardeners in the hot southern states and the cold northern regions can grow a larger variety of fruits and nuts, including the dwarf kinds. Spray materials will be on the market that are safer and easier to use. Nonorganic gardeners will find chemicals available that will thin the fruit, make it hang on the trees longer, help it color earlier, and even control the size of the tree.

While it is fun to imagine what's ahead for us home orchardists, there is no promise that fruit growing in the distant future will be any more enjoyable or the fruits more tasty then they are right now. So carpe diem!

APPENDIX

Botanical Names of Fruits and Nuts

This list may be useful for determining the different families of fruits for budding, grafting, plant breeding, and pollination.

		GENUS	SPECIES
TREE FRUITS	Apple	Malus	sylvestris
	Apricot	Prunus	armeniaca
	Cherry, Sour	Prunus	cerasus
	Cherry, Sweet	Prunus	avium
	Grape, American	Vitis	labrusca
	Grape, European	Vitis	vinifera
	Nectarine	Prunus	persica
	Peach	Prunus	persica
	Pear	Pyrus	communis
	Plum, American	Prunus	various
	Plum, Damson	Prunus	institia
	Plum, European	Prunus	domestica
	Plum, Japanese	Prunus	salicina
	Quince	Cydonia	oblonga
BERRIES	Blackberry	Rubus	various
	Blueberry	Vaccinium	various
	Elderberry	Sambucus	canadensis
	Raspberry	Rubus	various
	Strawberry	Fragaria	various
NUTS	Butternut	Juglans	cinerea
	Chestnut, Chinese	Castanea	mollissima
	Filbert	Corylus	avellana
	Hazelnut, American	Corylus	americana
	Hickory	Carya	ovata
	Pecan	Carya	pecan
	Walnut, Black	Juglans	nigra
	Walnut, English	Juglans	regia

Treats from Nancy's Winter Kitchen

Fruit tastes best, of course, plucked fresh from your own vine, tree, or berry patch. But since our love for fruits continues far beyond their prime season, each year we hoard any surplus. The following are some of the favorite recipes we use so that we can enjoy home-grown produce year-round.

Each fall, in addition to the large number of apples we store in the root cellar, we freeze an extra supply of raw cooking apples by peeling, slicing, and packing them tight in plastic bags. Whenever the recipe calls for "fresh apples" the frozen ones can be substituted. (We use a microwave oven to thaw all our frozen fruits just enough to break them apart.)

APPLE UPSIDE-DOWN CAKE

This is a long-time favorite of Vermonters.

2 cups sliced apples	Spread in bottom of buttered 8 × 8-inch pan.
3 Tbsp. shortening 1 Tbsp. butter or margarine	Melt together.
½ cup brown sugar firmly packed 2 Tbsp. milk	Add to shortening and spread over apples.
¼ cup shortening ¾ cup sugar	Cream thoroughly in bowl.
1 egg, beaten	Add to mixture in bowl.
1¼ cups flour 1½ tsp. baking powder ¼ tsp. cinnamon ¼ tsp. nutmeg ¼ tsp. allspice	Sift together.
½ cup milk	Add to mixture in bowl alternately with dry ingredients.

Spread batter over apple mixture and bake for approximately 1 hour in 350° oven. Serve warm with maple syrup and milk.

DUCHESS APPLE PUDDING

This recipe has also come down to us through several generations.

2 cups flour 4 tsp. baking powder 2 Tbsp. shortening	Sift together flour and baking powder, and cut shortening into mixture.
1 egg ¾ cup milk	Beat together and add to dry ingredients.
3 or 4 large apples	Slice as for pie.

Spread dough in greased 9-inch-square pan and cover with sliced apples. Cover apples with sugar and sprinkle lightly with nutmeg. Bake at 375° for 20–25 minutes. Serve warm, cut into squares, with sauce:

¾ cup sugar 1 tsp. butter ¼ tsp. salt ¾ cup boiling water	Mix in saucepan.
2 tsp. cornstarch 2 Tbsp. cold water	Dissolve cornstarch in water and add to saucepan, cooking until thick.
1 tsp. vanilla	Stir into mixture.

APPLE CROW'S NEST

Newcomers to Vermont are often surprised by the name of this dish, but everyone loves it. It's nothing but 5 or 6 large apples cut up into a 9-inch-square greased baking dish, topped with biscuit dough, and baked until the apples are soft. The crowning glory is a pitcher of rich milk with maple syrup and nutmeg added. The sweetened milk is poured over the "nest," and is it good!

FRESH APPLE CAKE

Our frequent contribution to local potluck suppers.

1¼ cups cooking oil 2 cups sugar 2 eggs 1 tsp. vanilla	Mix well.
1 cup raisins 3 cups chopped, peeled apples 1 cup chopped walnuts	Add to oil mixture.
3 cups flour 1 tsp. salt 1 tsp. soda 2 tsp. cinnamon	Combine and add to mixture.

Pack into 9 × 13-inch cake pan and bake at 350° for approximately 1 hour.

APPLE MACAROON

When time is too short to make a full-fledged apple pie, this is a superb substitute.

Approximately 4 large, tart apples	Slice in bottom of 9-inch pie plate.
½ cup sugar Cinnamon to taste	Sprinkle over apples.
1 egg ½ cup sugar ½ cup flour ½ tsp. baking powder 1 Tbsp. melted butter	Stir together, and pour over apples.

Bake 40–45 minutes at 375°. Serve warm, with or without whipped cream.

APPLESAUCE

We freeze lots of thick applesauce and thaw it into Aunt Margaret's delicious and easy-to-create dessert sauce; or bake it into nutritious soft cookies, applesauce cake, or tea bread.

APPLESAUCE DELUXE

5 Tbsp. butter	Melt butter and add sugar.
4 Tbsp. sugar	Amounts can be varied
4 cups applesauce	proportionate to amount of
	applesauce.

Approximately 1½ cups	
finely crushed graham	Add to butter mixture
cracker crumbs (or crushed	until mixture is rather dry.
macaroons or breadcrumbs)	

Just before serving, spread one layer of applesauce on the bottom of an 8 × 8-inch pan, then one layer of crumbs, and repeat, with crumbs on top. Decorate with whipped cream and top with dots of red jelly. Can be assembled in individual dishes, according to amount of sauce desired. Serves 8.

APPLESAUCE COOKIES

⅔ cup cooking oil	
1 cup brown sugar	Blend ingredients.
¼ tsp. vanilla	
¼ tsp. salt	

1¼ cups applesauce	
½ cup chopped dates	Add to first mixture.
½ cup chopped walnuts	
4 cups rolled oats	

Drop by teaspoon on greased cookie sheet. Bake at 350° approximately 20 minutes, or until well browned. Cool on sheet. Yields 3–4 dozen.

APPLESAUCE CAKE

2 scant cups white sugar 1 cup butter or margarine	Mix with pastry blender.
2 eggs	Beat the eggs, then beat them into sugar mixture.
3 cups flour 1 Tbsp. baking soda 1 Tbsp. cinnamon 1 tsp. cloves 1½ tsp. nutmeg ½ tsp. salt	Sift together.
2½ cups applesauce 2 Tbsp. dark corn syrup	Mix together, and add to wet mixture alternately with sifted dry ingredients.
1 cup raisins	Add to batter.

Bake at 300° for 1½ hours in a 9 × 13-inch pan.

APPLESAUCE TEA BREAD

1 ⅔ cups sifted flour 1 ¼ cups sugar ½ tsp. baking powder 1 tsp. baking soda ½ tsp. salt 1 tsp. cinnamon	Sift together.
1 cup applesauce 2 eggs, beaten ½ cup soft shortening ⅓ cup water	Mix together and add dry ingredients, beating only until moistened.
½ cup nuts and/or ½ cup raisins (optional)	Add to mixture.

Bake in wax-paper-lined loaf pan at 350° for approximately 1 hour. Cool in pan 10 minutes and remove to cooling rack.

SPICED APPLE PICKLES

Here's our heirloom recipe.

Approximately 9 lbs. Duchess or other cooking apples
Whole cloves

Wash, halve, and core apples, but don't peel them. Stick 2 cloves in each piece.

---

2 lbs. brown sugar
1 cup maple syrup
1 cup white sugar
1 quart cider vinegar
4 cups water
2 tsp. salt
8 sticks cinnamon

Bring to a boil, allowing cinnamon sticks to float freely. Place apple halves in spiced liquid and simmer, one layer at a time. Watch closely for doneness. They should be tender but not mushy.

Pack into sterilized jars and pour liquid over them to nearly fill jars. Seal. Yields approximately 12 pints. Wait at least 2 months before eating. By then they will have developed a spicy flavor.

SPICED CRAB APPLES

These give a festive touch to holiday meals.

15–20 ripe but firm red crab apples

Remove blossom ends but leave stems on. Prick each apple with darning needle or fork (at least twice).

⅔ cup sugar
½ cup water
8 whole cloves
1 stick cinnamon
Large strip lemon peel

Mix together in saucepan.

Place apples upright in pan and cover loosely. Cook for 10 minutes over low heat without stirring. Do not overcook. Remove from heat. Cool and pack into airtight freezer box, so that second layer fits between stems of first layer. Pour strained juice over apples. Let stand overnight in refrigerator and then freeze.

We like to freeze plums too, by washing, halving, removing the pits, and then packing them raw in airtight freezer bags.

TART PLUM COFFEECAKE

This coffeecake can be made with either fresh or frozen plums.

¼ cup shortening 1¼ cups sugar	Cream together.
2 eggs	Beat well, and add to sugar mixture.
1½ cups flour ¼ tsp. baking soda 1 tsp. baking powder Pinch salt	Sift together.
½ cup buttermilk	Add to sugar mixture alternately with dry ingredients, mixing well.

Pour batter into well-greased 9 × 9-inch pan and top with thawed plums or halved and pitted fresh ones. Sprinkle them freely with brown sugar and cinnamon, and bake at 375° for approximately ½ hour.

BAKED PEARS MERINGUE

Pears which have been stored in the root cellar are excellent in this dish.

4 pears
Sugar
Butter
2 egg whites

Cut pears into halves. Scoop out the cores and fill each cavity with ½ tsp. sugar and a dot of butter. (Use brown sugar with Seckel pears.) Bake in 300° oven until tender but still firm (about ½ hour). When they are done, cover them with egg whites beaten stiff and sweetened. Raise oven heat to 400° and return to oven to brown. Serves 4.

STREUSEL FRUIT CUSTARD

We make this favorite with either fresh or canned peaches.

Sliced peaches to cover bottom of
8-inch ungreased pan (6–8 medium
fresh peaches or quart jar canned
peaches, drained)

¼ cup sugar ¼ scant cup flour 1 cup dairy sour cream 2 eggs, beaten 1 tsp. vanilla	Blend ingredients until smooth, and pour over fruit.
¼ cup butter or margarine ¾ cup flour ½ cup brown sugar ½ tsp. cinnamon	Cut butter into other ingredients until crumbly. Sprinkle over fruit mixture.

Bake at 350° for 30–45 minutes and serve warm with whipped cream or ice cream. Serves 8.

COUNTRY STRAWBERRY SHORTCAKE

No dessert can surpass a good strawberry shortcake. "Good" to farm house-wives means using a rich biscuit dough instead of angel food cake mix.

2 cups flour ⅓ cup sugar 2 tsp. baking powder ¼ tsp. salt	Sift together.
½ scant cup shortening or butter	Cut into sifted mixture.
1 egg Approximately ⅓ cup milk	Beat egg and add to mixture. Then stir in milk, a little at a time, until dough sticks together.

On pastry board, roll dough *lightly* into size that fits into 9-inch-round cake tin. Bake in 425° oven for 12–15 minutes. Cool slightly. While still warm, split biscuits into 2 layers and cover bottom layer with crushed, sweetened fresh or thawed berries. Put the second layer on top, turning upside down so that the soft side is up. Cover it with another layer of berries long enough before eating so that the juice will soak in well. Then cover with thick, sweetened whipped cream.

BLUEBERRY BUCKLE

Blueberries (frozen raw, straight from the bush) often go directly from our freezer into blueberry buckle. We eat it warm, with milk poured over it, for dessert or as a rich coffeecake.

½ cup sugar ⅓ cup flour ½ tsp. cinnamon ¼ cup margarine	Cut margarine into other ingredients and set aside for topping.
1 egg ¾ cup sugar ½ cup margarine	Cream together.
2 cups flour 2 tsp. baking powder ½ tsp. salt	Sift together.
½ cup milk 1 tsp. vanilla	Add to creamed mixture alternately with dry ingredients.
2 cups blueberries	Fold into batter.

Pour into 9-inch-square greased pan and cover with topping. Bake at 375° for approximately 45 minutes.

GREEN MOUNTAIN GOOSEBERRY PIE

A corner of our freezer is always reserved for several bags of gooseberries (frozen raw) to go into this dish.

3 cups gooseberries 1 cup sugar ¼ cup water	Cook until berries are tender.

½ cup sugar 3 Tbsp. quick-cooking tapioca Dash salt ½ tsp. cinnamon ⅛ tsp. cloves ⅛ tsp. nutmeg	Stir into cooked fruit and cool.

Line 9-inch pie plate with pastry. Fill with fruit mixture, dot with butter, and arrange lattice strips on top. Bake at 450° for 10 minutes, and reduce heat to 350° for 20–25 minutes longer. When almost brown, remove from oven. Place a marshmallow in each diamond-shaped opening and finish browning.

WASHINGTON'S BIRTHDAY CHERRY PIE

In February we look forward to this special cherry pie.

Approximately 4 cups pitted frozen or canned pie cherries	Drain and save liquid.

⅓ cup cherry liquid 2¼ Tbsp. quick-cooking tapioca 1 tsp. lemon juice ¼ tsp. almond extract ¼ tsp. salt	Mix together.

1 cup sugar	Add to mixture, along with cherries. Let stand while making pastry.

Line 9-inch pie plate with pastry. Fill with cherry mixture. Sprinkle with ½ cup more sugar and dot with butter. Moisten rim with water and top with lattice crust, fluting edges high. Sprinkle top with sugar. (To keep edges from browning too much, fold strip of aluminum foil loosely around edge of pie.) Bake in 425° oven for 10 minutes and reduce the heat to 350° for 20 minutes longer.

247

RASPBERRY ICE CREAM

Occasionally we go on a calorie binge and, even in the winter, indulge in home-cranked raspberry ice cream.

Approximately 2 quarts berries 2¾ cups sugar	Mash thawed berries and sprinkle with sugar to rest for ½ hour. Strain to remove seeds. Juice yield should be 3½ cups.
4 cups heavy cream 1 tsp. salt	Add ingredients to juice in can of crank freezer and complete process as you would for any ice cream. Yields ½ gallon.

Several years ago we began to question why we were drinking so much tropical fruit juice when our own New England fruits were so good. We have since remedied that situation by freezing lots of apple juice and cider, and berry juices. Crab apple, plum, elderberry, raspberry, strawberry, and even rhubarb juice are especially delicious. We usually cook the fruit briefly, as if for making jelly, and strain it through a jelly bag or wire strainer. We next add honey or sugar to taste and heat the mixture slightly. Then we chill it quickly and pour it into plastic freezer containers, leaving plenty of headroom so that it doesn't spill when freezing. During the winter we drink the thawed juice "straight," in combinations with other homemade juices, or with orange juice. For a sparkling Christmas punch we add ginger ale or club soda. (If we are too busy to make juice during the harvest season, we freeze the raw fruit and make it later.)

HOMEMADE GRAPE JUICE

A fine use for surplus grapes, and a treat for nonimbibers.

Approximately 10 lbs. grapes 1 cup water	Heat in saucepan until pulp and stones separate. Strain through jelly bag.
3 lbs. sugar	Add to juice and heat to boiling. Freeze or bottle.

Makes about 1 gallon. Dilute with equal amount of water before serving.

RASPBERRY SHRUB

This was a tingly drink enjoyed by the local farmers when haying, in summer days gone by. We find it delicious year-round, and make it with frozen berries as well as fresh.

1 quart raspberries (fresh or frozen) 1 cup white vinegar 1 cup water	Cover berries with half-strength white vinegar (dilute with water), but not enough to let berries float. Let stand for 24 hours, then squeeze through strainer or cheesecloth.
Approximately 3 cups sugar	Measure juice, and add an equal amount of sugar. Then boil for 20 minutes. Cool, and either freeze or bottle. Yields 1 quart.

Dilute to use, adding approximately 3 tablespoons to a glass of water, orange juice, lemonade, iced tea, or ginger ale. We use it as a punch base too.

RED LAKE CURRANT SHRUB

The favorite drink of one of our gourmet neighbors.

Currant juice Water Sugar	Mash currants and strain through strainer or cheesecloth. Measure juice, adding an equal amount of water and half as much sugar. Chill, and serve with chipped ice.

FRUIT SHAKES

Frozen strawberries, raspberries, and blackberries make superb milkshakes. We toss a handful of whole raw berries (it's not necessary to thaw them if you can get them apart by prying) into the blender along with a cup of milk. Add ice cream or sugar if you have a sweet tooth, or use skim milk if you're watching your weight.

MAPLE BUTTERNUT FUDGE

We refuse to count the calories in the best candy we've ever eaten.

3 cups maple syrup 1 cup milk	Boil in saucepan to soft ball stage (when ½ tsp. dropped into a cup of water can be shaped into a soft ball with your fingers) or about 236°. Remove from heat and cool to lukewarm. Then beat until mixture is creamy.
½ cup chopped butternuts or walnuts	Add to maple cream and spread mixture in 8-inch buttered pan. Mark it into 16 squares and, if you wish, place one nutmeat on top of each.

Some of each of our surplus fruits go into preserves for the pantry. Among our favorites are thick plum jam, rich elderberry jelly, and uncooked strawberry jam that we store in the freezer. We ignore any exotic directions for making them, and have good luck with the simple instructions on the pectin box or bottle. We like to add special ingredients, however, in the following recipes.

SPICED GOOSEBERRIES

2 quarts red or green berries	Remove stem and bottom end of berries.
1 cup cider vinegar 4½ cups sugar Juice of 1 orange and ½ tsp. grated rind ½ tsp. powdered cinnamon ½ tsp. powdered cloves	Add to gooseberries and let stand for several hours.

Bring slowly to a boil and simmer in enamel kettle about 2 hours or until mixture becomes thick, stirring frequently. Taste, and add more sugar if needed. Pour into clean, hot glass jars and seal immediately. Yields 3–4 pints.

NEW ENGLAND APPLE BUTTER

15 cups thick, unsweetened
    applesauce
8 to 12 cups sugar (to taste)
4 scant tsp. cinnamon
2 scant tsp. allspice
1 box pectin

Bring to full rolling boil and boil hard for 1 minute, stirring constantly. Remove from heat, fill sterilized jars, and cover with paraffin. Yields approximately 8 pints.

Agricultural Extension Offices in the United States

STATE	CITY	ZIP CODE
Alabama	Auburn	36830
Alaska	College	99701
Arizona	Tucson	85721
Arkansas	Fayetteville	72701
California*	Berkeley	94720
Colorado	Fort Collins	80521
Connecticut	Storrs	06268
Delaware	Newark	19711
Florida	Homestead	33030
Georgia	Athens	30601
Hawaii	Honolulu	96822
Idaho	Moscow	83843
Illinois*	Urbana	61801
Indiana	Lafayette	47907
Iowa	Ames	50010
Kansas	Manhattan	66502
Kentucky	Lexington	40506
Louisiana	University	70803
Maine	Orono	04473
Maryland	College Park	20740
Massachusetts*	Amherst	01002
Michigan*	East Lansing	48823
Minnesota	St. Paul	55101
Mississippi	State College	39762
Missouri	Columbia	65201
Montana	Bozeman	59715
Nebraska	Lincoln	68503
Nevada	Reno	89507
New Hampshire	Durham	03824
New Jersey*	New Brunswick	08903
New Mexico	Las Cruces	88001
New York*	Ithaca	14850
North Carolina	Raleigh	27607
North Dakota	Fargo	58102
Ohio*	Columbus	43210
Oklahoma	Stillwater	74074
Oregon	Coryvallis	97330
Pennsylvania	University Park	16802
Rhode Island	Kingston	02881
South Carolina	Clemson	29631

STATE	CITY	ZIP CODE
South Dakota	Brookings	57006
Tennessee	Knoxville	37901
Texas	College Station	77840
Utah	Logan	84321
Vermont	Burlington	05401
Virginia*	Blacksburg	24061
Washington*	Long Beach	98631
West Virginia	Morgantown	26505
Wisconsin	Madison	53706
Wyoming	Laramie	82070

* *States marked with a star are leading producers of fruit and have excellent bulletins on the subject.*

United States
    Publications Division
    Office of Communication
    U.S. Department of Agriculture
    Washington, D.C. 20250

Canada
    Horticultural Research Institute
    Vineland Station, Ontario, Canada
    Central Experimental Farm
    Ottawa, Canada

The names of companies, nurseries, books, magazines, and organizations given in this section and elsewhere in this book are merely to save the reader time and inconvenience. In no way does it represent an endorsement or recommendation of the companies or products. Write to the firms that supply the items you are interested in, study their literature carefully, check any available consumer guides, then make your own decisions.

Fruit Organizations and Magazines

American Fruit Grower, 37841 Euclid Ave., Willoughby, Ohio 44094. Monthly magazine about fruit growing.

American Pomological Society, 103 Tyson Building, University Park, Pennsylvania 16802. Information on old and new varieties.

Brooklyn Botanic Garden, 1000 Washington Avenue, Brooklyn, New York 11225. Booklets for home gardeners.

Good Fruit Grower, 11 South 7th Avenue, Yakima, Washington 98901. Information for western fruit growers.

New York State Fruit Testing Cooperative Association, Geneva, New York 14456. Information about old and new varieties; also trees for sale.

North American Fruit Explorers, c/o Robert Kurle, 10 South 55 Madison Street, Hinsdale, Illinois 60521. Exchange of fruit-growing ideas.

Northern Nut Growers, 4518 Holston Hills Road, Knoxville, Tennessee 37914. Excellent source of nut-growing information.

Organic Gardening and Farming, 33 East Minor Street, Emmaus, Pennsylvania 18049. Monthly magazine of gardening information.

Pomona Book Exchange, 33 Beaucourt Road, Toronto 18 Ontario.

Nurseries

The following is a list of some of the nurseries in various parts of the country that issue a catalog or price list and are willing to ship plants and trees. Look for the letters indicating the types of nursery stock in which you are interested and contact those firms.

A. Tree fruits
B. Small fruits
C. Nuts
D. Old-time fruits
E. Dwarf fruit trees
F. Supplies
G. Will sell in large quantities for commercial growers
H. Rootstocks for grafting
I. Fruits for Zones 3 and 4
J. Fruits for Zone 9

J. Herbert Alexander, Middleboro, Massachusetts 02346
      B-G-I
W. F. Allen Co., 1175 Green Street, Salisbury, Maryland 21801
      A-D-E-I
Baum's Nursery, Route 2, New Fairfield, Connecticut 06810
      A-D-E-I
Bountiful Ridge Nurseries, Inc., Princess Anne, Maryland 21853
      A-B-C-D-E-F-G
Burgess Seed and Plant Co., Galesburg, Michigan 49053
      A-B-C-E
W. Atlee Burpee Co., 5395 Burpee Building, Warminster, Pennsylvania 18974
      A-B-C-E-F
C & O Nursery, Box 116, Wenatchee, Washington 98801
      A-B-C-E
California Nursery Co., Niles District, Fremont, California 94536
      A-B-C-E-G-H-J
Columbia Basin Nursery, P.O. Box 458, Quincy, Washington 98848
      A-E-G-H
Cumberland Valley Nurseries, Inc., McMinnville, Tennessee 37110
      A-B-D-E-G

Farmers Seed and Nursery Co., Faribault, Minnesota 55021
 A-B-C-E-F-I

Henry Field, 407 Sycamore Street, Shenandoah, Iowa 51602
 A-B-C-E-F-I

Dean Foster's Nurseries, Hartford, Michigan 49057
 A-B-C-D-E-F-I

Fowler Nurseries Inc., 525 Fowler Road, Newcastle, California 95658
 A-B-C-F

Hertel Gagnon R.R. 3, Compton, Que.
 A-B-E-I

Louis Gerardi Nursery, R.R. 1, Box 146, O'Fallon, Illinois 62269
 C (nut trees)

Grand Isle Nursery, South Hero, Vermont 05486
 A-D-E-F

Grootendorst Nursery, Lakeside, Michigan 49116
 H

Gurneys Seed and Nursery Co., Yankton, South Dakota 57078
 A-B-C-E-F-I

Hansen's New Plants, Fremont, Nebraska 68025
 A-B-I

Interstate Nurseries, Hamburg, Iowa 51644
 A-B-E-F

Merrill W. Jewett, Hyde Park, Vermont 05655
 B

J. W. Jung Seed Co., Box 434, Randolph, Wisconsin 53956
 A-B-C-E-F-I

Kelly Bros. Nurseries, 940 Maple Street, Dansville, New York 14437
 A-B-C-E-G-H

Lakeland Nursery Sales, Hanover, Pennsylvania 17331
 A-B-C-D-E-F

Henry Leuthardt Nurseries, Inc., East Moriches, Long Island, New York 11940
 A-B-D-E (also espaliered fruit trees)

Lundy's Nursery, Route 3, Box 35, Live Oak, Florida 32060
 A-B-C-E-J

J. E. Miller Nurseries, Inc., Canandaigua, New York 14424
 A-B-C-D-E-F-I

Mr. Gardener, Inc., Niagara Stone Road, Virgil, Ontario, Canada
 A-D-E-G

New York State Fruit Testing Association, Geneva, New York 14456
 A-B-C-D-E (also special grafts to order)

Rayner Bros., Inc., Salisbury, Maryland 21801
 B-C-E-G

Savage Farm Nursery, P.O. Box 125, McMinnville, Tennessee 37110
 A-B-C-D-E

R. H. Shumway, Rockford, Illinois 61101
 A-B-E-F

Southmeadow Fruit Gardens, 2363 Tilbury Place, Birmingham, Michigan 48009
    A-B-D-E-H-I
Spring Hill Nursery, Tipp City, Ohio 45371
    A-B-C-E-H
Stark Brothers, Louisiana, Missouri 63353
    A-B-C-D-E-G-I-J
Stern's Nurseries, Geneva, New York 14456
    A-B-C-D-E
Striblings Nurseries, Inc., 1620 West 16th Street, Merced, California 95340
    A-B-C-E-H
Traas Nursery, 24120 48th Avenue, R.R. 7, Langley, British Columbia, Canada
    H
Van Well Nursery, Wenatchee, Washington 98801
    A-D-E-G
Waynesboro Nurseries, Box 987, Waynesboro, Virginia 22980
    A-B-C-D-E-G

The following sell fruit seeds to grow into seedlings for grafting: Bountiful Ridge Nurseries and Striblings Nurseries (see addresses above). Herbst Bros., 1000 North Main Street, Brewster, New York 10509, sells fruit seeds as well as nut seeds.

Old-time orchards that sell scions for grafts: St. Lawrence Nurseries, Heuvelton, New York 13654, and Worcester County Horticultural Society, 30 Elm Street, Worcester, Massachusetts 01608.

For a complete list of nurseries in any state write to the state Department of Agriculture, which is usually located in the capital city. There is often a small fee for such a list.

Sources of Orchard Supplies

Department stores, garden centers, nurseries, hardware stores, and even general stores are possible places for you to buy supplies and equipment for your orchard. If you cannot locate a local source, the following firms may be of help.

Agway Farm Stores has retail outlets in many cities and towns; sells tools, fertilizers, spray and spray materials, weed killers, mouse poison, and much more.

A. M. Leonard Company, P.O. Box 816, Piqua, Ohio 45356, sells tree paint and sealers, grafting supplies, pruning tools, sprayers, electric bug killers, soil test kits, and harvesting equipment. Catalog.

Day Equipment Corporation, 1402 East Monroe, Goshen, Indiana 46526, sells commercial cider-making equipment.

Friend Manufacturing Corporation, Gasport, New York 14067, sells commercial orchard equipment of all kinds.

Garden Way Research, Charlotte, Vermont 05445, sells garden supplies, hand cider mills, and books.

Montgomery Ward has retail and mail-order stores in many cities. Its farm and garden catalog lists fencing, sprayers, pruning tools, bug killers, compost bins and shredders, bee equipment, bees, home fruit-processing equipment, soil test kits.

Manufacturers of Orchard Chemicals

These companies can supply information on the various fertilizers, insecticides, fungicides, and herbicides that they make or distribute, and can suggest where you can purchase them locally.

Agway, Inc., Fertilizer Chemical Division, Syracuse, New York 13201

American Cyanamid Co., Box 400, Princeton, New Jersey 08540

Chemagrow Agriculture Division, Mobay Chemical Corporation, Box 4913, Kansas City, Missouri 64120

Dow Chemical, Ag Organics Department, Midlands, Michigan 48640

E. I. Dupont de Nemours and Co., Inc., Bio Chemical Division, Wilmington, Delaware 19898

F.M.C. Corporation, Agricultural Chemical Division, Middleport, New York 14105

Merck Chemical Division, Agricultural Products, Rahway, New Jersey 07065

Rohm and Haas, Philadelphia, Pennsylvania 19105

Stauffer Chemical Co., Agricultural Chemical Division, Westport, Connecticut 06880

Uniroyal, Inc., Chemical Division, 59 Maple Street, Naugatuck, Connecticut 06770

Dwarfing Rootstocks Used in Propagating Fruits

Since many catalogs now give their readers a choice of dwarf rootstocks as well as varieties, this information is provided to help you make a better decision about which kind to order, if a choice is available. Heights are approximate, since they will vary according to soil, climate, and light conditions as well as the variety that is grafted upon them.

APPLE DWARF ROOTSTOCKS

The most common dwarf rootstocks used in propagating dwarf apples have been developed in England at the Malling experiment station. They are identified by numbers and the letters EM (East Malling) or MM (Malling Merton). Roman numerals were formerly used, but many nurseries are now using the Arabic numbers.

EM 2 (II). Semi-dwarfing to 10 feet. Does well on loams but not on clay soil. Does not anchor tree as well as some, so may need staking.

EM 4 (IV). Early bearing, heavy producer, widely used in Europe. Tends to root one-sided and therefore may lean in later years.

EM 7 (VII). Widely used semi-dwarf stock, 8 feet. Anchors the tree well and suckers very little. Tolerates heavy soils and is early bearing.

EM 9 (IX). Very dwarf (about 6 feet). Good for espaliers, living fences, and small areas. Susceptible to aphids and fire blight. Staking is recommended in windy areas as wood is very brittle.

EM 26 (XXVI). Slightly larger growing than EM 9, but smaller than EM 7. Often gets winter injury. Needs staking.

EM 27 (XXVII). Most dwarfing of all, even more than EM 9. Patented. Hardier than most Mallings but susceptible to fire blight. Needs well-drained soil.

MM 13A (XIII). Semi-dwarf. Productive but tends to take longer to bear than many dwarfs. Does fairly well in wet soils.

MM 104 (CIV). Semi-dwarf. Vigorous but cannot tolerate wet soils. Grows to 11 feet. Not early bearing.

MM 106 (CVI). About 9 feet. Resistant to aphids but may have trouble with collar rot in the Northwest. Sometimes is damaged by early autumn freezes. Needs well-drained soil.

MM 109 (CIX). Semi-dwarf, well anchored, nonsuckering. A good producer.

MM 111 (CXI). Vigorous, drought-resistant, productive. Aphid-resistant. Does especially well in warmer climates. Widely used in commercial plantings.

From Sweden

ALNAP 2 (A2). This rootstock was introduced to meet the demand for a hardier dwarf. Medium size (to 11 feet), drought-tolerant, and grows fast when young. Still under trial; has not yet been tried under all conditions.

From Canada

ROBUSTA NO. 5. Fast-growing understock that is somewhat dwarfing in cooler climates. Widely used in Canada and the Upper Northeast, especially for grafting apples of the McIntosh group. Not so good for regions that have long seasons, as growth may start too early in the spring. Budding them at least 2 feet high is recommended in order to utilize the extreme hardiness of the stock.

PLUM, PEACH, AND CHERRY DWARF ROOTSTOCKS

The stone fruits are usually grafted on one of these:

PRUNUS BESSEYI. This is the native western sand cherry. It produces a tree only about 6 feet tall, and they often begin to bear at about half that size. Especially good for tiny yards, large tubs, planters, roof gardens, and espaliers.

PRUNUS TORMENTOSA. The Nanking cherry grows about the same size and shape as the besseyi but is hardier and less vigorous. It would probably be selected if only hardiness were a factor.

PRUNUS FRUITICOSA. The native ground cherry is used occasionally for dwarfing cherries, particularly the sweet varieties.

NORTH STAR CHERRY. This is a naturally dwarf variety of sour cherry. Full-size rootstocks are grafted to North Star and allowed to grow a year, then are grafted or budded to the variety wanted.

Metric Equivalents

LENGTH

1 centimeter	= .39 inch
1 meter	= 39.37 inches
1 inch	= 2.54 centimeters
1 foot	= .3048 meter

WEIGHT

1 kilogram	= 2.20 pounds
1 pound	= .45 kilograms or 454.5 grams

CAPACITY

1 liter	= 1.056 quarts (liquid)
1 liter	= .908 quart (dry)

INDEX

A NOTE ABOUT THE AUTHOR

Lewis Hill was born in Greensboro, Vermont, where he
still lives. For over thirty years he has raised fruits and
berries as a hobby and, in 1947, started a mail-order
nursery specializing in hardy fruits and ornamentals.
Although selling by mail has been discontinued, he and his
wife, Nancy, continue to operate Hillcrest Nursery and to
grow old-time fruits. Mr. Hill has been president of the
Vermont Plantsmen and has tested new fruits for various
experiment stations for many years. He contributes
frequent articles to *Organic Gardening* and *American Nurseryman*
and writes gardening columns for local newspapers.
He is the author of *Pruning Simplified.*

A NOTE ABOUT THE TYPE

The text of this book was set in Compano, the film version
of Palatino, a type face designed by the noted German
typographer Herman Zapf. Named after Giovambattista
Palatino, a writing master of Renaissance Italy, Palatino
was the first of Zapf's type faces to be introduced to
America. The first designs for the face were made in 1948,
and the fonts for the complete face were issued between
1950 and 1952. Like all Zapf-designed type faces, Palatino
is beautifully balanced and exceedingly readable.

The book was composed by CompuComp Corporation,
Hoboken, New Jersey.

Typography and binding design by Susan Mitchell.